1000 Dresses

The fashion design resource

1000 Dresses

The fashion design resource

TRACY FITZGERALD
and ALISON TAYLOR

Foreword by Stephen Faerm

A QUARTO BOOK

First edition for North America
published in 2014 by Barron's
Educational Series, Inc.

All inquiries should be addressed to:
Barron's Educational Series, Inc.
250 Wireless Boulevard
Hauppauge, New York 11788
www.barronseduc.com

ISBN: 978-1-4380-0328-3

Library of Congress Control Number:
2013948147

QUAR.FBTD

Conceived, designed, and
produced by:
Quarto Publishing plc
The Old Brewery
6 Blundell Street
London N7 9BH

Project Editor: Victoria Lyle
Art Editor: Emma Clayton
Designer: Lisa Tai
Copyeditor: Claire Waite Brown
Proofreader: Aruna Vasudevan
Indexer: Helen Snaith
Picture Researcher: Sarah Bell
Art Director: Caroline Guest

Creative Director: Moira Clinch
Publisher: Paul Carslake

Color separation by Pica Digital Pte
Ltd, Singapore
Printed by Toppan Leefung Pte, China

9 8 7 6 5 4 3 2 1

Contents

Foreword

Whether you are a student, professional, or considering a career in the fashion industry, *1000 Dresses* offers a comprehensive overview of one of fashion's primary—and highly popular—areas of apparel design: The Dress. Following a historical and contextual overview of the dress, individual chapters showcase the key silhouettes employed throughout modern history. Readers may review each chapter's categories and sub-categories sequentially, or in any order that fits their needs. No matter where in the book the reader lands, they will find extensive information about the world of dresses, including design inspiration, textile knowledge, and detail development, seasonal variations, styling considerations, diverse aesthetics, and many other informative areas about dresses. Each category provides readers with historical examples for context alongside a wide range of traditional and interpretive design examples of the silhouette. Throughout *1000 Dresses*, the versatility and timelessness of The Dress is fully illustrated.

To succeed in today's competitive and highly accelerated fashion industry, students and professionals must acquire a tremendous amount of knowledge and skills quickly and thoroughly. *1000 Dresses* contributes significantly to this knowledge by giving readers a deeper understanding and literacy of fashion design, thus supporting the ability to solidify one's own unique and innovative vision for fashion design.

Steven Faerm
Assistant Professor, Fashion Design
Parsons The New School For Design

About this book

This is an indispensable source of inspiration for the practicing fashion designer, stylist, fashion buyer, fashion and textiles student, dressmaker, and anyone with an interest in the creative side of the fashion industry. The book offers a dictionary of ideas that can be used as a springboard for your own unique dress designs.

Each chapter focuses on a different dress genre, explained in articles that place the garment in its fashion and social context, and ones that identify its key design features. The dress genre is then organized into a multitude of variations—for example, the coatdress includes the subcategories tailored, housecoat, wrap, and cape. Each subsection contains a multitude of images that comprise the directory.

DIRECTORY

The directory is beautifully illustrated with a wealth of photographic images that enable comparisons, aid understanding, and inspire creative design thinking. Captions to each dress analyze, contextualize, and, above all, nail what it is about a particular design that makes it desirable.

IN CONTEXT

Each style is introduced with historical information on the development of the cut, and key historic events, designers, or dresses are discussed.

In context

Historic photographs of iconic dresses

Tabs on the right-hand side indicate the section

DESIGN CONSIDERATIONS

Design considerations—such as silhouette, length, fabrics, fastenings, embellishment, necklines, sleeves, lining, details, and shaping—are clearly explained, and simple annotated artworks show the dress construction.

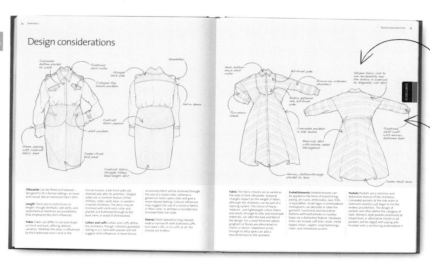

Design considerations

Annotations point out technical details

Illustrations showing the front and back of two extremes of the style

Boho

Enlargements give a close-up view of garment details

Drawings show design alternatives inspired by dress

Beautiful color photographs of 1000 dresses

Captions for every dress analyze each design

Key characteristics of the style are called out in bullet points

Use this book as inspiration for silhouettes, fabrics, and details.

Create a mood board to communicate your inspiration and vision.

The design process

The design process is centered on research, experimentation, and innovation, combined with analysis and development. Trial, error, and intuition are all part of the equation. Taste, aesthetics, trend, and who is wearing the dress and why must also be negotiated. Understanding the customer and market is crucial to getting the right balance between creativity, wearability, innovation, and commerciality.

To create a collection you need a solid foundation in design practices and an understanding of construction and make. You will also need to communicate effectively with the customer who, in turn, buys into the look. This originates from your inspiration—based on theme, muse, and defined trend—and develops into a creative narrative that tells the story of your brand. Understanding what other designers have done successfully in the past and exploring a variety of possibilities is vital to jumpstarting your own design process.

To help you do this, this book consists of a comprehensive directory of dress silhouettes. Easy to navigate text discusses style, form, cut, proportion, and construction and informative artworks illustrate these. Cataloged and presented in straightforward, accessible sections—including a useful glossary for easy reference—the information is intended to provide the means to broaden design knowledge and technical understanding.

Use the book as a starting point, as a reference for ideas. You may wish to concentrate on the specific categories, though mixing and matching design details across other dress styles is also an option. Altering the neckline, changing the length of the skirt, or adding volume can dramatically alter a look. Varying the textile can also change the aesthetic, for example, transforming a day dress into evening wear.

This book is intended as a starting point for your own unique interpretations. Discover a myriad of design possibilities, and use this book as a library of sources to assist you in your design process.

Customer profile Have an idea of who you want to create your work for. Who is your customer? What does she do and why does she need your garment? Navigate the book to help pinpoint what your customer might want to wear and use this to originate or bounce ideas.

Muse Your chosen muse is the ideal person who you are designing for. She can be a well-known personality or simply the ideal figure or style icon that would wear your dress. This gives you a focus, and you and your customer will both find the muse inspirational.

Market research Investigate what competitors in your market are doing so that you do not replicate what is already out there and can authoritatively predict what should be offered next. The book presents alternative dress styles by a wide range of designers, across numerous categories.

Inspiration Gather inspiration from a number of sources as a starting point for design development. Use this book, along with the Internet, magazines, books, exhibitions, and film, to gather relevant images that fit with your theme, customer, muse, and market. Your own photographs and drawings, fabric swatches, vintage garments, found objects, and ephemera are also good foundations for ideas. See the list (page 9) of other sources of inspiration.

Fabric sourcing Collect swatches of fabrics that fit with your collection and best express your theme. In the initial stages this might be snips for color referencing. You may wish to create small samples of

Use rough sketches to generate ideas and troubleshoot problems.

Final drawings are used to sell your idea to your customer.

seams or pockets with certain fabrics to fully understand the performance qualities and allow you to construct the look you want. Use the book to help you understand what fabric is best suited for any silhouette.

Color stories Decide what color palette suits your collection and fits with the story and mood that you want to create. You may wish to consult a color-forecasting company to help you predict the trends for the particular season in mind. Colors can be developed through your research, looking at nature or vintage textiles, for example. Use Pantone references to communicate and match your chosen colors. Look through this book to see how other designers use color to communicate ideas.

Mood boards Create a mood board to set the scene for your ideas. Collect fabrics, pages from magazines, photographs, postcards, etc.—anything that fits your theme, and can motivate and inspire you to further design development. The mood board is a good form of communication, in order to make sure that the design team are on the same page.

Drawing To generate and communicate ideas, drawing is an important part of the design process. From recording and generating original research and

inspiration, through to the development of design ideas, and the creation of rough sketches of garment silhouettes and details. Final illustrations can communicate and promote your collection to your customer.

Design development Decide what sketches work best and refine and edit, cutting out elements that don't work, and designing into gaps within the collection. Fabric choices, color, and pattern balance are all important considerations. Finishings, fastenings, and trims must all function, as well as aesthetically balance.

Edit final choices The collection must work as a whole and, therefore, the final edit will prioritize the collection and help to build range, allowing for coordinated looks.

Working drawings Create flat drawings showing back and front views as well as complicated side views or detailed areas, such as pockets. The drawings will communicate construction details, finishing requirements, and final fabric selection. These specifications will give accurate, detailed measurements that will help you to create your muslin and form the basis for the specification packs sent to the manufacturer when going into production.

Muslin development Create prototypes in calico or muslin, translating the paper designs into a three-dimensional garment using the working drawing as a blueprint for measurement and scale. Working on the stand or tailor's dummy allows you to check for fit and analyze the overall silhouette and finishing details. The toile should always be worn on the body for the final fit to check for ease of movement. Any adjustments can be resolved at this stage in the process before making the sample in final fabrics.

Final garment samples Cut in final fabrics using authentic fastenings and trims. Garment samples are now ready for the fashion show, photo shoot, and saleroom!

OTHER SOURCES OF INSPIRATION

☑ Historical garments
☑ Fashion shows
☑ Street fashion
☑ Fine art
☑ Popular culture
☑ Craft techniques
☑ Other cultures
☑ Nature
☑ Technology

DAY DRESS

The essential of any woman's wardrobe, casually worn for leisure and comfort or formally dressed for boardroom and status, the day dress comes in many guises, serving a multitude of functions.

Diagonal lines are emphasized by the sash inserted into parallel raglan-styled seams. Contrast textures are achieved by utilizing both sides of the silk satin.

In context

This elegant yet understated fitted day dress by Christian Dior features a square neckline that shows off the feminine collarbone and neck. The curved neckline forms the sleeves that are kept short and semifitted. The neckline also mirrors the proportion of the hat.

n the early 1900s, Paul Poiret abandoned tailoring and pattern cutting for a more experimental draped silhouette, inspired by a more natural female form. This paved the way for the changes in the 1920s, when women were liberated by the silhouette of the day dress, which elongated the body's proportions by dropping the waistline and shortening the length to midcalf. By the 1930s, the day dress was becoming more practical as women led more active lives, a phenomenon that Chanel exploited by developing sports-inspired, easy-to-wear jersey dresses. The austerity measures necessary during World War II resulted in fabric shortages. Manmade fabrics, such as rayon and synthetic jersey, took over from luxury cloth at a time when wool was used for uniforms and silk for parachutes. The unadorned silhouette was cut narrower and shorter for cost and economy. Post war, ordinary women were able to find employment outside of domestic service, and the day dress adapted to suit their new roles, with ready-to-wear dresses

making style affordable and accessible and allowing women to keep up to date with new fashion trends.

In 1947, Dior launched his New Look, with its glamorous nipped-in waist and longer, fuller skirts, which women embraced. Modern kitchen appliances allowed women to shake off their domestic ties and free their time for more fulfilling roles in the workplace. Givenchy introduced the sack dress in 1958, liberating women from the cinched waist and hourglass figure and paving the way for the shift dress and mini of the 1960s. The silhouette softened and lengthened in the 1970s, to midi and maxi. Laura Ashley, Bill Gibb, and Perry Ellis explored a more ethnic and romantic styling, as did Ossie Clark and Celia Birtwell, with their floral prints. The padded-shouldered power dressing of the aspirational 1980s epitomized that decade's obsession with status and success and translated easily into the day dress through formal business and office wear.

The iconic model Suzy Parker jauntily wears this fitted white linen dress. A novelty neckline calls attention to her collarbone and softly sloping shoulders while a matching belt emphasizes her small waist.

Design considerations

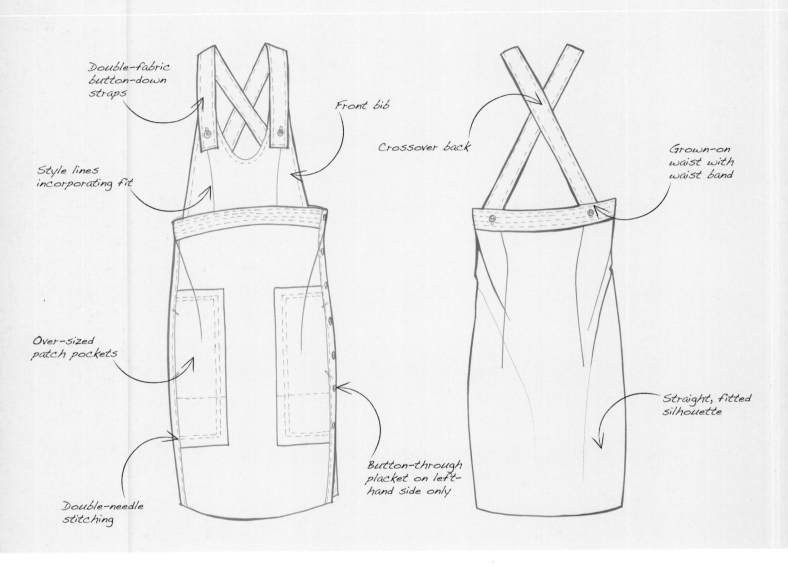

Double-fabric button-down straps

Front bib

Crossover back

Grown-on waist with waist band

Style lines incorporating fit

Over-sized patch pockets

Double-needle stitching

Button-through placket on left-hand side only

Straight, fitted silhouette

Versatility The day dress is defined by the intention that it is worn during the day. However, it is a versatile piece of clothing that can be dressed up or down depending on the event and can transcend into evening. As an alternative to casual wear separates, the day dress can function as a single item of clothing that can be "thrown on" as an easy-to-wear no-fuss option. Alternatively, the pinafore can be teamed with a shirt or fine-gauge knitwear for a relaxed informal aesthetic. Choice of fabrics, dress length, sleeve style, neckline, and silhouette determine its character.

Style The broad array of day-dress styles means there is one for any situation. Typically, the formal day dress can be worn in the workplace and provides a more feminine alternative to power dressing. Often teamed with a jacket, the dress can be softened by a cardigan and accessories and worn during a night out.

Silhouette The figure-enhancing fit-and-flare silhouette translates well with the wrap styling, and it suits casual and formal dresses. Casual and less formal circumstances require comfortable, unstructured dresses that are less figure hugging.

Length Length may be the obvious indicator of the day dress, traditionally at knee length, it works well with flat pumps, heels, or boots; however, there

Jersey rib-trimmed neckline and armholes

Faux apron front in crepe applied onto jersey-dress base and left to hang loose from waist

Multistitched, woven waist tie

Cut-away armholes

Jersey, maxi-length, straight dress

Finely gathered front panel

are no rules, and from maxi through to mini the variations are endless.

Fabrics Spandex combinations and new synthetics offer easy-care, crease-free options that are particularly useful for the busy working woman, and also great for traveling. Sportswear fabrics such as wool and cotton jerseys and sweats offer ease of movement and are great for layering for home and weekend living.

Fastenings The opportunity to select from a broad range of fastenings allows for diversity of styling and detailing. Contrast-color thread, multistitch detail, and contrast-color piping inserts can also provide design interest. Fastenings and hardware can be prominent features on casual dresses with chunky metal or plastic zips and elaborate zip pulls. Buckles and braces, rivets, eyelets, and press-studs reflect work-wear references and can be seen on pinafores and overalls.

Functionality and convenience demand pockets, which can be concealed within the garment seams or applied for a more decorative effect.

Formal

Every woman needs a dress that is sophisticated, maybe understated, and possibly practical, which she can effortlessly wear in order to create an impression. This dress has a polished aesthetic, which means it can be worn at an interview or business meeting. Semifitted, tailored, and structured in woven fabrics or gathered and flared in softly draping fabrics, the formal day dress sends out a strong message of authority, capability, and glamour. Minimal lines and neutral color tones with interesting yet subtle detailing exploit femininity yet, at the same time, mean business.

Modern blended, easy-care fabrics are an ideal choice, making the dress hardwearing and crease resistant and able to withstand the rigors of the working day while maintaining the appearance of effortless chic.

Often designed to be worn with a matching jacket or coat, the formal day dress can be short-sleeved or sleeveless, though long or three-quarter-length sleeves provide a more covered look more suited to the working environment. The formality of the dress suggests a longer length to just above knee level, varying in length to the calf. A shorter length, within reason, can be acceptable, however, for a younger market. Necklines seldom offer exposed cleavage and can range from the simplicity of a round neck to the exploitation of a range of collars. Shoulder pads and strong shoulder lines echo the power dressing of the 1980s and emulate a masculine silhouette.

KEY CHARACTERISTICS

- ☑ Sophisticated, smart, functional
- ☑ Semifitted, tailored, structured
- ☑ Minimal lines and neutral colors
- ☑ Easy to wear, hardwearing, practical

The black side panels flatter the body shape, while the white vertical **center-front panel** elongates the body, giving the impression of a slimmer silhouette. The **front** neck has a simple placket opening.

Alternative neckline and sleeves: Funnel neck and set-in short sleeves

The simplicity of the sleeveless round-neck, knee-length, fitted dress with center-front and -back seams is the perfect shape for the bold monochromatic animal print.

1 Grown-on, cap-sleeved day dress with a high V neck and a tulip-shaped peplum over a fitted pencil skirt. 2 Body-conscious, cap-sleeved dress. The high, square neckline reflects the angular cut and three-dimensional detail on the hips. 3 Semifitted dress with a square neckline and stand collar that sits away from the neck. Darts to the waist and bustline create shape and fit.

4 Vertical and horizontal black-on-white detailing of inset panels establishes a graphic symmetry to this semifitted, op art-inspired dress. 5 Slash-neck, pinafore-style dress with hourglass-shaped center-front panel that accentuates the curves of the body. The fluro-green piping defines the outline of the shape. 6 Fine, wool dress with grown-on boatneck. The bodice is fitted to just

above the bust point, where a circular-cut flared skirt is attached. 7 Elbow-length magyar sleeves, a simple rounded neckline, and a tied waist—this day dress is cut to give minimal flare at the hemline. 8 Fluid silk jersey with a bodice cut generously to give a blouson effect above the waist seam. Long fitted sleeves and a tighter cut in the skirt contrast to give a more body-conscious effect.

Formal (continued)

> The graphic white and sheer **cutouts** of the dress are the primary attraction on the otherwise simple **slash-neck**, semifitted dress with straight sleeves. The look is at once athletic and feminine.

Alternative neckline, sleeves, and paneling: Scooped round neckline and cap sleeves

A slash-neck, semifitted dress with raglan short sleeves that have a wide **turn-back cuff** opening, which is wrapped and cut higher at the front to form a **cape effect** at the back. The simple silhouette of the main body allows the interesting sleeve detail to be the main focus.

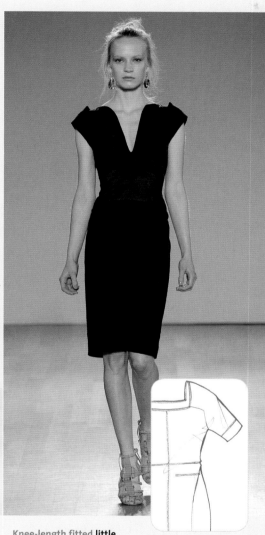

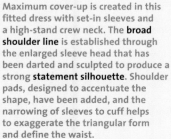

Maximum cover-up is created in this fitted dress with set-in sleeves and a high-stand crew neck. The **broad shoulder line** is established through the enlarged sleeve head that has been darted and sculpted to produce a strong **statement silhouette**. Shoulder pads, designed to accentuate the shape, have been added, and the narrowing of sleeves to cuff helps to exaggerate the triangular form and define the waist.

Knee-length fitted **little black dress** with deep waistband in **contrast satin**, suggesting a cummerbund and defining the waist. The sculpted silhouette, created at the shoulder profile and neckline, interrupts the formality of the dress.

Alternative neckline, armhole, and sleeves: Square neck, saddle shoulder, and short sleeves

The **white piping** contrasts with the black to create vertical and horizontal lines that dissect the dress at center front and waist. The round neck and armholes are faced, in keeping with the simple uncomplicated shape. Falling just above knee length, the dress is fully lined. Piped pocket openings at the hip reflect the **horizontal waistline** and continue the monochromatic effect.

Formal (continued)

> The use of varying weights of white woven fabrics in panels creates contrasting density. Deep shoulder straps create a **halter neck** that stands around the neck edge; contrast binding is used to face and trim the armhole. The high **sweetheart neckline** is accentuated by the deep split at center front.

Quirky, printed, soft woven dress that has the main bodice and sleeves cut in one piece. Fit has been achieved through the addition of **horizontal tucks** along the neck edge and shoulders that form the sleeve head. The sleeve hem is shaped, cut away at the front and left to drape loosely at the back. In contrast to the feminine style, the main focus of this dress is a **bold eye-like appliqué** exposing the torso. The appliqué is also reflected in the contrasting trim on the skirt hem.

Fitted to the **body contours** and simply finished with facings at the round neck and armholes, this is the perfect dress to transcend occasions. The **side split** at hemline breaks up the monotony of the black, creating a sexy and sophisticated aesthetic, perfect for accessorizing.

A long, lean silhouette is created in this long-sleeved dress, which hits just above the knee. The **squared padded shoulders** give a severe masculine appearance, which is feminized in the **cutout keyhole panels** at the bust with sweetheart neckline. Though revealing some flesh at the chest, the look is still demure and so maintains an aspect of formality.

A strong silhouette with **curve-cut three-quarter-length sleeves**, tulip-shaped knee-length skirt, and cowl-front neckline. The leather tie belt adds interest to the expanse of solid-color fabric. All elements of this design use exaggerated curved seams to highlight the **drapery in the neckline**.

Alternative neckline and sleeves: Low cowl neck and grown-on cap sleeves

1 The symmetry of this V-neck dress is emphasized by the contrasting color side panels and prominent center-front seam. 2 Body-conscious dress with pencil skirt and empire-line bodice. Bust suppression is achieved through tucks on the bodice that are left open at the neck edge. 3 An extended shoulder line creates a broad V-shaped silhouette that is mirrored in the A-line knee-length skirt. The center-front stripe and contrasting shoulder yoke and pocket flaps accentuate the shape. 4 The exaggerated tulip-shaped skirt is constructed from multiple layers of laser-cut shapes that are stitched at one edge to a foundation skirt, creating a three-dimensional effect. 5 Tabard-style, sleeveless dress with button fastening at the shoulders. 6 Layers imitate separate garment pieces: A fine, cotton overlayer is gathered at the side seams then brought forward with a tie belt. 7 A dipped-dye effect tops and tails this silk fitted column dress. The neckline is almost off the shoulder but high above the cleavage. 8 The design interest of this understated sheath dress is focused on the deep U-shaped neckline and capped sleeves.

Formal (continued)

The **magyar sleeves** are the focal point of this dress with self-fabric tucks inserted into the seam of the sleeve and running continuously from elbow to center-front neckline. This creates the split collar, which stands from the neckline, and silhouettes the curve of the sleeve, creating an **exaggerated sweetheart shape.** The cuff and underarm sleeve gusset are cut in one piece, as are the side dress and top of the sleeve.

The dress is fitted to the contours of the body with gathered fabric at the bust dart, **accentuating the curves** and giving a softer shape. The bodice yoke, in aubergine latex, provides a sharp contrast and an unexpected, **contemporary twist.**

Alternative neckline and sleeves: V neck and saddle shoulders with short sleeves

The dress has a minimalist quality, with a **heavy duchess-satin base** contributing to the formal aesthetic. With references from **Japanese geisha,** the front contrast panel at the center of the bodice has decorative embroidered and appliquéd graphic floral motifs. The high waistline, three-quarter-length sleeves, and neckline continue the strong, feminine-yet-puritanical look.

Pinafore

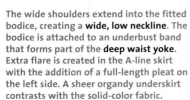

A sleeveless dress designed to be worn over a blouse or sweater, the pinafore dress is derived from the apron, which is worn to protect the garments underneath it.

The pinafore dress can be opened and fastened at the back with buttons or a zipper, which mirror the traditional apron. It can, however, be opened and fastened at the shoulder, by a front placket of variable length, or buttoned or zipped through the front from neck to hem. It can also double as a shift and be pulled over the head but is defined by the fact that it is worn over other layers. For ease, the dress may have a side zipper fastening or symmetrical underarm placket and buttons on both sides. The neckline would generally be low enough to reveal the blouse or sweater underneath, with variations from V to round neck, or perhaps a sweetheart shape.

Due to the work-wear and protective connotations of the apron, the pinafore dress will invariably have pockets, whether patched on the front or invisible at the side seam. Lining is essential, but some designs with a yoke might be faced at the yoke and unlined at the skirt.

The wide shoulders extend into the fitted bodice, creating a **wide, low neckline**. The bodice is attached to an underbust band that forms part of the **deep waist yoke**. Extra flare is created in the A-line skirt with the addition of a full-length pleat on the left side. A sheer organdy underskirt contrasts with the solid-color fabric.

The shaped waist, in contrasting **leather panels,** leads the eye to the metal chain strap that supports the skirt, forming a **halter-neck style**. The shaped hemline, with curved border, and the self-fabric band, left to hang from the skirt hem, reflect the shaped waistline and chain strap.

KEY CHARACTERISTICS

- ☑ **Derived from the apron**
- ☑ **Worn over other layers**
- ☑ **Sleeveless**
- ☑ **Reveals garments underneath**

1 Shift-style pinafore dress giving a sporty feel. The multiple color-blocked linen panels are defined by a strong outline of black tape and allude to the traditional apron shape. **2** Pinafore dress cut under the bustline with integrated bra cups threaded through the dress to form the shoulder straps. **3** Inserts of mesh are outlined by swirls of three-dimensional corded embroidery on this ditsy tie-print dress. The combination of fabric and shape gives an athletic twist. **4** Trapeze-shape pinafore dress pleated into a band above bust level, with shoulder straps. The deep border at the hem spreads the pleats to increase the volume. **5** Asymmetrical bodice styling, two different capped sleeves, a soft, flared A-line skirt, and a fitted waistline. **6** Simple color blocking in a 1960s-inspired pinafore dress with deep, circular cutout armholes from shoulder to hipline. **7** A round neckline and deep cutaway armholes. The heavy embellishment softens the look and contrasts the black with the white underlayered accessories. **8** This fitted-bodice, sleeveless dress has an exaggerated envelope neckline that complements the knee-length flared skirt.

Overalls

From classic Great Depression styling through to World War II army girls, the overalls dress is a derivative. Following the styling details of the bib-and-brace denim work-wear tradition, originally worn to keep garments underneath clean, the overalls dress copies the same durable vibe, creating a casual statement. Since the 1960s, different colors and patterns have been adapted into the dress, often with one of the straps worn loose or unfastened along the side and under the arm. The skirt is tight with a back split for ease of movement, and commonly worn above the knee for a younger look.

The bib-overalls fashion trend among American youth culture peaked in the latter half of the 1970s, and again in the late 1990s. Ralph Lauren, in particular, adopted this trend, which has been adapted and translated over many years.

Traditionally, this style of dress has five pockets and crossover back straps that pass over the shoulders to buckle to rivets on the bib front. Diagonal side openings with rivet-buttoned fastenings reinforce the dungaree function. Denim-jean style seaming and topstitching are common features. Fabrics include denim, corduroy, and cotton twill. Sanding techniques give wear and tear to areas of the garment for a distressed look, and other treatments, such as sandblasting, creasing, and stone washing, are also employed. Dyeing and bleaching add to the well-worn look.

Often worn over T-shirts or checked or plain cotton shirts, the dress can also be teamed with a more feminine white blouse for a prairie feel.

High-shine and paper-thin, this **plastic-coated fabric** has been translated into a **dropped-waist minidress** with deep V-notched neckline and metal dungaree clip fastenings on the shoulder straps. The skirt has been gathered into the waist seam, giving a softer, feminine feel to this usually more aggressive fabric.

Wide straps buttoned onto the bodice form the focal point of this design, creating a deep, scooped V neckline. The loose-fitting, straight-cut dress is easy to wear and uses **color blocking** to define the body's proportions. A large contrast-color pocket creates an informal, asymmetric style.

KEY CHARACTERISTICS

- ☑ **Derived from denim work-wear overalls**
- ☑ **Bib front, crossover back straps, diagonal side openings**
- ☑ **Tough, durable, casual look**

1 Needle-cord dungaree dress with deep waistband and A-line skirt with center-back fastening. The bib front has wide straps that cross over the back and button at the back waistband. **2** A shirt has been deconstructed to inspire this quirky minidress. The main body of the shirt has been taken away, leaving only the lower part of the sleeves, collar, and placket. **3** The crossover bib front is extended from the grown-on waist skirt with origami-like folds and tucks that give volume and drape to the wrap skirt. **4** Wide, short straps that end in a pronounced angle function as a visual emphasis on the shoulders. **5** The bodice has no shaping, creating an androgynous feel, though the buttons, binding, and motif give a more feminine aesthetic. **6** Textured straps reinforce the delicacy of the print and call attention to the full width of the shoulder. **7** The delicate two-color straps suggest a slip and bra, the bare essentials for a hot summer day. **8** Authentic "bib-and-brace" buckles support this shift-like bodice. The inverted V inserts reflect the V-shaped dropped waistline, to which a contrast fabric skirt is attached.

Wrap

The wrap dress was made popular by American designer Diane Von Fürstenberg in the 1970s, and DvF still produces variations of it today. Although categorized as a day dress, the relaxed, longer version—reminiscent of the housecoat—can be grouped with the caftan style. The shape is flattering and suits the hourglass figure: The skirt is fitted into the waist then tapered over the hips and flared to the hem.

A jersey or stretch fabric gives the dress a fluid drape, but equally a crepe or woven fabric with a spandex mix gives a similar effect. Traditionally, the wrap dress has no buttons or zippers; instead the internal wrap is tied to the right-hand seam inside the dress then tied at the left side as the dress crosses over. Sometimes the ties are taken through a buttonhole opening at the left side then wrapped around the body and tied at the front. It is a simple and chic style that can be worn to any occasion, day or night.

The sleeve would normally be fitted to the body to continue the fitted upper-body silhouette, though sleeveless or capped sleeves are options. A drop armhole shape and shorter turned-back deep sleeves can be applied to give a more relaxed look. The wrap will generally create a V neck, the depth of which can be determined by the cross of the wrap.

This style works best to the knee or just above but is also flattering at calf length. A longer maxi length takes this style into the evening, where choice of fabrics can change the look from understated sophistication to full-on glamour.

Effective use of **color blocking** is underlined in this simple wrap style. The sleeveless garment has wide shoulders that continue into the bodice and wrap across the body to a dropped waistline, to create a **low V neckline**. The uncomplicated fitted miniskirt reflects the overall modern feel.

Soft jersey wrap-over dress that fastens at the right hip with a tie, then buttons at the left-hand side. The front wrap facing conceals the buttonhole, giving the below calf-length dress a **streamlined** appearance.

KEY CHARACTERISTICS

☑ Front panels wrapped and often secured with ties or buttons to one side or belted

☑ V neckline

☑ Fabrics with fluid drape

1 A 1920s-inspired sheer silk-chiffon wrap dress with kimono-style elbow-length sleeves. The loose wrap-front bodice is secured into a dropped waist seam. 2 Charming wrap-front minidress with a young, fresh appeal belying its vintage inspiration. 3 Mini-length loose-fit halter-neck sundress with a plunging V neckline. The tie, at hip level, creates soft drapes across the body.

4 The silk satin fabric has a metallic foiled print that drapes to give a soft liquid effect. Deconstructed finishes, such as the overlocked edges and the open underarm seam, give a lingerie styling. 5 The wrap ties of this silk satin dress create shape and drape to otherwise rectangular shapes. Circular flared sleeves echo the soft drape at the hemline. 6 Two separate

contrast-print garment panels wrap around the body and attach at the hip forming a low V neck. 7 The wrap is secured by double-breasted buttons on a deep-fitted dropped waistband. The fitted waistband contrasts with the softly gathered skirt and the drape of the magyar sleeves. 8 The deep scallop-edged V neck gives detail and decoration to an otherwise plain dress.

Wrap (continued)

> With no shoulder seams, this dress is cut in **one piece** from front to side panel, draped around the neck to form the **draped cowl** at the back, then continued to the other side panel. The front wrap panels are pleated at the ties and tied at the left-hand seam to provide further draping.

Alternative sleeves: Raglan armhole with butterfly sleeves

Maxi-length wrap dress constructed from **scarf squares** in fine cotton lawn, to give a tiered, layered effect, making the loose caftan shape ideal for summer. The scarf squares are fixed at the shoulder by a fine shoestring strap and again at the cuff, leaving the top of the sleeve open to **expose shoulders** and upper arms. The bodice is wrapped to form a V neckline and a self-fabric belt defines the waist and closes the wrap.

Asymmetrical wrap dress with **kimono references**. The exaggerated shape provides a large canvas for the painterly print. The **diagonal hemline** is created by corners of the rectangular side-front panel.

An elegant wrap-front dress that finishes just below knee length. The inherent drape in the fabric is shown to its best advantage with **fluted, tiered short sleeves**. The wrap creates a low, plunging V neckline that leads to a contrasting tied belt that defines the waistline. The stylized tulip print achieves a **contemporary feel** with its expansive use of background color.

This relaxed pinafore wrap is constructed in a woven tartan cotton. The bodice is cut on the bias, and excess fabric is softly pleated into the shoulder seam and the armhole facing. The **additional fabric** is wrapped across the waist and extended in a loop before returning. The skirt is **pleated** at the hip into a deep yoke from the waist seam.

Alternative sleeves and neckline: Elbow-length dolman sleeves with asymmetric revere collar

Fitted-and-flared

The **print design** is integral to the shape, and the print mimics the center-front yoke panel, defines the waist, and edges the hemline. The bodice is darted to fit, disguised within the print, and the deep return side pleats create the **A-line flare** of the skirt.

The dramatic use of **monotone jersey stripe** creates an avant-garde silhouette. The addition of volume and flare to the skirt changes the direction of the stripe, accentuated by the uneven hemline that dips at the side views. The **solid-color, square neckline** provides structure.

The fitted-and-flared day dress is a feminine, pretty, and often flirty style that has a semifitted bodice and waist that gradually flares out from the hip level to create a fuller skirt at the hem. Modified from the A-line shape, the flare of a fitted-and-flared dress is usually evenly distributed around the body, creating a softer and less dramatic silhouette. It flatters the figure, accentuating the waist and is a versatile style that works just as well for special occasions as for day wear.

Often able to absorb the latest prints or garment details, the fitted-and-flared style can be translated easily into most fashion trends and is continually reinvented by designers every season. Style variations are endless, depending on the source of inspiration, with necklines ranging from V, scooped, and horseshoe to those with collars. Lengths are variable, from mini through to knee length and maxi. It is often designed with front button-through fastenings or concealed side zippers, though the options are limitless.

Soft woven fabrics that have drape work best for this style because they maintain the gradual flare of this silhouette, though more structured versions in heavier-weight fabrics will create a defined, strong shape.

KEY CHARACTERISTICS

☑ Semifitted bodice or fitted bodice

☑ Skirt flares out from hip level

☑ Varied lengths, necklines, details

1 Strapless dress to midcalf length in lightweight woven fabric. Cut as a separate bodice and skirt, both on the bias to create stretch and flare.
2 The yellow neck detail and inserts into the bodice add interest to the neat fitted-and-flared dress. 3 A flirty fitted-and-flared strapless sundress with built-in-apron effect in contrast stripe and floral print. 4 The heart-shaped neckline that

forms a wrap opening reinforces the pretty and feminine shape of the fitted waist and flared skirt.
5 An exaggerated shoulder detail sits on top of a traditional set-in sleeve and extends past the natural shoulder line, forming a grown-on stand collar at the back and leaving the front neckline exposed. 6 Cute, fitted-and-flared dress layered over petticoats. A sash emphasizes the waistband

and establishes the 1950s silhouette. 7 The bodice design gives the impression of a strapless dress but remains appropriate for day wear when combined with the shirting neck feature.
8 The complex embroidery and the shapes within the pattern have been placed to define the fitted bust, the waist, and the flare of the skirt.

Body conscious

The body-conscious day dress represents female strength and power. This potent style defines body contours, often creating an hourglass figure and making the most of the bustline, waist, and hips. Its pedigree is in the long, lean, sheath-like silhouettes that skimmed the contours of the body in the 1950s, where complicated construction produced the appearance of simplicity. The contemporary body-conscious dress also cleverly incorporates fit and shaping in style lines and paneling that flatter the figure, concealing curves where they are not needed and accentuating those that are. Fabrics are usually medium- to heavyweight structured woven and often have an elastic content to help achieve a perfect fit and comfort. Style lines and paneling can be highlighted with contrast-color piping to create a sportier vibe and are often color blocked for a more youthful feel.

An empowering style, bringing confidence to the wearer, the versatility of the body-conscious day dress makes it an ideal choice for office wear in black, grays, and more muted tones, as personified by the much-imitated Galaxy dress by Roland Mouret in 2005. The very fitted silhouette defines this style, though the neckline, sleeve styles, and skirt lengths can vary depending on the design influence. Wide, open square necklines exposing the chest area work well, with short and capped-length sleeves and interestingly cut sleeve heads to soften the overall look. Lengths work best at around knee length, either finishing slightly above or below.

The figure-hugging dress to the ankle gives an elongated **column appearance** with a split up the center front to thigh. The front panel has a separate piece that is stitched to side seams after it has been twisted, to form a **draped effect** that flatters the stomach area.

Body-hugging sheath dress. A side slit allows for ease of movement and reveals a **show of leg.** The diagonal white abstract print breaks up the column of black. A **cutout insert** strategically integrated into the print, with set-in power mesh, shows a flash of body.

KEY CHARACTERISTICS

- ☑ Fitted, hourglass silhouette
- ☑ Style lines and paneling that flatter the figure
- ☑ Woven fabric with stretch combinations

1 Cutout, raglan-shaped armholes and a round neckline create a sporty feel. Curved dart shaping from armhole to waistband create style lines that emphasize the contours of the bodice. 2 Body-contouring panels are trimmed with neon yellow. Curved seams that extend from front to back panels avoid the need for side seaming. 3 Contrast color fabrics combined with a mesh print define the panels and trims within this body-conscious minidress. 4 A plain-black shift-shape dress is enhanced with black-and-white and rainbow body-conscious style lines. 5 Leather piping trims the shoulder, the armhole, and the bodice seam, which mirrors the boatneck. 6 Strips of tie-dyed fabric run horizontally around the body, fixed by vertical knitted loops that continue to form a halter neck and shoulder straps. 7 Excess fabric is draped and gathered into the seams of the skirt to create a ruching effect. The soft gathers are contrasted by angular points that overlap the shoulder. 8 Paneled sections emphasize the curves of the body. The print reinforces the style lines and create a visual play with the lacing at the shoulders and thigh.

SHIFT DRESS

The shift dress is a versatile wardrobe staple, with universal appeal that transcends all seasons. Androgynous and ageless, the shift can be styled up or down for casual and evening wear, adapting easily from office to party.

White shift dress with short, set-in sleeves and V neck. The printed, graphic image of a sundress with a chevron stripe caricatures the body, giving the illusion of a slimmer silhouette.

In context

The shift can be sophisticated and elegant, as exemplified by this white linen tunic and underskirt by Givenchy, worn by Audrey Hepburn.

The shape of the shift dress allows for freedom of movement, making it easy to "shift" around in. However, the term also signifies a shift in culture and attitude, reflected in the radical changes in fashion in the 1920s, when the emancipation of women demanded a more flexible style of clothing. The 1920s flapper or Charleston dresses evolved through the revolutionary designs of Coco Chanel. The shift style became popular with American youth culture in the 1950s, then translated into the sack dress shown in Cristóbal Balenciaga and Hubert de Givenchy's 1957 Paris collections. In the 1960s, reflecting the age of space travel, new technology, and the sexual revolution, the shift was popularized by Mary Quant, Pierre Cardin, and André Courrèges. Icons such as Jackie Onassis, Audrey Hepburn, Twiggy, and Jean Shrimpton have famously worn the shift.

The mood of the photograph, the setting, and the fashion are all stereotypically "swinging sixties." Young women wanted to emphasize their youthful exuberance, not look like their mothers. These shift dresses, in bright bold colors and graphics, are shapeless, creating a girlish figure with a flat chest and no hips.

Design considerations

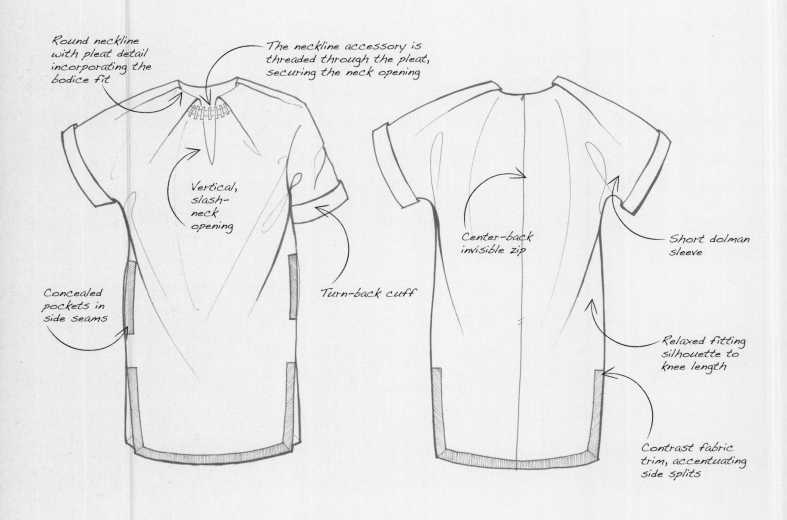

Round neckline with pleat detail incorporating the bodice fit

The neckline accessory is threaded through the pleat, securing the neck opening

Vertical, slash-neck opening

Concealed pockets in side seams

Turn-back cuff

Center-back invisible zip

Short dolman sleeve

Relaxed fitting silhouette to knee length

Contrast fabric trim, accentuating side splits

Versatility The timeless silhouette is extremely versatile. It can be adapted to fit a variety of shapes and sizes and is suitable for all ages. The easy-to-wear attributes of the shift dress make it an ideal garment for casual wear. The shift can transcend day into evening, can be dressed up or down, and is an ideal blank canvas for accessorizing or for showing off large and colorful print stories.

Silhouette Its loose and easy cut allows the shift dress to hang from the shoulders, though it can be adapted to allow for back and front yokes. The silhouette can be straight or A-line, permitting ease of movement. There is minimal or no waist definition, with the dress often concealing the shape of the body. If sleeveless, the loose shape can be worn over a sweater or T-shirt.

Length Usually sits above the knee, with variations at knee length or below. The mini length epitomizes the shift-dress style.

Sleeves Sleeveless or short sleeved and rarely below three-quarter length. Armholes offer design variations from set-in to raglan, and sleeve heads also provide scope for styling possibilities.

Neckline Typically a high round neck or boatneck, though neckline variations, such as V, can be considered. Assorted collars, such as a Peter Pan or Nehru, can also be applied.

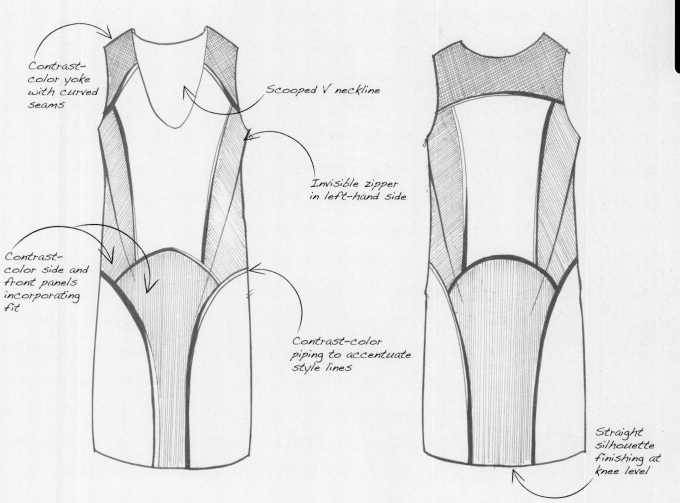

Contrast-color yoke with curved seams

Scooped V neckline

Invisible zipper in left-hand side

Contrast-color side and front panels incorporating fit

Contrast-color piping to accentuate style lines

Straight silhouette finishing at knee level

Fastenings Depending on the design of the shift, openings and fastenings can include side, center-back, and front zippers, or alternatives such as buttons or popper-stud fastenings.

Darts and seams The shift normally requires fit around the bust in the form of darts, which can be manipulated to form style lines. The dress also has side seams, unless design considerations dictate otherwise.

Fabric Fabric choices are key to this style. The shift works best with a structured woven, heavyweight jersey or stretch woven fabric in order to stand away from the body. The fabric consideration can often dictate the usage of the dress; for example, day wear/work wear or occasion/evening wear. The simplicity and versatility of the shift, however, can often transcend categorization.

Lining The shift can be lined or unlined depending on the choice of fabric, occasion, and season.

Details Historically, the shift is plain, to conform to its work wear origins, though design details and functionality considerations, such as concealed or patch pockets, can be applied.

Shift

The shift dress signifies youth culture; however, because its style flatters a range of figure types, it has been adapted and worn by women of all ages.

Choice of fabric can dramatically affect the look. Plain black or white fabric can provide a sophisticated canvas to dress with accessories. In contrast, the simple shape is an ideal background to show off vibrant, colorful prints.

The easy cut allows the shift dress to hang loose with little waist definition, designed to conceal feminine contours yet expose legs and arms. Traditionally simple, short, and above the knee, it can be sleeveless or short sleeved, often sporting a high neckline or typical boat-neck collar. Various modifications to length can reinvent the youthful aesthetic to give a more sophisticated, grown-up appeal. The bust is usually fitted with darts, and the skirt is either straight or A-line, with shoulder and side seams.

For formal day wear the androgynous shift is an ideal substitute for the masculine trouser suit, worn under a jacket for power dressing. The dress can be worn straight from the office to evening events and restyled for a more glamorous and feminine vibe.

A classic sleeveless shift in a large tweed with contrast **Peter Pan collar**. **Fabric roses** are applied to form a deep textured hem.

The **column effect** of this monochrome dress is accentuated by the black-and-white striping running **horizontally** around the bodice. The binding on the neck and armholes also runs down the side seam and matches the dimension of the stripe.

KEY CHARACTERISTICS

- ☑ Fitted bust
- ☑ Little waist definition, skimming the body
- ☑ Straight skirt above or to the knee level
- ☑ Sleeveless or short sleeved

1 Contrast fabric and color blocking give the suggestion of a pinafore style. **2** The dress is pleated to the yoke, controlling the fullness above the bustline, then tapers to the short hemline. The bold print, square neckline, and three-quarter-length sleeve create a 1960s aesthetic. **3** The metallic sheen of the silver fabric and interesting asymmetrical keyhole cutout add glamour to an otherwise simple dress. **4** Horizontal contrast panels of floral cotton and chintz brocaded prints set against nude seersucker give a ribboned bandeau effect. The placement of the bands is designed to edge the hemline and cuffs and to define the yoke and bustline. **5** Geometric vertical and horizontal color blocking gives definition to the shift and the illusion of a dropped waistline. **6** Straight vertical and horizontal asymmetrical panels juxtapose with the organic curves of the black-and-gray tonal brocaded print. **7** Studs are used to control the pleating on the neckline and to reinforce and define the strong, curved, dropped shoulder line. **8** Contrast matte and shine add interest to a simple yet strong shape. Laser-cut edging and minimal detailing create a sharp look.

Shift (continued)

> Short and sleeveless red dress with an abstract print. The styling emphasis is on the neckline, where a bias-cut, **self-fabric scarf tie** knots around the neck and drapes down the center front. The abstract diagonal shards of the print work with the **bias of the cut**.

Grecian styling is created using **two different fabric layers**. The body-conscious underlayer forms the foundation for the shift, which is established by the bias cutting of the second layer of soft fabric draping as a **cowl at the front**. The cowl is attached to the raglan-shaped neckline, which defines the straps of the sleeveless yoke.

Evoking 1950s styling, this sophisticated shift has a grown-on **funnel collar** and short set-in sleeves. The simplicity of the uncluttered shape is a perfect blank canvas for the bold jewelry-motif print, designed with a **strategic border** running around the hemline.

Alternative sleeves: Short puff sleeves, gathered into fixed bands

The rounded front panel **crosses and intertwines** with the rounded neckline then curves to the underarm. This is mirrored in the **curved hemline** that scoops to the side seams toward the hipline. The full sleeves softly gather to the cuff and again at the armhole shoulder.

Alternative neckline and sleeves: Funnel neck and raglan short sleeves

The bold, photographic, enlarged floral print on a **semitransparent fabric** is the main feature of this simple shift. The cuffs of full sleeves are gathered into a binding that is also used to edge the neckline. One sleeve is left unprinted to give an **asymmetrical twist** to the story.

1 Organdy layers are used to create a color-blocked, geometric, large placement pattern. The shapes are defined by a combination of French seams, decorative stitching, and bindings. 2 Soft suede and black leather panels contrast in color and texture. The inserted V yoke panel is mirrored by the hemline. 3 A twist on a simple shift with deep, asymmetrically placed double pockets on the left hip. 4 Diagonal panels in contrast fabric, with a drop shoulder and deep, round neck, are designed to mimic a separate garment. 5 The placement of the bold pattern emphasizes the cut of the dress. The kangaroo pocket forms an envelope shape and places focus at the front of the dress. 6 A beautifully understated shift dress that allows the detailing of the finish to become the focal point. The bound neckline curves through to the dropped armhole that translates into a capped sleeve. 7 The diagonal of the raglan armhole continues into the neckline, which enables a green yoke to be inserted for contrasting interest. 8 This archetypal, uncomplicated shift shape enhances the heavily bead-encrusted and embroidered fabric.

Shift (continued)

In contrast navy and white, this shift has **nautical references,** reinforced with a boatneck. Falling just above knee level, the design emphasis is placed on the front **placket opening** at the hemline in contrast navy-with-white topstitching. The navy capped sleeves, edged with a deep white binding, echo the theme of straight and curved shapes.

The large mirror-image **placement print** with heraldic references sits on an ombré background that fades to the hemline. Elbow-length sleeves have inverted pleats to cuff and set-in armholes that help to reinforce the symmetry of the print. The simple square neckline, cuffs, and hemline emphasize the **uncomplicated cut** and give prominence to the print.

Monochrome blocked panels give **architectural influence** to a shape that has clean, formal lines. The lack of symmetry is reinforced in the side-split front. The **decorative seaming** incorporates darts and shaping and cleverly conceals the pocket openings. The asymmetrical color blocking on one sleeve distorts the balance of the dress.

Shift (continued)

The fabrication of the dress is **layered and sculpted** to define the suggestion of body contours, and it incorporates shaping and style lines without compromising the traditional shift silhouette. Laser cutting and bonding—cleverly forming and stitching together contours—connect vertices with flat, triangulated, and curved shapes, which almost create a **three-dimensional surface** and give the impression of articulated joints.

Contrasting fabrics are used to distinguish the yoke panel of this simple shift. The bust suppression has been incorporated into the seam and the grown-on stand collar and capped sleeves keep additional seams and **style lines to a minimum.**

Oversized shift dress with a wide **dropped shoulder** and deep armhole that can be belted through the front to create waist definition. The scale of the dress provides a **large canvas** to showcase the dynamic placement print. Contributing to the caftan-like style of the dress, the back hangs loose to create volume.

1 Placement of the print is completely mirrored to create perfect symmetry. The padded shoulders give definition to an otherwise simple silhouette. **2** A chic sleeveless shift with black and white contrast accentuating the cut. The bust suppression is disguised within the bib-front paneling. **3** Cream-and-black contrast blocking cuts the dress at the waistline. Pattern is created by bold graphic black paneling down the front bib. **4** The lace bib yoke trims the silk satin shift dress. Full rounded sleeves gathered at the cuff and sleeve head help create a soft cocoon silhouette. **5** Crew-neck felted-knit raglan-sleeved mini-length shift. The softness of the fabric and the rounded silhouette counterbalance the geometry of the asymmetric pattern. **6** The simple shape is a perfect canvas for displaying the painterly, geometric print that graduates in tone toward the hemline. **7** Short-sleeved shift dress in Aertex fabric creating a sportswear feel. **8** The graphic, color-blocked center-front panel of this shift is softened by the lighter side panels. With its wide boatneck and elbow-length split sleeves, this simple shape achieves a feminine feel.

1 Knee-length shift dress with monochromatic tessellated shapes patchworked to give a dynamic pattern with a three-dimensional effect. 2 A simple shift with a patch pocket—perfect for accessorizing. 3 The placement of the geometric print creates borders at the hemline and gives the illusion of side panels. Interest is focused on the bodice, where the zigzag seam is accentuated with embellishment. 4 An enlarged placement print of botanical florals is the centerpiece of the front panel of the dress. The contrasting white deep shoulder straps mimic a pinafore style. 5 The pared-down, clean simplicity of the white dress is interrupted by a contrast bib-fronted panel, layered from the yoke seam. 6 Simple shift with high round neck, grown-on cap sleeves, and trimmed with gold zip-fastened pocket openings at hip level. 7 The matte wool skirt contrasts with the sheen of the leather drop-waisted bodice, creating a pared-down aesthetic. 8 Generously cut gathered sleeves and deep side pockets accentuate the curve of the silhouette of this pretty minidress.

9

10

11

12

13

14

15

16

9 Geometric patterns and different densities of tone and color are created through multilayering of organdy, leaving some single layers for transparency. **10** Almost clashing two garments, the right- and left-hand sides differ in fabric, color, and proportion. The staggered geometric paneling tapers in steps toward the shoulder and drops lower at the hemline. **11** This shift is traditional in styling, made in a textured stone linen for a simple aesthetic. **12** The asymmetrical styling is created by contrasting panels of color and mixing different weights and textures of cloth. **13** The subtle double layering of white fabric implies an overalls shape that integrates with the neck facing and is inserted behind the yoke panel. **14** A panel of contrasting fabric inserted down the center front, intersecting with jagged seams that are echoed at the hemline, gives the impression of an apron with a bib. **15** Heavy duchess satin gives weight to this shift, which is divided by a dropped waist. The neckline is edged with metallic binding. **16** Featuring a round neck and drop shoulder with short, wide sleeves, the generous silhouette is gathered at the hemline with a drawstring.

A-line

The A-line shift shape is easily recognized. The silhouette is flared from a narrow shoulder line to the hemline, with the increase in dimensions occurring at the side seams, rather than distributed equally around the circumference as seen in the trapeze shift dress. Courrèges defined the A-line dress in the 1960s as the triangular shape that we associate with the term, which was widely used as a silhouette by Mary Quant. The style represents the 1960s ideology of space age, and can be seen in a number of sci-fi movies of the time, characterized as the dress of the future.

The shape is flattering and easy to wear for a number of body shapes since it doesn't hug but skims the body. It works well with fabric that has a medium- to heavyweight structure and is ideal for heavier jersey or wovens. The simplicity and geometry of the style make it ideal for minimal use of color, or strong, bold geometrics.

The dress works best with a simple collarless neckline and sleeveless armholes cut as rounded or scooped, or accentuating the geometry as a V or a square cut. Variations and subversions with collars and sleeves can be added to create diversity. Fastenings and trims, such as pockets, zippers, or buttons, can be used to break up the blank canvas of the simple shape. It is traditionally worn above the knee to mini length.

KEY CHARACTERISTICS

- ☑ **Triangular or A shape:** Narrow shoulder line, wide hemline
- ☑ **Flared silhouette increasing at side seams**
- ☑ **Knee to mini length**

Microgeometric-patterned, **jacquard**, sleeveless shift with contrast-fabric center placket, collar, and underbust band. The white **contrasting color** and scalloped edge of the collar feminizes this traditionally menswear jacquard pattern.

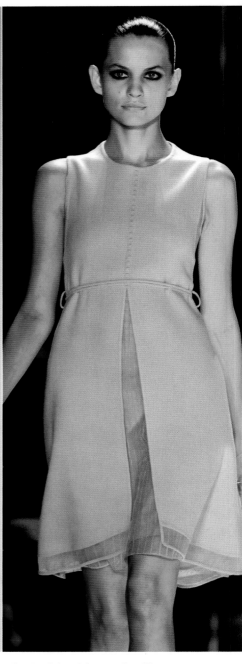

The simplicity of the round neckline and deep armholes creates a sophisticated feel. The A-line of the skirt from **empire-line** seam is helped by the deep inverted box pleat at center front. The contrast of **transparent fabric** at the hemline and center insert creates interest.

1 Printed, round-neck, mini-length A-line shift with contrast fabric full sleeves that are gathered into the sleeve head. The long sleeves have a deep shirred cuff. **2** Dropped-shoulder, mini-length shift with center-front inverted box pleat that creates fullness in the skirt. The short sleeves are heavily gathered and flared. **3** Checks, stripes, and color blocking define the bodice and create a deep border at the hemline. The A-line shift is created from back and front panels of heat-set pleating that excludes the need for bust suppression.

4 A 1960s-inspired shift, with an oversized Peter-Pan collar, detailed bodice trim, and button front. **5** Simple, 1960s mini-length A-line shift with a slightly wide round neckline. The full-length set-in sleeves have buttoned shirt cuffs. **6** The graphic impact of the main dress is complemented by the solid-color collar and deep hem band. **7** This simple shape has a slightly flared hem and a large self-fabric bow placed diagonally across the chest at the neckline. **8** Sleeveless mini-length shift with contrast piping that accentuates the A-line shape and pocket placement. Shoulder piping directs the eye to the center-front corsage.

1 An oversized-check shift dress with short puffed sleeves. The wide round neck, hem, and underbust band have been cut on the bias to contrast the direction of the check. 2 This exaggerated, structured A-line silhouette combines contrasting fabrics of solid and transparent to create design interest on the bodice and hem. 3 Mini-length, structured shift dress with a wide scooped neckline and narrow sleeveless shoulders. Double rows of solid black trim run along the underbust seam and hem. 4 Sleeveless dress with a grown-on stand-funnel neck. Jet pockets are trimmed with black binding, and black piping runs down each side of center front and along the hemline. 5 The deep V-shaped neck yoke and vertical style lines on the bodice draw the eye to the box-pleated skirt. The horizontal waistband accentuates the dropped waist. 6 The mix of fabrics with contrasting sleeves and curved neckline is designed to mimic a pinafore dress. 7 The lace, drop-waisted bodice suggests a two-piece, but a pleated skirt is attached and layered to create a day dress. 8 A simple A-line shape incorporates the shaping into the bodice panel.

< Quintessential 1960s-inspired sleeveless shift. The wide neckline and armholes are highlighted with a **contrast binding** that frames the uncomplicated A-line silhouette. The strong style lines and **large pocket details** are also emphasized by the binding.

Exaggerated **short puffed sleeves are** gathered at the cuff and pleated into the armhole to create maximum volume. The hot pink reinforces the **feminine aesthetic**. The side seam pockets help to define the trapezoid shape.

Alternative neckline and sleeves: V neckline with jabot frill and double-layer, fluted sleeves

A-Line (continued)

1920s-inspired shift with dropped waist, featuring **color-blocked, rectangular, diagonal-stitched,** and appliquéd fabrics on the bodice with a square neckline and short capped sleeves that continue the geometric theme. The layered skirt again reinforces the **flapper inspiration.**

The **cutwork and appliquéd** large-scale pattern cleverly creates a **scalloped edge** and defines the profile of the neckline, capped sleeves, and the hemline. **Contrast fabrics** and stitching help to outline the pretty, floral-inspired motifs.

The combination of **vertical and horizontal lines** is the distinctive feature of the sleeveless trapeze dress in a black and white geometric textured fabric with a **shirt collar** and placket in contrast black. The yoke and top of the patched pocket are edged with the black fabric, and the dress is cut short to reveal the black underskirt.

1 A-line sleeveless dress with a no frills aesthetic. The center-front opening has invisible fastenings. Deep inset pockets, cut diagonally, are attached at the side seam. 2 Enlarged broderie anglaise A-line shift dress in sugary pastels. The oversized embroidered collar contrasts with the plain white organdy yoke and sleeves. 3 Emphasis is placed on the deep plunge V neck, cut to reveal a shaped, curved undercorset. Volume is created in the exaggerated A-line skirt. 4 The fabric has been heat set in fine pleats to create movement and give structure to the simple boatneck and A-line silhouette. 5 The angles created by the stand shawl collar inserted into the square neckline and the diagonal of the capped sleeve counterbalance the A-shaped skirt. 6 The A-line shape is created partly on the bias, with diagonal panels bonded together using needle-punched felting. 7 The bejeweled V neckline creates a point at the center of the waistline. The points of the folded origami panels also join at center front, creating an envelope effect. 8 Transparent black layers of organdy create a two-tiered A-line effect. The black is punctuated by the deep V neckline.

A-Line (continued)

The dress is simple, with the focus on the **hemline and cuff.** The black lining is visible where the back of the dress is longer than the front, and in the binding at the front hemline. Long set-in sleeves, with a little fullness at the head on a slightly dropped shoulder line, taper to the petal-style wrap cuff, also exposing a **black lining**.

The perfect canvas for a bold **1970s-inspired print,** this archetypal trapeze minidress has a number of **traditional features. With** a wide funnel neck and set-in three-quarter-length sleeves with a turned-back cuff, the dress is also embellished with reflective silver disks that decorate the front panel and collar.

Black and white contrast panels give a modern feel, while the satin silk fabric is more formal, allowing the dress to **transcend day to evening. The** round neckline and armhole suggest a prim aesthetic, but the **V insert** at the bustline offers a glimpse of cleavage and adds an element of sensuality.

Alternative neckline and sleeves: Slash neckline with extended shoulder seam and wide cap sleeves

The wide, **deep V neck** plunges at the bust and is cut wide toward the armhole, almost giving a strap effect at the shoulder, with the front panel designed to give the illusion of a **slimmer silhouette.**

< The trapeze is combined with the shirtdress, evidenced in the hemline with a **shirttail** effect. This also creates the suggestion of layered garments, where the hemline dips lower at the back to reveal the **black lining.** The black also borders the front hemline and the armhole.

Trapeze

In contrast to the basic shift dress, where the shaping is added to the side seams to create an A-line shape, the flare of the trapeze shift is increased throughout the dress by dividing, slashing, opening, and spreading, therefore enhancing the width of the hemline of the front and back pattern pieces to create volume. Like the A-line shift, the trapeze is narrow at the shoulder and flares out toward the hem and does not define the waistline. The volume in the dress creates drape and allows the hemline to swing freely. Contemporary versions can be customized with belts and gathered to create a soft, blouson look.

The term *trapeze* is taken from the geometric shape known as the trapezoid. The trapeze shape is often favored in maternity and children's dresses with baby-doll dresses a derivation of this shape. The trapeze shape became a major fashion trend after the launch of Yves Saint Laurent's 1958 collection for Dior, and was a distinctive contrast to Dior's previous heavily structured New Look garments. The trapeze shape found its way into mainstream fashion in the 1960s with the shorter minidresses of Mary Quant and has remained a core garment silhouette ever since.

A long-sleeve, jersey, turtle-neck trapeze shift with a very wide skirt hem. The **weight and drape** of the fabric increases the movement and impact of this style. This pattern has been slashed from the hem to the bust and **fullness added**, keeping the shoulder and cross-chest area fitted to maintain a flattering shape.

A formal, sleeveless wool shift that finishes just above the knee. The center-front panel is grown-on at the neckline to create an unusual **semifunnel shape**. Fullness has been added on the dress panels from below the bustline, gradually increasing to the hem to create the trapeze shape.

KEY CHARACTERISTICS

- ☑ Trapezoid shape: Narrow shoulder line, very wide hemline
- ☑ Flared increase in silhouette throughout dress to create volume
- ☑ Unstructured look without waist definition and free hemline

1 A casual trapeze with long sleeves that are full and flared at the hem, reflecting the flare of the dress hem. 2 A bold style, maximizing graphic impact with opposing-direction black and white stripes. The fluidity of the solid-color fabric helps to balance the strong shoulder line. 3 This sunray-pleated silk trapeze, with short balloon sleeve and an open slotted neckline, is a feminine interpretation of the shift style. 4 This archetypal trapeze has a young, retro feel. The high round neck balances the flirty short hemline and small cap sleeve. 5 An unusual trapeze shift, with a wide stand collar, cape-effect sleeves, and a modern self-fabric bow. The cape sleeves are left loose, wrapping around the arm into a center-front yoke. Flare has been created in the skirt from below the yoke seam. 6 The printed geometric border adds interest to this simple knee-length trapeze. The gathered round neckline is reflected in the cuffs. 7 Florals and tartans in a wool fabric are mixed to create a border print. 8 The solid, wide straps of this dress help to highlight the trapeze shape. The fitted bodice is a stark contrast to the full midthigh-length skirt.

Trapeze (continued)

> Abstraction of shape and disproportionate cutting subvert the notion of the trapeze. Circular cutting is implemented, wrapping the body, mixing gathered **tiered borders** of varying depth that attach on top and under the main dress panel.

Maximum fullness is created with the combination of **circular cutting** and yards of lightweight silk habotai, which enable **fluidity of movement.** The manipulation of placement prints, derived from postage stamps, adds a touch of **humor.**

Blue **leather** cut in panels integrate the shaping to create a distinctive trapeze silhouette. The **side curved vent openings** have a contrast orange gusset, adding to the sporty feel.

Alternative neckline and sleeves: Keyhole neckline and low, raglan cap sleeves

The high round neck and slightly extended, sleeveless shoulders of this trapeze create an informal balance with the **diagonal dissecting paneling** and asymmetric hemline. The contrasting sheer-and-matte stripe chiffon fabric accentuates the diagonal style lines, creating a delicate **cobweb-like effect** that complements the full, uneven hem.

The trapeze shape is accentuated by the **horizontal panel** above the bust and the **braided fabric** detail that expands in width toward the hem. The braided fabric straps at the shoulder and the fitted knit sleeves only serve to emphasize the voluminous hem.

Tent

The tent dress has similarities with the A-line and trapeze shift dresses, but is recognizable for having greater volume. The silhouette can also be called a pyramid flare. The tent flares out from the chest and envelops the whole body, achieving a smock effect. This is a difficult style to wear for women with large busts, since these can push the dress farther away from the body, causing it to resemble maternity wear; however, it can be worn with a skinny belt to cinch the waistline. The dress can incorporate gathered tiers, creating even more fullness. Strategically placed pleats or sunray pleats are a popular feature.

Fabric choices are generally lightweight, to accentuate the movement of the dress. Large prints work well and plain colors offer scope for costume jewelry. The tent has potential for voluminous asymmetrical shapes and is favored by avant-garde designers who want to envelop rather than accentuate the body. This is an ideal shape for hot weather, since it doesn't stick to the body.

The dress can be styled with or without sleeves, and although an ideal shape for spring/summer, it can work well for winter, with solid pantyhose or leggings. The length works best to the knee or several inches above it. Too short and the dress would be classified as a baby-doll. The tent also works well as maxi length, falling into the realms of the caftan.

Voluminous layers of black transparent-over-solid fabrics shroud the body, disguising the contours. Flesh-colored power mesh set into four rows of **V-shaped banding** stripe through the negative space of the neckline, keeping the shoulders of the dress from falling.

Circular cutting rounds the short hemline of the caftan shape. The painterly black and white tribal print is engineered around the body, defining and mocking a yoke and creating borders around the hemline and cuffs. The soft fabric and volume combine to create **movement and drape**.

KEY CHARACTERISTICS

- ☑ Tent shape: Narrow shoulder line, extremely voluminous hemline
- ☑ Envelops the body
- ☑ Lightweight fabric

1 The body is enveloped in this knee-length dress cut with magyar sleeves. Shoulder padding creates a straight, strong shoulder line. **2** Color-blocked stripes emphasize the geometric cut. Chiffon pleating softens the hard lines. The dress is fixed at the waistline, giving some definition to the shape. **3** With drop shoulders and wide set-in sleeves, volume is added to the already overblown cocoon-like shape. **4** Floor-length dress with an austere feel and a robe-like quality, broken by the deep V neckline. **5** A printed panel at the front of the dress suggests a slim column silhouette. This is contradicted by pleated chiffon side panels flaring at the hemline, making a tent-like shape. **6** Folded handkerchief triangular shapes are created from rectangular panels to create sleeves and armholes integrated into front and back panels of the dress. **7** Enveloping the body, abstract pleated shapes create asymmetrical pattern pieces. Edged with strapping, the dress has a deconstructed look. **8** Circular cutting is evident, and gathering into the bodice creates a trapeze silhouette, but turning back on itself, the hemline transforms into a tulip shape.

Tent (continued)

The oversized shapes are created by cutting rectangular pieces of contrasting silk satin, which are **folded and seamed** into corners and joined at the center front and back. The striped fabric gives an indication of the **grain** and helps to explain how the pieces have been cut. The excess fabric is allowed to form the drape at the front, adding to the volume of the dress.

Many features of the dress suggest a **caftan shape**, such as the round neckline split at the bodice, and the volume and length. The shapes, however, are more rounded, and circular cutting, rather than rectangular shaping, is evident. The overall aesthetic is **cocoon-like**, particularly apparent at the armholes and the cape effect at the back.

The dress is cut with greater volume at the left-hand side, which **pleats** at the shoulder, creating drape at one side. The side of the dress seemingly folds into the hemline to give the impression of a **continuous** piece of fabric.

1 Abstract shapes are achieved through the crossover wrapping effect, where two halves of different-shaped garments seemingly collide.
2 Colored stripes in varying proportions punctuate the oversized tent shape. The horizontal band at the waist gives a slimming effect. 3 Silk is gathered into a contrasting knitted-rib panel, which divides the dress at the bodice to give a blouson effect. The deep V neckline and the side split reveal the body. 4 Lightweight sunray-pleated chiffon fabric is held in place with a brass neckpiece, then cascades down the body. 5 Circular shapes at front and back are joined at the top of the sleeve to create a caftan shape. The deep slashed neckline is grown on from the front panel. 6 Simple oversized dress in wool and linen mix. The neck and opening are trimmed with a black leather binding, which is also used for the lacing down the front. 7 Generously proportioned shift with turned-back caftan sleeves, button-through side panel, and shoulder seam. 8 Oversized tent dress with wide sleeves that are pleated into the dropped shoulder, creating a curved silhouette.

Tunic

The tunic shift dress is usually worn over layers of other garments such as leggings, thick pantyhose, a sweater, or a shirt. Simple in style, reaching from the shoulders to a length somewhere between the thighs and the ankles, it is based on an Ancient Roman garment worn by both men and women. A tunic describes military and ecclesiastical garments, and the term is often used to define protective garments that are worn over other clothes. The tunic dress is generally sleeveless, if designed to be worn over a T-shirt or a sweater, and may have front, back, or shoulder fastenings. If the dress is cut loose then it can be pulled over the head with no need for fastenings. The neckline needs to accommodate the undergarment, and so a round, scooped, V, or square-cut neckline is an ideal choice.

Variations such as asymmetrical cutting or scalloped edgings to a neckline may also be echoed in the armhole shaping. Zippered or buttoned center or side-front panels with a split hemline can be applied to reveal an underlayer of leggings or thick pantyhose, and statement feature pockets may add to the work-wear aesthetic of the tunic dress.

A slightly oversized, relaxed-fit, sleeveless check shift with a wide round neckline that complements the **front yoke seam**. Finishing at knee length, the dress has a deep **inverted pleat** that starts from the yoke seam and continues to the hem.

A very loose-fit dress, with grown-on shoulder seams that allow the garment to hang from the shoulders. The front neck yoke extends to the armholes, which accentuates the **boxy feel**. The dress has a concealed center-front button placket that develops into a pleat at skirt level to create more fullness to the hem. **Deep pockets** are inserted into the long diagonal bust darts.

KEY CHARACTERISTICS

- ☑ **Derived from ancient military and ecclesiastical clothing**
- ☑ **Designed to be worn over other garments**
- ☑ **Generous, loose fit**
- ☑ **Knee length or shorter**

1 Loose-fitting, sleeveless, ankle-length dress. Piping highlights the neckline and thigh-high side splits. 2 Heavy cotton dress with wide round neck, elbow-length sleeves, self-fabric belt and jet side pockets giving a utilitarian air. 3 This tabard-style shift has a wide boatneck with sheer, contrast-fabric shoulder straps. Sheer fabric side panels are inserted to create fit. Side splits and a deep border hem accentuate the large side pockets. 4 Combining tunic and coatdress styling with a deep V neckline and button-through center-front opening. Large patch pockets and pocket flaps are positioned at the side hips. 5 Rectangular cutting, influenced by the kimono, breaks up the dress into sections of monochromatic print and solid black with colored horizontal stripes accenting the bodice, waist, and hemline. 6 This shift displays traditional shirting references, which include the curved shirttail hem and traditional shirt cuffs. 7 Navy-on-white diagonal panels create a wrapped stole effect. The shapes are defined by contrasting topstitching. 8 Loose-fitting tunic dress with minimal shaping. The wide boatneck gives a deconstructed look.

SHIRTDRESS

The shirtdress is a good fashion basic for building a wardrobe and, because of its potentially simplistic nature, is an ultimate standard to layer with other garments or to mix with accessories. The crossing of boundaries between masculine and feminine allows for versatility of shape and style.

The flat shirt collar and layered shirttails define this dress, placing it firmly in the shirtdress category. The exotic stamp-inspired design has been carefully placed for maximum impact. The sharp crisp cotton lends itself well to the oversized silhouette and large kimono sleeves.

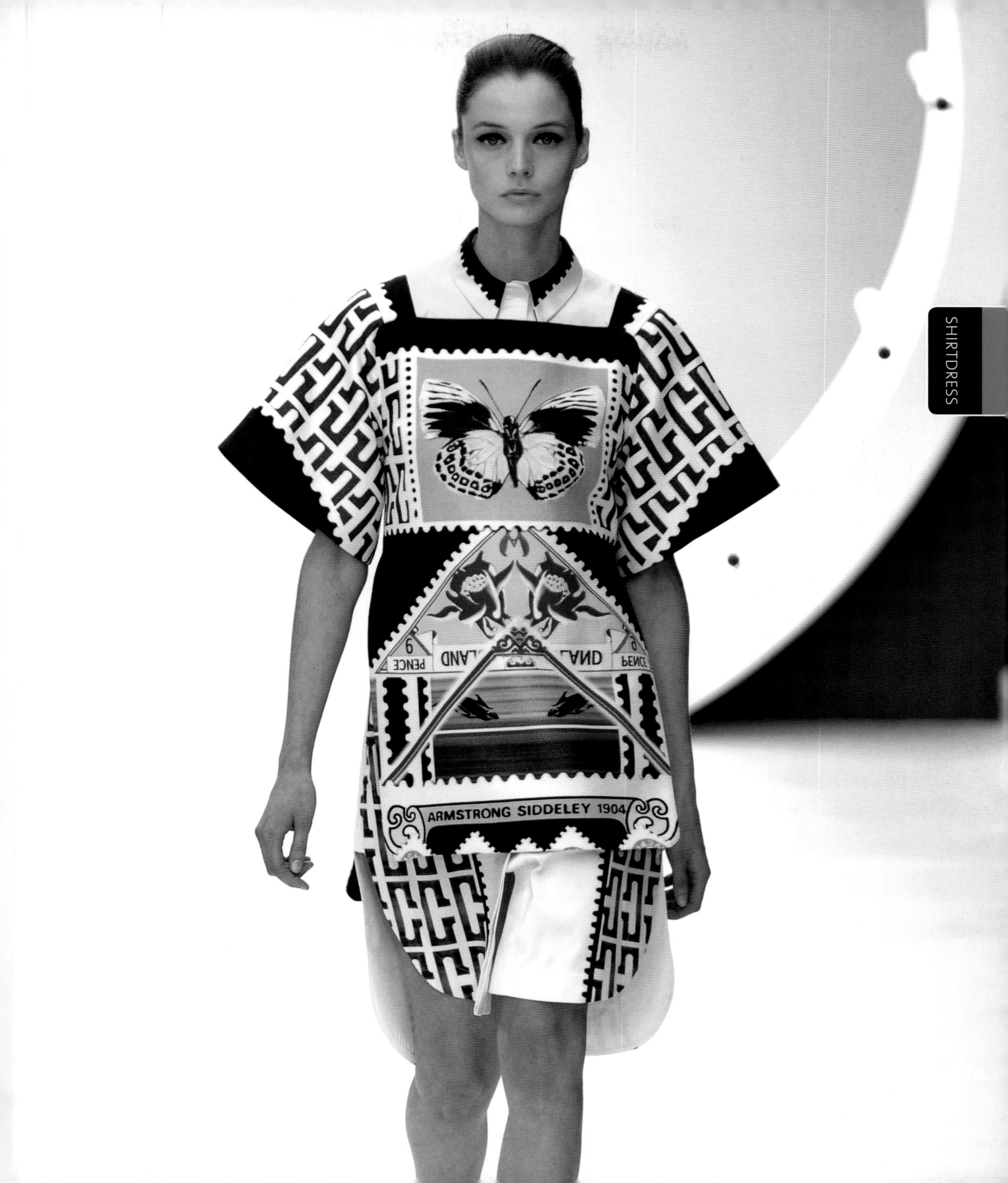
PENCE
LAND
ARMSTRONG SIDDELEY 1904

In context

The iconic 1960s model Twiggy wears a shirtdress with an exaggerated Henley collar and flap pockets. The effect of the shapeless shift on the petite model is one of a child wearing an adult shirt. Youthful exuberance and naiveté matched the era of exploration that so typified the 1960s.

The shirtdress, as the term implies, is derived from a traditional man's shirt, with separate button placket, double-layer back yoke, and collar stand, through to the more formal dress shirt with the winged collar, bib front, and turned-back cuffs and cuff links. The dress gives the impression of a lengthened shirt and can be oversized and worn loose or belted. The dress can also be seamed at the waist, with a separate bodice and skirt, otherwise known as a shirtwaister. The shirtdress can be androgynous and masculine or, by sharp contrast, feminine and pretty, as seen in the shirtwaisters of the 1950s, typically worn by Doris Day.

Dior's post-World War II New Look defined the shirtdress, where the silhouette included very full skirts and a nipped-in waist, and often featured a notched collar and elbow-length sleeves with cuffs. In the 1950s, American popular culture adopted the shirtdress as part of its uniform, and housewives made their version of the housecoat dress respectable. Influences have also been derived from military uniform/safari and work wear, with a revival of the shirtdress in the 1980s.

As women entered the workforce in earnest throughout the 1970s and 1980s, they needed clothes that they could feel comfortable in and would make them look great. This shirtdress by Calvin Klein has a dirndl skirt, sashed waist, and a jacket-like collared neckline that is both sexy and reminiscent of the man's dress shirt it is imitating.

Design considerations

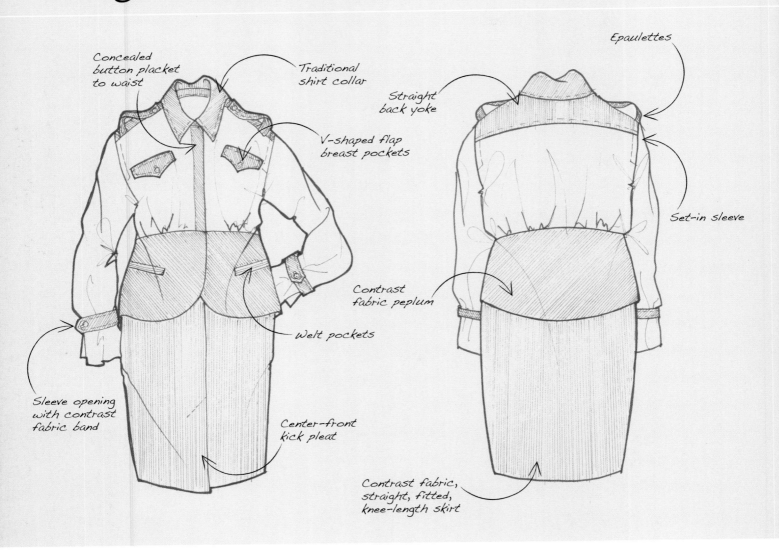

Concealed
button placket
to waist

Traditional
shirt collar

Straight
back yoke

V-shaped flap
breast pockets

Epaulettes

Set-in sleeve

Contrast
fabric peplum

Welt pockets

Sleeve opening
with contrast
fabric band

Center-front
kick pleat

Contrast fabric,
straight, fitted,
knee-length skirt

Silhouette Can be fitted and tailored—designed to fit a formal setting—or loose and casual, like an oversized man's shirt.

Length There are no restrictions on length, though shirttails, side vents, and asymmetrical hemlines are possibilities that emphasize the shirt influences.

Yokes Yokes can differ in size and shape on front and back, offering distinct variation. Whether the dress is influenced by the traditional man's shirt or the formal tuxedo, a bib-front yoke will dramatically alter its aesthetic. Shaped yokes are a common feature of the military, safari, work wear, or western-inspired shirtdress. The dress may be trimmed with shirt-neck collar and placket and buttoned through to the bust, hem, or waist if shirtwaisted.

Collars and cuffs Collars and cuffs define the shirtdress, though collarless granddad styling or a V neck with placket will still suggest shirt influences. A more formal, structured effect will be achieved through the use of a stand collar, whereas a grown-on revers open collar will give a more relaxed feeling. Cultural references may suggest the use of a stand or Nehru or Mao collar, or perhaps a rounded lace-trimmed Peter Pan style.

Sleeves Short sleeved to long sleeved; wide or narrow fit with buttoned cuffs; turn-back cuffs, or no cuffs at all: the choices are endless.

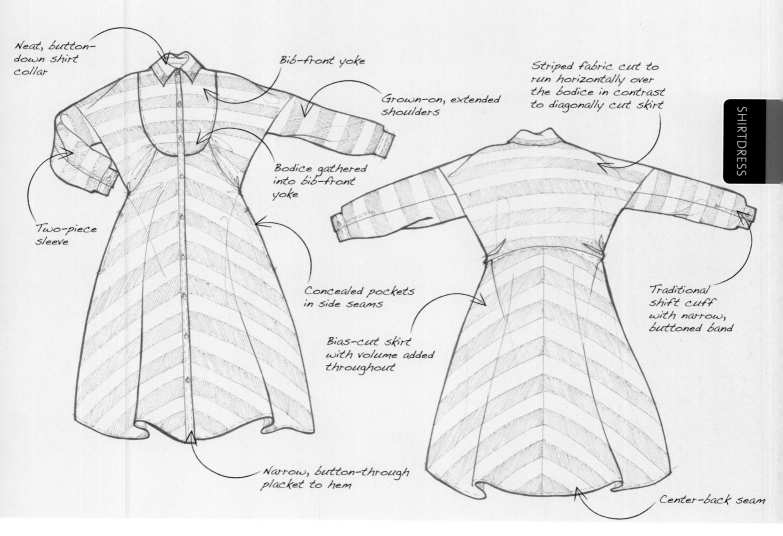

Neat, button-down shirt collar

Bib-front yoke

Grown-on, extended shoulders

Striped fabric cut to run horizontally over the bodice in contrast to diagonally cut skirt

SHIRTDRESS

Two-piece sleeve

Bodice gathered into bib-front yoke

Concealed pockets in side seams

Bias-cut skirt with volume added throughout

Traditional shift cuff with narrow, buttoned band

Narrow, button-through placket to hem

Center-back seam

Fabric The fabric choices are as varied as the style of shirt silhouette. Seasonal changes impact on the weight of fabric, although the shirtdress can be part of a layering system. The choice of heavy-, medium-, and lightweight cotton linens and wools, through to silks and manmade materials, can alter the look and feel of the design. For a more feminine option, gingham or florals are alternatives to checks or denim. Statement prints through to ditsy spots can add a new dimension to the aesthetic.

Embellishments Embellishments can be applied in the form of topstitching, piping, pin tucks, embroidery, lace, frills, or epaulettes. Small logos or embroidered monograms can decorate or label the garment. Functional and decorative buttons with buttonholes or rouleau loops are a distinctive feature. Hardware trims can include cuff links, studs, metal-tipped collars, zippers, snap fastenings, rivets, and rhinestone accents.

Pockets Pockets are a common and distinctive feature of the shirtdress. Concealed pockets at the side seam or oversized varieties just begin to list the endless possibilities. The design of pockets will often define the category of style. Western-style pockets positioned at breast level, or alternative mouth or jet pockets, will be edged with piping and finished with a reinforcing embroidered V.

Shirt

The shirtdress design can derive from numerous sources of inspiration, such as safari, lumberjack, western, regatta, and rugby shirts. They are rooted in tradition, born out of the menswear classic shirt, and can be reworked to provide a versatile, utilitarian, and often simple chic appeal in their classic form, combining utility and elegance.

This classic dress style is usually defined by time-honored design features, such as back yokes and, sometimes, front yokes, depending on the inspiration; double-needle stitching on the side seams and underarm sleeve seam; collars that can set the tone of the style and can range from rounded, button-down, and straight point to wing and Nehru; shirttails topstitched with a rolled hem, often with a gusset in the side seams; and cuffs that can be buttoned or cuff linked.

The shirtdress can be a hard-working basic that you can dress up or down, and is often accessorized with a self-fabric belt, usually tied, not buckled. For formal wear, the collars and cuffs can be cut in contrasting color fabric. Suitable for all climates and occasions, the shirtdress can be made in traditional lightweight woven cotton poplin and broadcloth, or be adapted in silk for evening wear, and wools for fall and winter.

Soft, relaxed, oversized, long-sleeved shirtdress to calf length with **side splits** to the knee and bound edges. The two-piece collar has a classic broad spread and top-button fastening. Other details include a forward shoulder seam and a **square pocket** applied at the left breast.

This dress combines a **trapeze-style** shift with shirt-style collar and front placket opening. The white cotton summer dress has a **sportswear feel** with contrast blue collar and V-shaped patch pocket and short sleeves. The piped front placket is fastened with rouleau and small buttons.

KEY CHARACTERISTICS

- ☑ Traditional men's shirt detailing
- ☑ Sometimes back and front yokes and placket
- ☑ Collars and cuffs
- ☑ Pocket features
- ☑ Run-and-fell seams on side seams and underarm sleeve seam

1   2   3   4

5   6   7   8

1 Drop-waisted shirtdress with box-pleat skirt. The bodice is seamed for fit with a two-piece 1970s-inspired pointed collar. **2** Silk and chiffon shirtdress softly gathered to the waist seam with belt tabs. The stand collar is cut on the bias and ties at the front neckline opening. **3** Contrast color neck stand and center-front placket. Details include front-pleated panels and side-seam pockets. **4** Sleeveless shirtdress with Peter Pan collar. The skirt is attached to a dropped waist and is cut from rectangles that extend the width of the waist measurement, falling as a handkerchief hemline. **5** High-waisted shirtdress with an A-line skirt. Full sleeves are gathered to the sleeve head and to a narrow, buttoned cuff. **6** Equal proportions balance the contrasting collar, cuffs, placket, and inverted V-shaped waistband. The matte dress contrasts with the shine sleeves. **7** Gingham shift dress with transparent sleeves and starched flat collar and cuffs. A wide V neck allows the collar to stand at the shoulder. **8** Fit-and-flare minidress with front placket opening to below bust. The front bodice darts split the shoulder into a keyhole opening.

Shirt (continued)

> Panels of ditsy floral prints are mixed together in this pretty shirtwaisted dress. Fullness is controlled at the bust, hip, and cuffs by a **smocking effect** using dirndl elastic. The large pointed flat collar lays flat against the garment. The front placket is faced with a **contrast print.**

Alternative sleeves: Gathered cap sleeves

A bold hexagonal print with a **vintage feel** is contrasted with a black collar, cuffs, and **patch pockets,** then finished with a black belt and decorative vintage-inspired buckle. The pockets and collar are embellished with lace panels that are in keeping with the retro feel of the dress.

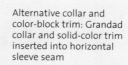

The **slim-line silhouette** of the shirtdress is exaggerated by the floor length, which elongates the body. Worn **unbuttoned to thigh** and again at the deep V neckline to give a sophisticated edge, this is an ideal garment to wear into evening or over separates for a more casual look.

The **lightweight fabric** of the spot print is an ideal choice for the shirtwaisted dress. The skirt is cut on the bias to create **volume and flare** to below the calf. Sharp contrast-color stripes edge the cuff and collar and run down to form the placket of the dress from neck to hem, and are used again to create the tie-belted waist.

Alternative collar and color-block trim: Grandad collar and solid-color trim inserted into horizontal sleeve seam

Crisp white cotton shirtdress with an **irregular cut**. The bodice is shaped diagonally to create two different silhouettes either side to the placket. The right-hand skirt is pleated and gathered into the waist seam on the lower side and forms a sharp A-line from the left side seam. The **asymmetrical hemline** and color blocking on one sleeve and opposite hemline help to create a shirtdress with a split personality.

1 Crisp, oversized boyfriend shirt with traditional attributes, such as two-part stand collar and patched breast pockets. 2 Sundress with a deep armhole and V neck tapering to shoulder straps with a flat shirt-neck collar. Worn layered over a contrasting print as a pinafore. 3 Maxi shirtdress in a floral chintz with contrasting collar and placket to the waist. A self-fabric rouleau cord is threaded through the shoulder, waistband, and hemline. 4 A traditional, button-through, shirt-waisted dress that flares out to the hemline. 5 The brocaded fabric, deep V neck, raglan armhole, and curved-to-pointed hemline suggest an elongated waistcoat. Worn layered over a chiffon blouse to create a pinafore style. 6 The oversized pinstripe and starched white collar are subversions of a traditional man's shirt. Back to front in appearance, the collar forms a boatneck. 7 Sleeveless shirtdress with halter neck to stand collar. The skirt is cut on the circle with excess pleated into the waist seam. The hemline is split at the side seams, forming a classic scoop shirttail. 8 Maxi-length shirtdress with a bold placement print from waist to hem.

Shirt (continued)

Positioned **off-center** on the left-hand side of the dress, the button-through placket is extended, turned back, and held down by buttons and buttonholes. The overall styling is relaxed, with short sleeves and a self-fabric tie belt. The fabric is embroidered with rows of tiny florals that give a **raised-slub effect** to create a dress that can be dressed up or worn casually.

The small, one-piece collar is stitched flat to the neckline with a button-through placket down center front with **numerous small buttons**. The wide waistband sits high below the bustline, falling at hip level. The bodice is gathered into a yoke panel and again at the waist.

Alternative sleeves and waist yoke: Batwing sleeves with V-seam detail reflecting the V-shaped waist yoke

The textured seersucker woven fabric allows for a **structured design.** Much emphasis is placed around the shoulder and neckline with a high but wide V neckline trimmed with a **shawl collar**. Yoke panels at armhole level incorporate two layers of sleeve with a capped sleeve layered over a short sleeve, giving an epaulette effect. The button-through separate placket runs to a dropped-waist seam where the flare of the skirt is controlled by **large box pleats**.

Shirt (continued)

Pretty, vintage-inspired shirtdress with a **bib-front panel** running from neck to hem, giving the impression of a placket opening where the buttons are purely decorative. Pleats run from the center panel around the dress, suggesting a gymslip. Black piping and decorative trim are used to outline the front panel and waist seam and define the **large one-piece collar** sitting flat around the neckline, with black cuffs and a border around the hemline to complete the look.

Sleeveless silk dress with a small button-down collar on a separate stand and a front button-through placket to a **dropped-waist** seam. A mock waistband is tied with a leather lace. Pleats in the skirt are fixed into the waistband and again at the hem, and stitched into the inside facing that binds the hemline and **deep scoop tail** with side splits.

The oversized shirt sports a **granddad collar stand** with a single button fastening at the neck. The center-front placket facing is cut on the bias and opens to below the bust. The crisp cotton check is a perfect summer weight, and with **side openings** and a deep-scooped tail, this is an ideal garment for layering over trousers.

Alternative front fastening: Bib panel with button-through placket and Nehru collar

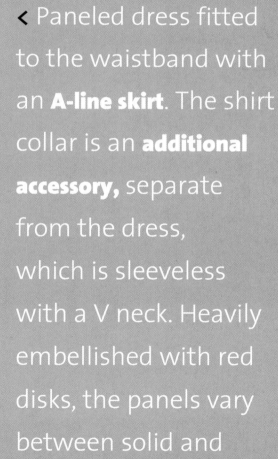

The inserted contrast red fabric **bib-front yoke panel** is the main focus of the dress with a large Peter Pan collar and decorative beads, jewels, and embroidery embellishing the seam. Three-quarter-length sleeves are edged with a cuff to pick up the collar detail. The striking large-scale subverted tartan and warm colors in **fine wool fabric** help to create an ideal dress for fall/winter.

< Paneled dress fitted to the waistband with an **A-line skirt**. The shirt collar is an **additional accessory,** separate from the dress, which is sleeveless with a V neck. Heavily embellished with red disks, the panels vary between solid and transparent.

Uniform/military

Inspiration from a wealth of sources can inform this style, including military, police, work wear, and school uniforms. Uniforms were designed to standardize dress, creating a distinctive garment intended for identification, belonging, and display while providing an air of authority and organization. Decadent and colorful for ceremonial occasions, through to functional and utilitarian for practicality, the looks can vary in aesthetic.

Key shapes are double-breasted with stand collars; single-breasted with large revere collars; shearling collars, Nehru, or Mao collars; fitted waists and full skirts, pencil skirts with back vents; pleated skirts and peplums; and A-line with inverted box pleats, dropped waistlines, or knife pleats.

Design features center around collars, pockets, and buttons, as well as epaulettes, embroidered insignia, badges, and ribbons. Multipockets are a strong theme, often with a mixing of styles and sizes. Reinforced areas, such as quilting and leather patches, will replicate the protection of armor, and self-fabric or leather belts and belt loops can emphasize form and add to the feeling of constraint.

Literal translations into fabrics such as wools, gabardine, cotton twill, and cotton drill are obvious choices, but silks, linens, finer cottons, and manmade fabrics can also accommodate the styling features. Colors such as navy, black, red, and khaki illustrate the theme, but subversions will take the dress into a less obvious realm. Stripes, camouflage, geometrics, and image prints will give added interest.

The **basic shape** has the features of military uniform, with shirt collar and front placket opening, breast pockets inserted into the yoke seam, and diagonal side pockets with stand. The **digital print** is strategically engineered to trim and define the pattern pieces.

This luxury, sanded-silk, **maxi-length** dress has an asymmetric button fastening on the left side that continues to the floor. There are oversized patch pockets at hip level, smaller patch **pockets** with flaps at the bust, a soft shawl collar, and long and lean set-in sleeves.

KEY CHARACTERISTICS

- ☑ Traditional military uniform detailing
- ☑ Collar, pocket, button, and epaulette design features
- ☑ Decorative embellishments, badges, insignia, and topstitching

1 Cotton shirtdress with inverted-pleat patch pocket with flap and exposed side pocket bags. The pinafore skirt panel and pockets are trimmed with mitered corners in contrasting colors.
2 Double-breasted dress with inverted-pleat pockets with flaps on the breasts and hips, epaulettes, strapping, and a double-buckle belt.
3 Collarless shirtdress with dirndl waist and front

placket opening concealing button fastenings. The inverted-pleat pocket and flap and shoulder epaulettes are trademark military features.
4 A fitted shift style with concealed-button placket on a high round neckline, contrasting leather epaulettes, and belted waist. **5** Multiple pockets in varying shapes are an eclectic mix, held together by the solid color of the fabric. **6** Shirtdress with

pared-down uniform styling. The front body is extended to form a concealed fly front with a single button revealed at the neck stand of the two-piece collar. **7** A short center-front zipper and low-luster fabric yoke and sleeves contrast with a suiting-fabric main body and white collar. **8** The applied breast pockets, with an inverted pleat and button-down flap, are distinctly military in feel.

Safari

The safari-style shirtdress is a classic that has been reinterpreted by a range of designers. It transcends fashion trends. While Yves Saint Laurent developed the safari dress in the 1960s, it was made fashionable in the 1980s by Ralph Lauren and Calvin Klein. The style is ideal for summer traveling and hot climates and was popularized by Meryl Streep in the 1985 movie *Out of Africa*.

Fashion takes the image of the romantic explorer and reinterprets it for the modern traveler, using traditional linens, khaki cottons, poplin or twill, or contemporary performance fabrics. Muted khaki, olive, or stone, with perhaps a camouflage print, are used to create an authentic safari look, although white is an ideal alternative. The use of a bright, trend-led summer palette can update the look, and a modern camouflage-inspired or animal print can also help to confirm the style.

Traditionally, the safari shirtdress is a cross between a military field jacket and a shooting jacket, with four bellow pockets, a belt across the middle, and a traditional point collar with epaulettes on the shoulder. Pockets were designed to carry ammunition, compass, map, and knives. The contemporary equivalent survival kit might consist of a cellphone and tablet computer, credit cards, passport, and shades, and may be the blueprint for designing the size and shape of the pockets. Alternatively, they can remain purely for decoration.

Loose-fit, georgette shirtdress, taking inspiration from camouflage prints. It has a button-through center-front placket leading to a traditional shirt collar. A belt creates a **softly gathered waist**. The **dropped shoulder** complements the relaxed style and the wide short sleeves are loosely secured back.

The left side of this dress has a **fitted bodice**, using princess seams to create shaping and fit over the bust into a nipped-in waist. In contrast, the right side has a **draped silk jersey** panel that creates soft folds as it wraps to the left, creating a deep wrap opening at the hem.

KEY CHARACTERISTICS

- ☑ **Cross between military field jacket and shooting jacket**
- ☑ **Four bellow pockets, belt across the middle, traditional point collar, epaulettes**
- ☑ **Khaki, olive, stone, or white color or camouflage print**

1 The oversized breast pockets and wide dropped shoulder sleeves match the generous proportions of this ankle-length dress. **2** The formal feel of the suiting fabric is offset by the self-fabric waterfall frill that begins under the collar on the right side and is inserted into the side seam. **3** Loose, short-sleeve shirtdress with front placket buttoned from neck to hem. The inverted-pleat patch pockets with flap fulfill the safari look. **4** This cool linen shirtdress has short sleeves, side splits, a grown-on collar, center-front placket, and inverted-pleat pocket with flap. **5** The loose-fit bodice has symmetrical patch pockets with box-pleat detail and button-down flaps. A full skirt is created by ample tucks at the waistline. **6** Button-through shirtdress with set-in sleeves with turn-back cuffs.

The bodice and skirt are separated by a waistband that gives definition to the waistline. **7** The use of khaki fabric and animal-print trim strongly suggest safari references. The asymmetrical design details and peplum subvert the traditional safari shirt. **8** This wide, horizontal stripe in high-shine silk satin creates a bold design, offset by the simple A-line shape and military-inspired pockets.

Safari (continued)

> **Body-conscious** shirtdress with traditional safari detailing that has been enhanced by the addition of a **metallic belt** and metal epaulettes.

Safari and trench-style shirtdress with off-set, button-through, double-breasted placket opening that continues around the hem with a mitered corner. **Double-needle topstitching** features around pockets and collars with a double storm-flap feature on one side. Three **applied pockets**, two at the hip and one on the breast, have box pleats, mitered corners, and contrast-color buttoned V flaps.

SHIRTDRESS

A self-fabric **drawstring tie** at the waist adds slight definition to the relaxed shape of this dress. The soft drape of the silk complements the **cape-effect shoulders**, while the sheer contrast-fabric chiffon sleeves add a subtle twist to the design.

Double-breasted button-through **trench-style safari dress** with storm flaps. The tie-dyed fabric suggests dappled sunlight, giving a **camouflage effect**. A leather belt defines the waist and adds to the utility aesthetic.

V-neck collarless and sleeveless shirtdress with button-through front placket opening. **Safari styling** is created with the application of deep applied pockets with curved flap at the hip and mitered pockets at the breast. A self-fabric belt is threaded through decorative leather **belt tabs** and tied at the waist.

Alternative pocket: Rounded bellow pocket with button-down flap

Tuxedo

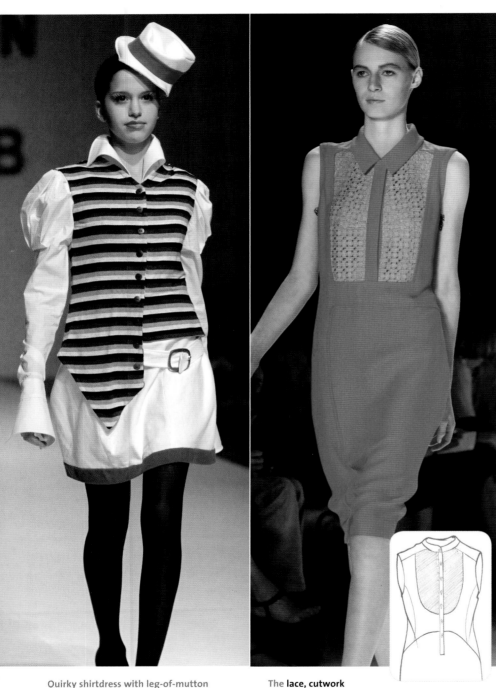

Derived from a formal man's dress shirt, the tuxedo-style shirtdress borrows from its distinctive design features. The style evokes formality and dress codes, although it can still maintain a relaxed vibe, suggesting boyfriend-borrowed chic. Strong features are the starched bib-fronted yoke and turned-back cuffs. Long sleeves may be rolled up to achieve a more casual feel. With the addition of a collarless stand left open, or with a wing collar added and buttoned to the neck, the effect will still be created.

Dickey front, detachable wing collar, cuff links, and button studs can help to authenticate the look. Pleats, pin tucks, or lace braid can decorate the dickey front, and a pull-on tab can be added at bottom center front of the bib panel. Rumba frills can also adorn the front shirt panel either side of the placket. Embroidery can be used for a decorative effect and monograms can replace the logo.

Long, curved shirttails and side vents can be used to vary the hemline, and lengths can be short and sexy or long and voluminous, maximizing cover-up. Pin-striped fabrics and white starched linen or cotton fabrics help to recreate the aesthetic, though shaping and details mixed with vibrant colors and patterns can still help to realize a subverted version. Styling combinations that integrate the tuxedo jacket with the shirt can develop a less traditional and more abstracted form.

Quirky shirtdress with leg-of-mutton sleeves that extend into an **exaggerated cuff**. The contrasting horizontal-stripe fabric gives the illusion of a separate vest. The **revers collar** stands high and curls away from the neckline. The mini-length hem has side splits and a solid-color border.

The **lace, cutwork panels** on the bodice are inspired by traditional dress shirts and give a feminine feel to an otherwise formal style.

Alternative collar and front panel: Grandad collar, curved bib front, and shaped waist seam

KEY CHARACTERISTICS

- ☑ **Derived from male formal dress shirt and dinner jackets**
- ☑ **Starched bib-fronted yoke**
- ☑ **Turned back cuffs**

1 Shirting collar details synthesize with oversized tailored jacket lapels on the bodice. This extends into a draped panel at the hip that continues into a straight skirt. 2 Shift-shape shirtdress with a low curved neckline and contrasting cuffs. A detachable stand collar and bib wraps and fastens at the neck. 3 Transparent undershirt with solid cuffs, collar, and bound hemline. A tuxedo layered-vest front has a circular-cut peplum and waterfall frill that cascades from the center placket. 4 Black and white suit and shirt details reference masculine formal dress. The faced collar and revers define the V neck, while mock jacket revers form a capped sleeve. 5 A dickey fly front with pleated tucks and a placket that extends to a pull-on tab define this drop-waisted, sleeveless dress. 6 A fitted, sleeveless bodice with a contrast-color, bib-effect panel with button-through opening to the waistline. 7 Wrapped shirtdress with revers collar and low front neck drop. Vertical welt pockets sit high on the loose-fit bodice and echo the tailoring influences of the revers. 8 Dickey bib-front yoke and rounded shirttails reflect a masculine dress shirt. Contrasting stand collar, placket and cuffs.

Tuxedo (continued)

> An asymmetrical, masculine dress shirt with **opposing features** on each side of the center-front placket. The left side is **exaggerated in scale**, no longer fitting the body, falling off the shoulder, and reaching the floor, creating a look that questions proportions and fit.

Elements of the shirt have been subverted to create a waisted dress in sharp cotton. The **bib front** crosses the waistband, extending to patch pockets with flap, front placket, and stand collar. The use of flesh-colored power mesh as a base gives **transparency** to the back and shoulders. The deep plunging cleavage combines feminine and masculine features.

Traditional tuxedo design details have been subverted and applied in **multiples** to different areas of the body to create this interesting garment. The **layering** of the contrasting sheer and solid fabric is integral to the design.

This duchess satin, **shift-shape** dress has contrasting sheer inserts that accentuate the style lines, reflecting the **oversized wing collar** detail.

Deconstructing the shirt and abstracting and layering have created an innovative statement dress. Although breaking with convention, recognizable elements of the shirt remain. The use of repetition reinforces the iconic value of the traditional man's shirt. Starching, bonding, and clever use of interfacing have been employed in order to achieve a **sculptural silhouette**.

SUNDRESS

This versatile wardrobe essential transcends occasions, making it an ideal style for day and evening wear. With a multitude of design options there is a sundress for every taste. It is an important inclusion in all spring/summer collections.

This digitally printed sundress has a fitted bra-cup bodice, wide shoulder straps forming a sweetheart neckline, and a full, gathered dirndl skirt. The bra cups are sandwiched into the skirt's waistband at the side views, exposing the center-front torso. The deep, solid-color horizontal band inserted in the skirt breaks up the busy print.

In context

So much of what was popular in the 1960s was about bright colors and bold graphics. These two Lilly Pulitzer shift sundresses were just that, yet they were also appropriate for wealthy socialites on vacation in warm climates. Their matching colored kerchiefs perfectly finish off the look.

A must-have for every warm-weather vacation, the sundress is a practical and easy-to-wear garment that can be worn all day in a warm climate. Worn long or short, it can be a great canvas for bold prints or for solid colors with accessories for evening wear. Designed to keep you cool in hot weather, the sundress is typically produced in lightweight jersey and woven fabrics, often in natural fibers appropriate for spring/summer. It can be worn strapless for an even tan during the day and combined with a shoulder cover for cooler evenings. The extensive range of styles, with varying hemlines, necklines, and sleeves, make it suitable for most occasions.

It is said that the origins of the sundress began in Palm Beach in the 1950s. American socialite Lilly Pulitzer is believed to have invented the sundress out of a need to disguise juice stains on her clothes while making her orange juice. The dresses were very colorful so the stains would not show. They were admired and sought after, leading Lilly into a new career in fashion.

Iconic American designer Claire McCardell also had functionality at the heart of her design ethos. The ready-to-wear designer produced simple, affordable clothes suited to most forms throughout the 1930s to the 1950s. Her celebrated bright, cotton, check sundress, a basic tent dress with a halter-neck top, belted to give shape, accentuated the female form, but could also be worn unbelted to accommodate different body types.

In the UK, ready-to-wear fashion company Horrockses came to epitomize the quintessentially British sundress of the 1950s. The dresses reflected the optimism of the time, with bright floral and bold stripe cotton prints, fitted bodices, and full skirts. In contrast, Emilio Pucci took the fashion world by storm with his lightweight textiles and dazzling psychedelic prints, abandoning heavy fabrics and traditional floral prints that were familiar at the time. These revolutionary new designs were ideal for his lightweight silk jersey and silk chiffon high-summer beach- and evening-wear dresses, which became an essential component of resort wear for the international smart set, and were favored by movie stars such as Elizabeth Taylor and Marilyn Monroe.

Emilio Pucci became known in the 1960s for his brightly colored graphic prints that were easy to wear and comfortable. This caftan sundress is ideal for a hot day on the beach or in town, all the while looking exotically chic.

Design considerations

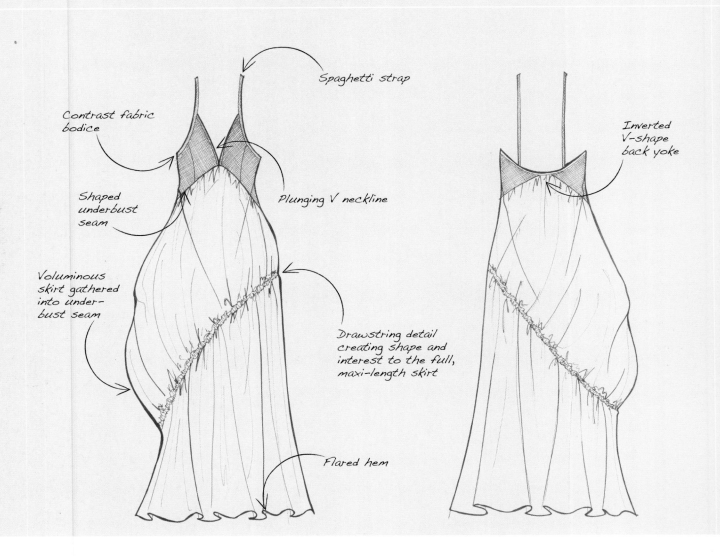

Contrast fabric bodice

Spaghetti strap

Shaped underbust seam

Plunging V neckline

Voluminous skirt gathered into under-bust seam

Drawstring detail creating shape and interest to the full, maxi-length skirt

Inverted V-shape back yoke

Flared hem

Influences The sundress draws upon a diverse range of exotic travel influences, such as the caftan, kimono, and sari, all worn by cultures in hotter climates.

Practicality Functionality is the crucial design consideration because the sundress must be comfortable to wear in warm weather. Ideal for vacations, the sundress is a versatile garment that can pack easily, produced in a crease-resistant fabric or intentionally creased for effect.

The sundress can be dressed down for the day and accessorized for the evening.

Silhouette Generally sleeveless, strapless, or with fine spaghetti straps, the sundress can be mini or maxi length, with variations in between. Taking inspiration from petticoat styles, the sundress is often bias cut, skimming the body and allowing for the natural stretch inherent in the woven fabrics. Alternatively, it is often loose and oversized, allowing for air

circulation, and sometimes intended as a cover-up from the sun, hanging loosely to avoid contact with the body contours. Gathers and tiers are a common feature, creating volume and silhouette.

Fastenings Fastenings are often kept to a minimum, with the intention that the dress be thrown on over swimwear. Fit can be achieved through shirring, smocking, or drawstring ties.

Traditional grandad collar

Extended center-front button-through placket

Drawstring detail creating a relaxed front yoke

Straight back yoke

Vertical drawstring with self-fabric tie giving shape to the hemline

Oversized, horizontal pleats at waist level

Full dirndl skirt gathered into horizontal pleat

Voluminous, loose-fitting silhouette

Deep hem band

SUNDRESS

Bodice Sundress designs are often influenced by foundation garments such as bras and corsets, accentuating the bust with integrated bra cups. Details such as eyelets and lacing or hooks and eyes are commonly used to define the bodice.

Fabrics Fabrics are often lightweight, soft wovens that can vary from transparent or translucent to solid. They have a mainly natural fiber content for breathability, such as linen cotton and silks, though

new manmade fibers allowing for non-crease and permanent pleating are often used. New technology has developed fabrics with wicking properties and sun-blocking features, adding greater functionality to the styling.

Seasonal styling The seasonal aspect of the sundress demands bright colors and bold prints. Embellishments, such as embroidery, beading, lace, and other trimmings, evoke the often bohemian

feel of the sundress. The sundress can transcend seasons through layering over garments in pinafore styling or accessorized with knitwear, jackets, and pantyhose.

Sun

The sundress is intended to be worn in warm weather, and is typically an informal dress made in print and solid-color fabric, such as lightweight cottons, or cotton combinations, and other natural fibers that are cool and breathable, such as linen. Associated with vacations and exotic travel, when the high levels of sunlight allow the wearer to be more ambitious with color and print, the dress features fabrics ranging from delicate ditsy florals to bold, graphic geometrics. Embroidery and embellishment are also key design details that can recreate an exotic, ethnic theme.

Sleeveless or with fine or spaghetti straps, the sundress is usually open-necked, exposing the shoulders, back, and arms, making it ideal for a walk on the beach or for pulling over swimwear. It is frequently designed with a keyhole back fastening with a rouleau loop and button or invisible zipper in the left side.

The neckline can be sweetheart, halter neck, wide scoop, or V. Designed for easy care, comfort, and ease of wear, shaping can be created through the use of darts, bias cutting, or smocking, so the dress can be pulled over the head without the need for fastenings. Appropriate for all ages and body shapes, the sundress works in a variety of lengths, from mini to maxi.

A sleeveless, V-neck, shift-shape, mini-length dress. **This simple style is an ideal canvas for very detailed fabric.**

Alternative neckline: Square neckline with wide straps and bow detail

1970s-style, hippie-inspired maxi sundress in fine cotton lawn. The high-waisted bodice is heavily embellished with **braiding and embroidery,** suggesting multicultural influence. The skirt is gathered into the waistband to create fullness, in keeping with the **boho aesthetic.**

KEY CHARACTERISTICS

- ☑ Lightweight fabrics often in natural fibers
- ☑ Ambitious colors and prints
- ☑ Sleeveless, usually with fine straps
- ☑ Various lengths and necklines
- ☑ Loose and relaxed fit

1 The volume of fluid silk creates impact. The straight neckline, simple shoulder straps, and solid color are balanced by the ornately embellished neck edge. **2** A-line, sleeveless shift with a boatneck. The underbust self-fabric band gives definition to the bodice. **3** An off-the-shoulder neckline with a contrast-fabric collar-effect detail. Darts from the waistline to the bust give shape. **4** Lively sundress with a fitted bodice and contrasting lace circular skirt. The horizontal style line above the bust creates a yoke-like detail and allows for two clashing colors to be used together. **5** The overlapping swags of fabric coupled with the warm colors reinforce the Indian-inspired jungle print, for an exotic appeal. **6** The diagonal neckline is bound and extended to the shoulder strap, creating a sarong-inspired sundress with minimal structure. **7** Sleeveless sundress with a scooped front neckline. Shoulders that divide into two add interest to an otherwise simple style. **8** A vest-shaped bodice creates a casual, easy-to-wear garment. An intricate, cutwork fabric adds interest to the full, flared skirt.

1 A length of cotton lawn is folded and gathered across the width and worn diagonally from armhole to shoulder strap. Excess fabric forms a draped sleeve. **2** Simple A-line shift minidress. The denim fabric suggests dungaree styling; however, the double-tiered frill at the bodice gives a softer feel. **3** High-waisted sundress with a sweetheart neckline and gathered skirt. Contrasting borders define the neckline, waistband, tie, and hemline. **4** Easy-to-wear sundress with an empire line, wrap-over bodice, and softly gathered, flared miniskirt. **5** Strapless sundress with curved bodice and integrated bust support. The simple shape allows the bold print to fill the dress panel. **6** Sleeveless minidress with tiered and gathered hemline. Circular keyhole cutouts around the neckline are trimmed with contrast ribbon. **7** Patchwork denim mini sundress, heavily inspired by western styling, such as double-needle stitching and contrast-color thread. The dress has an open-ended center-front zipper and faux jean waistband on a dropped waistline. **8** A geometric stencil print is echoed in the cutout ladder straps at the back of the dress.

9 Fit-and-flare sundress with a wide, square neckline that forms the shoulder straps and yoke. Panel seams are accentuated with bright piping. **10** The peplum and fishtail hemline create a Victorian-inspired silhouette that enhances the hourglass figure. **11** Maxi tent dress with exaggerated volume increasing from the hip. Deep side pockets are in keeping with the oversized proportions. **12** Maxi dress in lightweight cotton. Built-in bra and cups with a sweetheart neckline give structure and shape to the strapless bodice. **13** A full skirt has been pleated into the bra-style bodice. Care has been taken throughout to cut the pattern pieces to maximize the print. **14** Fitted, strapless bodice and pencil skirt with a curved peplum. A front bib panel, inserted into the waist seam, creates a high neckline over the strapless bodice. **15** Chiffon halter-neck sundress with a deep V neckline that appears to extend around the arms to create a faux off-the-shoulder effect. The full skirt has godets to add more flare. **16** This sundress is based on simple sarong styling and handkerchief shaping, taking the corners of the rectangle to create the halter neck.

Sun (continued)

> Tiered, short **skater skirt** attached to a dropped-waist bodice gathered by a drawstring to create a soft blouson effect. The **gathered frill** around the neckline and down one side of center front to the waist accentuates the peasant look. The cotton muslin produces a fluted edge on the layered flounces.

The archetypal sundress with **fitted bodice** to the waist and gathered and flared hem. The sweetheart neckline, wide shoulder straps, and shaped cups are all iconic features of the **1950s-inspired sundress**. The gathering has been confined to the hips and back, keeping the front panel flat to give a more flattering shape.

The full, gathered, tiered, **prairie-influenced skirt** contrasts with the fitted, sleeveless bodice with wide **square neckline**. The waistline is accentuated by the addition of a short, gathered, circular-cut peplum, and the busy print is balanced by tiers of larger-scale complementary prints at the hemline.

Fit-and-flare sleeveless sundress with V neck and halter-neck straps that extend from underarm side seam and cross over to back neck. The **pussycat bow** at center-front neckline creates a feminine decoration. The **lightweight** woven fabric flares to below the knee.

Diagonal seamed panels create structure and suggest origami-inspired pleating and folding. The **shibori-dyed print** continues the theme and complements the three-dimensional folded panels.

Sun (continued)

Pretty, lightweight, cotton minidress with retro 1970s-inspired geometric print. **The crochet lace** of the collar and the front placket and pockets continues the **eclectic vintage feel.**

References to Japanese origami and **packaging** are evident in the design of this dress. Vertical and horizontal lines intersect the center front and waistband, almost packaging the body with ribbons and ties. Shoulder ties in contrast color strongly suggest a **dungaree style.**

Simple A-line sleeveless shift dress with separate bodice with round neck, center-front placket, and deep-cut armholes. The simple shape is subservient to the **bold floral print** of the cotton dress.

1 Contrast-color blocking defines the proportions of the dress. The drop waistband elongates and disguises the contours of the body. 2 The dress is worn dungaree style over a sleeveless vest, which gives the body-contouring shape a sportswear feel. 3 Enveloping the figure, the oversized proportions are gathered at the yoke and drawn in at the hemline. The bodice suggests a bandeau-wrapped effect. 4 A large frill, gathered into the yoke above the bust, curves and dips lower at the back, creating volume, in sharp contrast to the closer-fitting, slimmer shape underneath. 5 Sophisticated sundress with zigzag silhouette cut into bodice seaming, giving strong suggestions of a tuxedo. This shape is echoed again at the hemline. 6 Lightweight, cotton, maxi-length sundress with Hawaiian print. Sleeveless with a deep round neck and drawstring waistline. 7 A floral print is cut on the bias, with a diagonal waistband and front yoke panel. Waterfall-draped panels, inserted from the waistband, hang to form draping. 8 Monochrome paneled dress with body-contour panels that give a slimming effect. The bra top is shaped into a deep sweetheart silhouette.

Smock

The smock evolved from traditional clothing worn by British shepherds and peasants as a protective work-wear garment. These smocks were decorated to achieve individuality, with design origins related to regions, families, and the wearer's occupation.

Traditionally made in linen or wool, the smock is an oversized T shape, finishing at the knee or calf, and often featuring a round flat collar or shirt collar with a short placket. The excess fabric at the shoulders and sometimes the bodice was pleated into unpressed folds and decorated with smocking embroidery in self-colored heavy linen thread. The smocking embroidery allows for a degree of stretch, making the garment easy to pull on and off. The reversible features of the smock meant the garment could be worn inside out when dirty. The smock was adapted to serve other occupations, such as fishing and painting, with large pockets to accommodate tools.

The smock dress has featured extensively in children's wear and is traditionally used for Christenings; it is also an ideal shape for maternity wear. In mainstream women's fashion, the smock has been translated in lightweight linens, silks, and cottons and embroidered with more contemporary threads in contrasting colors. The smock dress has evolved through the decades, taking on a more bohemian look, adopted by the hippies of the 1970s. Smocking is now used to embellish other areas of the garment, such as sleeves and cuffs, where gathering is required.

KEY CHARACTERISTICS

- ☑ Oversized T shape
- ☑ Knee or calf length
- ☑ Round, flat collar or shirt collar with short placket
- ☑ Pleated, unpressed folds at shoulders or bodice
- ☑ Gathering, shirring, and smocking

Wide, elasticized neckline and **cap sleeves** that can be worn either on or off the shoulder. The dress has **two skirt layers** under the bust. The front of the outerlayer is left open to expose the contrast-printed underskirt.

Alternative bodice: Spaghetti straps with elasticated, smocked empire-line bodice

The white kerchief and long, flowing, smocked dress, with a **shirred neck** and side slits, suggests a Greek holiday and the **exotic peasant styles** popular in the late 1960s. One can imagine this dress against sun-bleached white Greek buildings and a crystal-blue sky.

1 The yoke has been extended with fabric bands that give the impression of cap sleeves. The yoke finishes above the bustline and the skirt is gathered into the yoke seam. **2** Shift-shape sundress with a square neckline. A detailed vertical panel of fine pin tucks on the center front continues to the dropped-hip seam. **3** The substantial fabric of this sundress is gathered and smocked into a single-shouldered band. **4** Extra volume is added with drawstring ties on the skirt's sides. A half-skirt with an oversized apple-catcher pocket is added at the waist. **5** Multiple vertical pin tucks on the bodice achieve fit to the waist and bustline. An exaggerated sweetheart neckline is created from twisting the bodice fabric to form straps. **6** An elasticized, gathered neck edge creates a flexible neckline. Voluminous, raglan sleeves are gathered into an elasticized cuff and reflect the capacious body. **7** The pleats, which start at the neck, create shape and texture and manipulate the graphic print. **8** The voluminous silhouette is achieved by an A-line bodice and additional fullness from the dropped waist seam. The bell sleeves echo the silhouette.

Petticoat

Influenced by lingerie styles, the petticoat sundress is made of lightweight woven fabric, often bias cut in linen and cotton, with spaghetti straps and lace trims.

The petticoat style can convey a variety of historical design references, from the narrow, sheath-like, sheer slips of the late 1920s to the full, tiered-ruffle, western-style prairie petticoats with broderie anglaise trim. Some subcultures have also adopted the petticoat style as part of their uniform, from the stiff layered net of the 1950s-inspired rockabillies and the romantic gathered flounces of Victorian-influenced new romantics through to the macabre mourning dress worn by goths.

Every decade fashion designers reinvent the underwear as outerwear trend, which was popularized in the 1980s by Madonna, although now the originally garish designs have taken on a more subtle and romantic feel. Contemporary petticoat-dress styles now integrate lingerie features, such as fabrics, pattern cutting, and trims, and are not defined by length, which ranges from very short to full length. Necklines, such as V, sweetheart, and halter, expose the chest and can vary in feel from demure to seductive. This is an ideal style for layering and juxtaposing with masculine tailoring or knitwear.

Grecian styling is evident in this dress, with two circular necklaces used as a base to fold, wrap, and thread lengths of fabric. **Layers of organdy** allow varying degrees of transparency and create different levels of hemline. The stitched waistband controls the fabric and creates fit to accentuate the waist.

This silk satin sundress is bias cut, creating a **body-skimming** fit. A contrast-color, more-structured overlayer on the bodice softly curves around the body from the underbust level on the front view to a full-length panel on the back. Fine **spaghetti straps** discreetly support the dress.

KEY CHARACTERISTICS

☑ **Influenced by lingerie styling**

☑ **Often bias cut in silk, linen, or cotton**

☑ **Spaghetti straps and lace trims**

1 Stripes run horizontally at the deep waistband and gathered tiered hemline. The direction of the fabric changes at the bodice and skirt, where the stripe runs vertically. 2 Body-skimming, bias-cut dress with a gradually flared skirt starting from hip level, a subtle cowl on the high neckline, and spaghetti straps. 3 This maxi-length dress has a fitted bodice and wide sweetheart neckline.

The bra cups and shoulder straps are reminiscent of swimming-costume styles. 4 All over-lace sundress with a fitted bodice and full calf-length dirndl skirt. The skirt is paneled to accommodate flare from the hip through to the hem. 5 Shoulder straps extend to the waistband and outline a heart-shaped panel at center-front bodice. 6 Delicate minidress with a wide, square neckline,

reflecting the horizontal, multistripe lace trim on the bodice. 7 The tubular shape of this simple mini sundress is emphasized by the vertically striped fabric. Compacted, circular-cut gathered frills at the hemline add interest. 8 A hand-painted image fills the canvas of the vintage petticoat; the surface decoration has been added after garment construction.

Petticoat (continued)

> Bias cutting and lace inserts accentuate the diagonal of the dress, creating a **V shape** at center front and back. The V shaping is picked up at the neckline, where a **lace** insert is positioned at the yoke and trimmed with pink silk binding, and at the handkerchief hemline.

This ethereal, calf-length sundress achieves impact through the use of a substantial amount of silk chiffon fabric. The simple, contemporary feel of the style is created by the **straight halter neck** and unusual diagonal direction of the spaghetti straps. The dress is circular cut from the neckline, with a **voluminous skirt** that falls longer at the back.

SUNDRESS

The dress is slashed from the hem to dropped waistline where bias-cut godets are inserted into the panels to create a **flared hemline**. The changes in the direction of the checked fabric create additional design interest. The structured **braided trim** at the deep neckline and armhole emphasizes the petticoat styling.

Sunray pleating is stitched down at the hip to create a fitted waistband; the excess fabric at the bodice is folded over to create a blouson effect. The thin binding around the neckline and armhole also forms the fine **spaghetti straps.**

The handkerchief hemline with **fringed border** gives an asymmetrical appearance and, together with the bold print on silk fabric, suggests a **vintage shawl**. Bias cutting avoids the need for bust suppression, and facing at the bodice creates a streamlined neckline. Thin spaghetti straps are tied at the shoulder and left to drape, providing additional decoration.

Petticoat (continued)

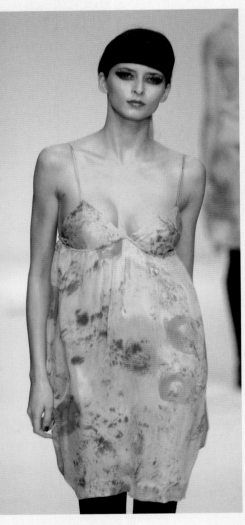

Simple, **tabard-style** minidress with a contemporary floral-pattern fabric. **Laser-cut floral motifs** have been heat-sealed and sandwiched between layers of organdy to achieve an interesting and contemporary version of a floral print.

The bodice and shoulder straps are cut all in one with an **asymmetric** V-shaped neckline, emphasized by a self-fabric tied bow. The neckline is balanced with the diagonal underbust seam and asymmetric, deep, circular frill hem. An additional, smaller, circular **frill bow** echoes the neck detail.

A typical **baby-doll** style of sundress in a silk chiffon fabric. The bra-cup bodice has solid-color straps reflecting the highlight color in the print design. The dress is fully lined, and the **chiffon skirt** is lightly gathered into the underbust seam, finishing above knee level.

1 Lines of elastic detailing on the bodice define the body's contours. Elasticized to the top hip, creating a dropped waistline, the skirt is softly gathered and flared. 2 Sheer, body-skimming sundress. The embellished fabric is contrasted with solid-color circular-cut frills at the neckline, hip, and hem to give a degree of modesty. 3 Uncomplicated, sleeveless maxi-length dress

with a high V neckline—an ideal canvas for the graduated border embroidery. 4 A bold placement print is the focal point of a simple shift-shape sundress. An elaborate beaded border trim complements the print. 5 Midi-length, sunray-pleated chiffon dress with delicate spaghetti straps and elasticized blouson waistline. 6 Broderie anglaise lace dress with a scalloped

hem and bodice. Cut as a shift, a deep ribbon is used to accentuate the high waist. 7 Supported by fine spaghetti straps, the neckline is fully gathered, forming draped cowls to hip level, with the underskirt draping to the hemline. 8 Sleeveless, scooped-neck sundress with asymmetric style lines incorporating volume in the panels to achieve drape in the bodice.

Sarong

The sarong can be traced to Southern Asia, and the term originally describes the lower garment worn by both males and females in Malaysia, Indonesia, and the Pacific Islands. It is usually formed from a length of fabric with a decorative panel of pattern or contrast color woven or dyed into it. Patterns are often created through batik dyeing and ikat weaving. Similar to the Indian sari, it features a length of fabric wrapped around the body to create the garment. This style has been adapted for beach and après beach, as well as finding a place in mainstream high-summer fashion. Mimicking the tying and wrapping techniques of the sarong, designers engineer the construction through clever pattern cutting and draping devices.

The style is flattering, sometimes exposing bare shoulders or wrapped and open at the hem to create a split effect to expose the leg. Necklines vary from halter to strapless, and the length can be from knee to floor. Borders are engineered to echo the traditional styling, and bold patterns and striking colors often define the sundress version of this style.

The sarong style of sundress epitomizes vacations in the sun, and its versatility as a garment transcends day to evening. Statement jewelry and flat sandals can accessorize this look and glamorize an otherwise simple style.

This maxi-length, chiffon sarong style has an asymmetric **tied and knotted neckline** that exposes the shoulders and arms. The dress falls from the gathered neckline, with a gradually flared skirt. Definition to the shape is created by a **simple rouleau tie belt** around the waist.

The deep plunging neckline is emphasized with **metallic foil highlights**, and the animal-inspired pattern graduates from **small to large** at the hem, increasing in scale with the increased width of the skirt.

KEY CHARACTERISTICS

- ☑ Mimics tying and wrapping techniques of traditional sarongs
- ☑ Exposed shoulders and split leg
- ☑ Bold patterns and striking colors

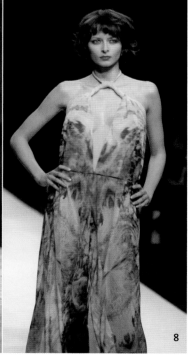

1 A traditional twisted-and-knotted neckline and asymmetric knotted hip detail maximize sarong styling. 2 The garment design has become subservient to the print artwork, with the print defining the strapless bodice and A-line silhouette. 3 With no cutting or bust suppression, the dress doubles as a canvas for a digital print. The dress is pleated into a horizontal bodice supported by V-neck shoulder straps. 4 The solid-color, wide shoulder straps wrap around the body and hold the unstructured fabric in place, creating a deconstructed look. 5 Devoré dress with semifitted bodice and full maxi-length skirt. A curved, strapless neckline is gathered into a deep, tucked neck stand. 6 An exaggerated cowl-front bodice is bias cut, creating drapery to the dropped waistline. The waistline has a contrast-color drawstring band and supports large external pockets. 7 A halter neck and inverted V-shaped yoke support a voluminous floor-length skirt, paneled to create extra flare. 8 Halter-neck sundress with a length of fabric integrated into the seam, which is wrapped around the body to imply a sarong.

Skater

Mini in length and inspired by American ice-skating dresses of the 1950s, this style has a young appeal, with a pretty and flirty sensibility. The style is usually defined by a fitted bodice, a waist seam, and a flared or pleated skirt; however, fit and flare can be achieved by inserting godets or circular cutting the skirt. Pleats can be constructed as box pleats, inverted box, sunray, or knife pleats inserted into a waist seam or yoke. Permanent pleating can be achieved through heat-pressing on manmade fabrics. Soft gathers are also an option, with varying length tiers a possibility. The style of bodice and necklines is limitless, and though generally sleeveless, the dress can have short or three-quarter sleeves.

This sundress is often designed with underpetticoats that accentuate the fullness of the skirt and create a more exaggerated silhouette. Soft wovens or jersey knitted fabrics are ideal for this style. Although the silhouette is predominantly feminine, it can also have a sportier vibe, as typically seen in the Norma Kamali 1980s version.

The fitted bodice, cinched waist, and short flared skirt are typical of the skater style. The curved **sweetheart neckline** is cut high and is accentuated by the deep split at center front. The wide **box pleats,** fixed sharply to the waistband, soften as they reach the hemline, due to the unpressed folded edge that doubles back as lining.

High-waisted **strapless bodice** with shaped panels at center front and inserted bows at neckline. The fullness of the gathered skirt is increased by a **layered petticoat**. Vintage-style printed florals with border hemline contrast with a tartan petticoat and braided trim.

KEY CHARACTERISTICS

- ☑ Fitted bodice with flared or pleated skirt
- ☑ Mini length
- ☑ Underpetticoats to accentuate the fullness of the skirt

1 Pinafore bib front with halter neck and waistband that amplifies the hourglass figure. The sharp box pleats sewn into the waistband contradict the unstructured folded hem. **2** The bodice is gathered into the waistband and cutout panels at the side seam exaggerate a slim waist. The gathered skirt and layered petticoat hemline complete the skater look. **3** Micro-minidress with flared skirt cut on the bias. The fitted bodice is faced with an integrated bra to create bust support and enhance cleavage. **4** A candy-stripe print runs horizontally, accentuating the fullness of the skirt. Style lines created by darts run on an angle from waist seam to bust. **5** Strapless drop-waisted bodice with boned panels that incorporate bust suppression and provide added support. **6** The scooped neckline and dropped shoulder, with keyhole opening and ties, reinforce the retro look. **7** Sundress with a princess-seam fitted bodice and mini length, full circular skirt. A vertical laser-cut design adds interest. **8** A busy microprint is used for a fitted bodice with open neckline, contrasting the larger-scale pattern used for the gathered full skirt.

Tea dress

Nothing epitomizes summer like a floral tea dress. Afternoon tea, a fashionable pursuit of the rich, was adopted as an aspirational activity of the lower classes of society. Taking tea required a new wardrobe, and the tea dress became an important symbol of this ritual. This style transcends fashion trends and is embraced and adapted by designers from season to season. Its versatility as a sundress and its wealth of historical references allows for reinvention while maintaining its vintage appeal. The tea dress is traditionally fit and flare, sometimes cut on the bias, and can have a variety of bodice styles and necklines and sport a variety of collar shapes and styles. Hemlines are traditionally to the knee, or variations of calf length, but can be subverted to mini length for a younger market.

Feminine and pretty, the sundress version would be made from lightweight wovens, usually printed in floral patterns, though geometrics, paisleys, and combinations of prints work well for a quintessential look. Embroidery and lace trims often embellish the bodice, with covered buttons and rouleau loops an additional feature. Gathered frills and circular-cut flounces can also add design interest. Bodice designs accentuate the feminine feel with pin tucks and underbust seams with softly gathered bra cups. Half-tie belts can be inserted into the side seams and tied in a bow to add interest to the back view. Side- and back-seam zippered fastenings are common features, ensuring the decorative interest on the front bodice and sleeve is not interrupted, since the dress is seen to its best advantage across a tea table.

Fitted bodice with dart suppression, wide V neck, and set-in capped sleeves. Shaped from the waist seam, the **A-line skirt** ends at knee length and fastens at side seam by an invisible zipper. The pretty print, in crisp medium-weight woven cotton, is complemented with an **asymmetrical belt** at the waist.

The V neckline draws attention to the **center-front seam** and the center-front, thigh-length split. The skirt has a **curved yoke** that balances the neckline.

Alternative bodice and sleeves: Wrap front with short kimono sleeves

KEY CHARACTERISTICS

- ☑ **Fit and flare or draped and gathered**
- ☑ **Feminine and pretty**
- ☑ **Knee or calf length**
- ☑ **Soft woven fabric, ditsy florals, and polka dot prints**

1 A basic semifitted shape with short, set-in sleeves and a subtle A-line skirt. Unusual oversized pocket openings add interest and drama. 2 Straps cross at the neck to create a halter neck. An opaque top layer of silk chiffon in a soft floral creates a feminine and fluttery look. 3 A simple fit-and-flare shape is offset by a geometric embroidered pattern and an elaborate beaded neckline.

The colors are bright, feminine, and summery. 4 Floral lace appliqué creates a delicate three-dimensional look that is balanced with the simplicity of a jewel neck and A-line skirt. 5 Deep V-neck, high-waisted sundress in cream silk with diagonally cut panels trimmed in red tape. The red-and-navy striped waistband reinforces the flag influence. 6 Ditsy-floral shirtdress with

scallop-trimmed collar, decorative lace-paneled yoke, and deep lace hemline border. 7 Fit-and-flare dress with button-through front fastening, wide neckline, and short puffed sleeves. The Peter Pan lace collar and lace appliquéd detail on the bodice and pocket trims add a quirky element. 8 Combinations of mismatched vintage prints create an eclectic layered effect.

KNIT DRESS

Whether figure hugging or oversized, the knitted dress has become an important fashion staple, crossing the boundaries of sportswear through to evening glamour.

Heavy-gauge, double-breasted coatdress with short, set-in puffed sleeves, fastened with a self-yarn tubular tie belt. An ornate ribbed revers collar is edged with a scalloped trim. The crinoline-style skirt creates volume to emphasize the small fitted waist. The garment shaping is created and disguised within the crochet-knitted stitch.

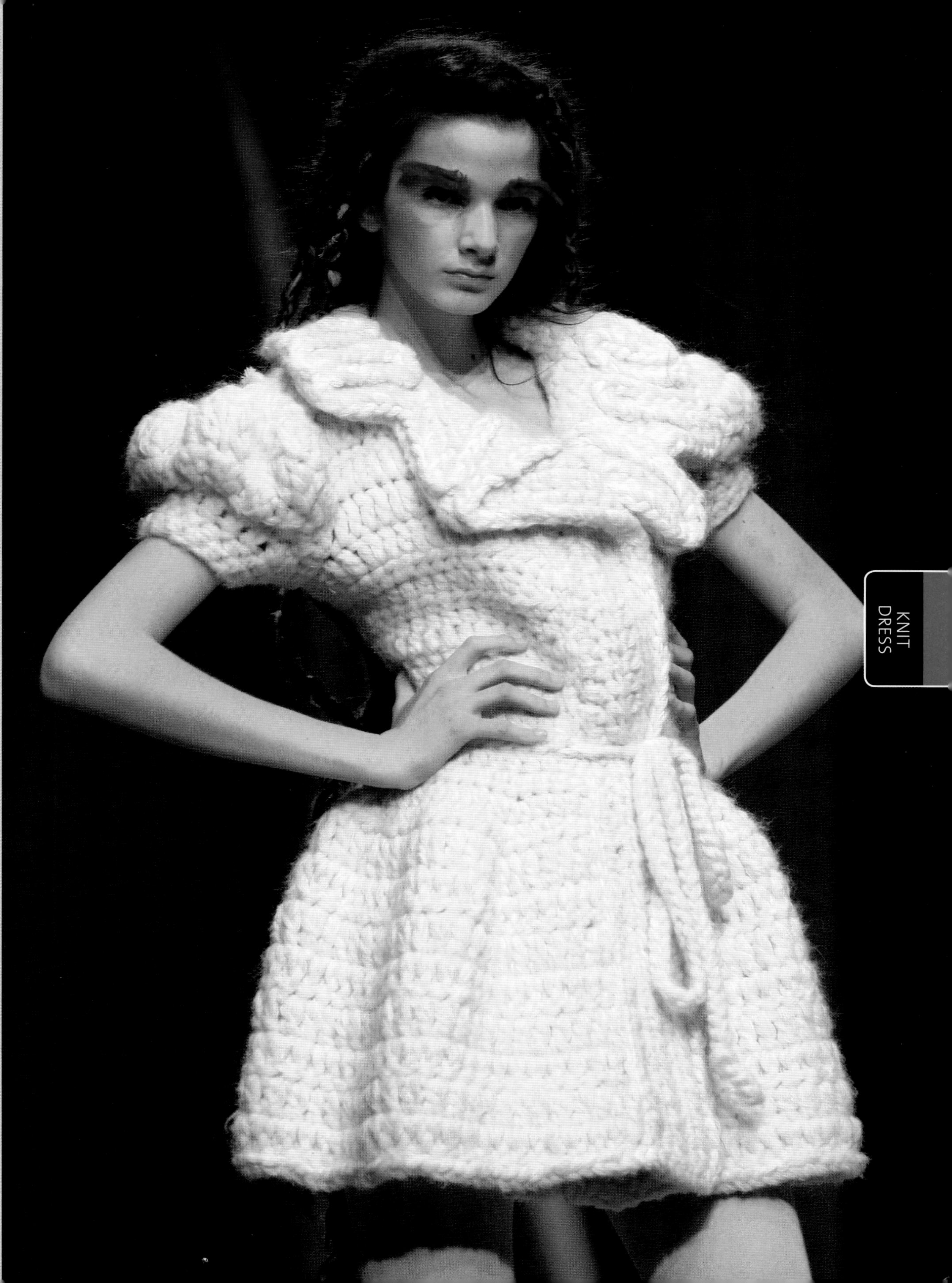

In context

The model Lauren Hutton epitomized the sexy 1970s, and Halston was an iconic designer known for his stunning yet simple knits. Here, silk jersey drips over Hutton in the form of a deep V halter with a fabric twist under the bust, and a high slit from the front hem.

nnovations in technology and the creative potential of knit structures have allowed the knitted dress to evolve from the humble origins of underwear to the prominence of the mainstream fashion runway. Knit's inherent elasticity, enabling the fabric to stretch, expand, and return to its original shape, allows for a relaxed ease of movement, which means that it can be worn casually in a sportswear context, meet the practical needs of office-to-home day wear, or be dressed up for body-conscious evening glamour.

The more relaxed silhouette of the 1920s saw tunic-shaped knits emerging, and Madeleine Vionnet's bias cutting, showing the contours of the body, translated through to the knitted dresses of the 1930s. The make-do-and-mend era of the 1940s encouraged women to hand knit dresses, the patterns for which were published in magazines, while, in contrast, Hollywood was inspiring the design of glamorous knitted full-length jersey dinner dresses. Coco Chanel came to epitomize the twinset, often including knitted dresses in her collection.

The skinny-rib sweaterdress of the swinging sixties was epitomized in Mary Quant's London collection, in parallel to Dorothée Bis and Sonia Rykiel in Paris. In the 1980s, the power dressing of body-conscious women in gyms encouraged designers such as Azzedine Alaïa to design body-conscious knitted dresses with references to corsets, and Norma Kamali to develop jersey-knit sportswear-inspired dresses. In the UK, Bodymap and Pam Hogg were designing dance-inspired jersey-knit dresses.

In the 1990s, Japanese designers, from Rei Kawakubo of Comme des Garçons and Junya Watanabe through to Kansai Yamamoto and Issey Miyake, pushed the boundaries of the design of the knitted dress. Issey Miyake's A-POC (A Piece of Cloth) range saw the construction of the garment from a single piece of cloth.

Comfort and agility are key attractions in knit dressing. While creating a slim and attractively clinging silhouette, the knit dress with Henley collar and slim, shawl-collar jacket allow for movement and ease.

Design considerations

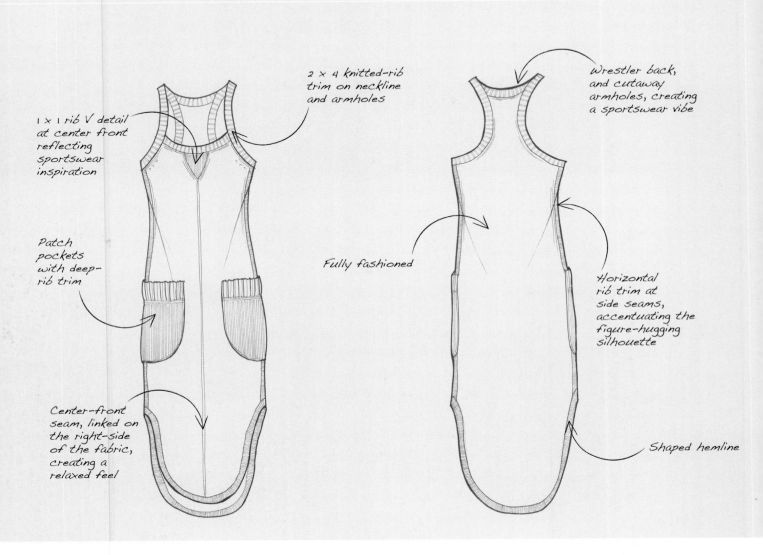

1 x 1 rib V detail at center front reflecting sportswear inspiration

2 x 4 knitted-rib trim on neckline and armholes

Wrestler back, and cutaway armholes, creating a sportswear vibe

Patch pockets with deep-rib trim

Fully fashioned

Horizontal rib trim at side seams, accentuating the figure-hugging silhouette

Center-front seam, linked on the right-side of the fabric, creating a relaxed feel

Shaped hemline

Versatility The versatility of the knit dress provides enormous scope for design expression, with the stretch performance qualities allowing for greater possibilities than a less forgiving woven fabric. Shaping can be factored into the design detailing, surface, structure, and decoration, removing the need for darts and other methods of compression.

Surface decoration Techniques, such as intarsia, jacquard, Fair Isle, cable, lace, weave, Swiss-darning embroidery, crochet, macramé, and dyeing, offer design versatility in pattern and surface decoration.

Fabrics Diversity of knit processes, from hand to machine, means a variety of stitch structures and textures are available, forming fabric types such as felt, fleece, rib, double or single jersey, plain or purl, and cloque or blister fabrics.

Qualities A variation of gauges determines the weight of fabric and density of the knit structure. The breadth of yarn qualities, from manmade to natural fibers, with combination blends and different finishes, presents tremendous scope for texture, drape, and handle. Bouclé or slub yarns can add texture and color, and dyeing techniques, such as ombré and space dyeing, can give an ikat appearance when knitted.

Rib polo neck

Saddle-shape full-fashioned armholes

V-shape front and back yoke

Cable stitch detailing on front view

Relaxed fitting silhouette finishing at mini length

2 x 2 rib cuffs and welt

KNIT DRESS

Fully fashioned Fully fashioned knitwear is engineered and shaped to size during knitting. The fashioning marks, or shaping, are evident at the point of increasing or decreasing. The welts and cuffs are integral, with only the collar or plackets added afterward. Linking is used as a joining method for shoulders and collars, which is a stitch-per-stitch joint. The garment sides, sleeves, and underarms are cup seamed, stitching the edges of knit pieces together. This method decreases wastage and is used for high-end garments using more expensive yarns.

Cut and sew The cut-and-sew technique is the quickest and cheapest method of knit construction, where garment pattern pieces are cut to size from lengths of knitted fabric from a flat bed or circular cloth. Seams are overlocked prior to sewing or linking to prevent stitches from unraveling, but they can look bulky. This method increases fabric wastage and is generally used in mass production.

Complete garment The complete-garment technique is the same as fully fashioned but without seams. Garment panels are knitted simultaneously on the machine together with cuffs, collars, and welts, with the body tube in the middle and two sleeves either side, each with a separate cone of yarn. The garment leaves the knitting machine completed.

Knit

The knit dress crosses all categories, from casual to formal, and can be worn during the day through to evening. New and exciting yarn developments allow the knit dress to be designed for hot summer climates and adapted for cold winter months. The designer has control over all aspects of the design process, from textile development to garment silhouette, with huge potential for cutting-edge and creative masterpieces.

Experimenting with combinations of texture, stitch, color, and pattern, Kenzo and Missoni are examples of design labels known for their production of exuberant knitted collections. Creative and glamorous, the fine gossamer knitted weblike structures of Julien Macdonald's signature dresses are fit for the red carpet. Mark Fast and Louise Goldin explore innovative techniques to develop exciting new garment shapes and stitch structures that continue to push boundaries. Celebrated for his originality and innovation, Azzedine Alaïa experiments with various manmade yarns to create ingenious, dense-yet-pliable knitted structures described as perforated, blistered, and pleated, that embrace complex tailoring techniques and enhance the female form.

Heavy-gauge jersey knit coatdress with scooped neckline, long sleeves, and front-placket opening. Two breast patch pockets and **oversized pockets** at hip level are trimmed with **large press-stud fastenings** with reinforced topstitching. Bound edgings feature strongly as well as the twin-needle topstitching.

Fine-gauge, knitted jersey, drop-waisted, **1920s-inspired** dress falling just below the knee. The contrast-color bold **graphic banding** adds interest and gives definition.

Alternative neckline and sleeves: Ribbed, knitted collar with raglan short sleeves

KEY CHARACTERISTICS

☑ Fully fashioned or cut and sew

☑ Fine to heavy gauge

☑ Textured stitches, cables, and ribs

☑ Fair Isle and intarsia patterns

1 Contrast chenille and rayon fit-and-flare dress. The dress is complemented by an exaggerated scarf-like striped neckline. **2** Exaggerated shoulders are further emphasized with a self-yarn waterfall frill. A similar frill creates a peplum effect on an otherwise body-conscious shape. **3** The fit-and-flare, houndstooth knitted pattern suggests a woven cloth, but shaping and volume have been achieved through full-fashioned knit shaping. **4** Fine-gauge jersey, drop-waisted dress suggesting a two-piece outfit. The pressed knife-pleated skirt finishes just above the knee, epitomizing "granny chic." **5** Openwork-lace patterning creates changes in scale and patterning throughout the dress. A picot edging trims the hemline, sleeves, and neckline. **6** Oversized shapes are created with a scooped neckline and dropped shoulder. Contrast exaggerated cuffs and patch pockets create graphic color blocking. **7** Tucking gives a seersucker effect, with contrasting tensions creating a blistering relief over a simple T-shirt shape. **8** Ribbed pinafore dress with contrast-color argyle-inspired pattern. The skirt is paneled to give flare.

Knit (continued)

> Gathered tiers in black-and-white striped horizontal bands, and contrasting **stockinette stitch and rib**, mimic a two-piece. Binding at the neckline and armholes also creates the shoulder straps of the dress.

Gathered **knitted tiers** are created and layered to form the hemline of the dress, contrasting with an **eyelet patterned knit.** On a smaller scale the tiers are used horizontally around the bustline and again to edge the neckline and to form short sleeves.

Mimicking a two-piece, the horizontal **knitted rib** is gathered to form a double layer of tiers at the **dropped waistline**. The gathered rib also creates a tiered hemline and decorates the pocket openings.

Alternative bodice detail: Square neckline with wide shoulder straps and knitted waterfall frill

Fine-gauge knitted dress shaped to fit and flare to knee length. The **scooped boatneck**, round armholes, and **open-lace effect** stitch combinations make this an ideal summer-weight garment.

Graphic gray-and-black striping runs horizontally and contrasts with a thinner stripe running vertically at the sleeves and side panel. Wide magyar sleeves are cut into a **racer-style** armhole and a deep black rib **accentuates the waist**. A vertical panel is set into the side seams to give a peplum effect.

1 Skinny, ribbed, turtleneck sweaterdress. The dress increases in volume at the hip toward the hemline, where it gathers into a knitted binding. 2 A plain jersey panel cuts diagonally through the middle of the dress from shoulder to hip, contrasting texture and color. 3 Graphic color blocking in panels give a body-conscious sportswear feel. The concealed pockets with zipper openings accentuate the active, athletic vibe. 4 This dress is cut as separate pieces and joined at the high waist seam to create a fitted bodice and flared skirt. 5 Full-fashioned knitted minidress with use of diverse stitch textures to define panels. 6 Fine-gauge, voluminous, relaxed maxi-length dress with variegated stripe mixed with Fair Isle-patterned panels. Style definition is achieved by drawstring knitted tapes that outline the shapes. 7 A tiered-lace gathered skirt is joined seamlessly with a knitted sweater bodice with polo-shirt collar and placket. 8 Use of strong color blocking delineates the drop-waisted silhouette. The stripe helps to create a sporty vibe, which is offset by the feminine lace-effect striped skirt.

Knit (continued)

Mixing tucks, lace, Fair Isle, and rib-knit patterns in multicolored horizontal stripes in fine-gauge linen and cotton. The mini-length dress is shaped to **flare out** at the hem and cuffs, but the waist and sleeves are fitted. The knit increases again at the bust and the top of the sleeve to give a ruched sleeve head. The applied lace neck placket is cut wide to give a **dropped shoulder**.

Heavy-gauge bouclé yarn gives the appearance of hand knitting, with four **cabled panels** running center front on a stockinette base. The cables split at the waist to suggest V shaping, while ribbing at the waist provides fit. The cable outlines the raglan shaping to reinforce the full-fashioned detailing.

Hand knitted and felted, the simple gray mélange sleeveless dress is **flared** to just above knee level. The cast-on hem, cast-off neckline, and unbound armholes maintain the pared-down aesthetic. Large three-dimensional **knitted and crochet** stemmed daisies decorate the hemline.

Sweater

A sweaterdress is an elongated version of the sweater and can be worn as an oversized garment or as a semifitted, body-skimming version. Traditionally, the sweaterdress is a fall/winter item in a heavy gauge, though finer-gauge versions are a consideration for spring/summer collections. Necklines and trims reflect the nature of the sweater, with versions such as the turtle, polo, crew, or V neck. Predominantly this style is long-sleeved with ribbed cuffs. Armholes and sleeve heads may be set in, raglan, saddle shoulder, dolman, dropped shoulder, or batwing. Knitted stitch structures, such as cabling, Fair Isle, and lace, can be applied, as well as intarsia and embellishment.

The sweaterdress made an appearance as far back as the 1920s but was often worn as an oversized twinset. During the beatnik 1950s, the exaggerated proportions of the sloppy-joe sweater, often borrowed from boyfriends' wardrobes and usually worn to the knee with capri pants or slimline ski pants, was the forerunner of the contemporary sweaterdress. The statement, skinny-ribbed sweaterdress, as epitomized by Mary Quant, Dorothée Bis, and Sonia Rykiel in the 1960s, was worn well above the knee, sometimes belted and accessorized with pantyhose or over-the-knee socks. The 1980s sweaterdress referenced the graphic impact of the 1920s styles and echoed the oversized silhouette of the 1950s, but with deeper armholes, wider sleeves, and emphasized shoulders, often using shoulder pads. Pictorial images using intarsia and embellishment were prevalent.

KEY CHARACTERISTICS

- ☑ **Elongated sweater**
- ☑ **Sweater necklines and trims**
- ☑ **Predominantly long sleeved**
- ☑ **Heavy gauge**

Body-conscious, mid-thigh bandage sweater dress. Individual bandages are knitted using the jacquard technique in alternating scales of **houndstooth pattern**. Hardware pieces are woven and sewn between each bandage, adding texture and dimension to the dress.

A bohemian feel is produced by the use of **braided fringing** knitted into the dress, running horizontally around the body. The bodice, turtleneck, and short set-in sleeves are knitted in a tuck stitch, and chenille yarns are used to create a **soft feel**.

1 Fleece-back sweat minidress with self-color 1x1-rib cuff and hem. A contrasting rib neck insert creates a turtleneckline. **2** This nautical-inspired boyfriend sweater with a deep V-striped front has rows of two different types of cable knits and a flirtatiously short hem. **3** Basket-weave, hand-knitted dress with a 3x2-rib turtleneck and stockinette-stitch set-in sleeves. The uneven hem fringing is achieved by knitted rouleau lengths and knitted strips to give a 1920s flapper silhouette. **4** Garter stitch is used to trim the neckline and cuffs and in a deep band at the hemline that extends the flare of the skirt. Inverted V pointelle patterning on the skirt emphasizes the A-line shape. **5** Casual, oversized sweaterdress in gray angora with dropped shoulder line, long sleeves, and cowl-neck collar. **6** Fine-gauge, mini-length sweaterdress with a soft, high-rolled polo neckline. Elongated sleeves have integral fingerless gloves. **7** Typical sweater minidress translated in a bold, wide horizontal stripe that has been carefully matched across the armhole and sleeve head. **8** An archetypal boyfriend sweaterdress. The deep and wide V neck falls off the shoulder.

Sweater (continued)

Soft gray, mini-length sweaterdress with contrast horizontal **chevron stripes** in blue chenille and gold Lurex yarns. The long sleeves have been set into the armhole and **gathered at the wrist** to create a blouson effect. The boatneck is finished with a narrow rib, but the hemline has been left as a simple cast-on edge.

Bold **intarsia-patterned** sweaterdress in heavy-gauge yarn. Diagonal shapes feature heavily in tribal-influenced geometric patterns. **Bright colors** give a stark contrast to a mirror-image design. The pattern has been designed to match the body and sleeves, and the drop-shoulder line is disguised within the pattern.

Sleeveless, horizontal **candy-striped** minidress with a high turtleneck. The heavy-gauge knit has been **felted** to create a dense, soft feel. The blue-and-gray stripe changes to gray and black at the bodice and again at the shoulder to give focus to the top of the garment.

Alternative neckline and sleeves: Split turtleneck with raglan short sleeves

<Lively hand-knitted sweaterdress with a **homespun craft aesthetic**, mixing varying weights and compositions of yarns and colors to create an individual, slightly **ad-hoc piece.**

KNIT DRESS

Fine-gauge silk-jersey sweaterdress with contrast color-blocked panel inserts. The focus is on the asymmetrical hemline created by a shorter front-panel insert, creating a **layered look.** Contrasting rust-colored inserts at front panel mimic a cardigan placket and create another layer at the front hemline. The heavy-gauge **ribbed turtleneck** collar extends to a circular yoke, adding to the layering story.

T-shirt

Named after the shape of the garment's outline, and universally considered to be a casual item with references to sportswear, the T-shirt dress can also sit in a relaxed evening-wear setting and can make an ideal blank canvas for costume jewelry or embellishment. It is always made in a jersey fabric in varying weights and compositions though can be either circular knitted or paneled with side seams. The fit can be oversized—sometimes belted to alter the silhouette—or cut in a more body-conscious manner. Dress lengths vary from mini to maxi, and sleeves from cap to cuff length. Jersey-ribbed trims are common on the neckline but can be added to the sleeves and the hem.

With its foundations in circular-knit hosiery manufacturing, the T-shirt dress evolved from the new streamlined silhouette of the 1920s. Based on the chemise, the T-shirt dress reflected the new athleticism and informal dressing of the age. With advancements in engineering, the speed of mass-produced fine-gauge knitting techniques, and cut-and-sew finishing, the T-shirt dress emerged as part of an ensemble or twinset.

Progressing through the decades, the dress was a feature of the beatnik subculture of the 1950s, and was heralded, then subverted, in the 1970s when punk established itself as an important fashion statement, and again in the 1980s when its blank canvas became a vehicle for political slogans and statements (such as in the work of Katharine Hamnett), as well as advertising and branding.

The silhouette of this T-shirt dress gives the impression of **two styles colliding.** For example, one slim-fitted, set-in sleeve contrasts with the drop-shoulder, wider T-shirt sleeve on the other side. The neckline is a combination of a V and a scooped, rounded neck, and is offset by the asymmetrical drape of the skirt.

Traditional tubular knit jersey, body-conscious dress with cap sleeves, taking direct reference from the **basic white staple** jersey T-shirt. The basic dress is an ideal **blank canvas** for substantial styling statements.

KEY CHARACTERISTICS

☑ **Elongated T-shirt**

☑ **Casual, with references to sportswear**

☑ **Jersey fabric**

1 Silk-jersey dress with cowl neck and asymmetric draped leg-of-mutton sleeve. Leather neck strapping contrasts with the drape of the fabric, creating a strong focal point. 2 Oversized, foil-printed, mini jersey dress. An exaggerated long sleeve, dropped shoulder, and deep scoop V emphasize the relaxed feel. 3 A sarong-inspired silhouette playing with cultural references within its asymmetric style lines of wrap and drape. 4 A young and sporty T-shirt dress with a dropped waist and gathered frill skirt. The rib-trimmed round neck and set-in short sleeves are a direct translation of the basic T-shirt shape. 5 An asymmetric, grown-on overlay, which ties at one shoulder, covers a deconstructed mini vest dress. Gathered fabric at waist level creates volume and drape. 6 Oversized dress with low- and wide-cut V neck with exaggerated drop shoulder and elbow-length kimono sleeves. 7 Mélange jersey fit-and-flare T-shirt dress—an ideal backdrop for graphic logos or slogan prints. 8 Liquid-jersey dress with a grown-on dropped shoulder line and a wide round neckline. The oversized fit accentuates the natural drape in the fabric.

T-shirt (continued)

> Magyar-style, long-sleeved, silk-jersey dress with boatneck and dropped waistline. The **nautical influences** continue with the bib-fronted, multibutton fastening. The hemline extends and doubles back to create an envelope-shaped, draped front, forming an overskirt effect.

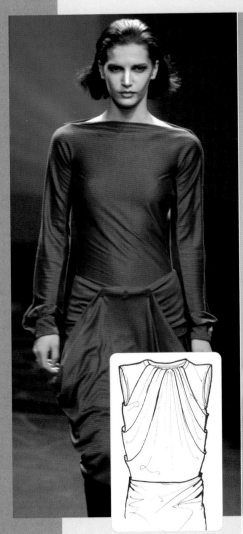

Alternative bodice and armhole: Sleeveless bodice with a round neck and draped fabric from the neckline, around the sides, to the center-back seam

Asymmetrical T shape, with a **twisted knot** at the neckline to give drape to the front of the dress. The dropped shoulder line forms a capped sleeve to continue the relaxed, **oversized silhouette.**

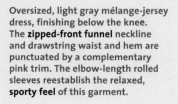

Oversized, light gray mélange-jersey dress, finishing below the knee. The **zipped-front funnel** neckline and drawstring waist and hem are punctuated by a complementary pink trim. The elbow-length rolled sleeves reestablish the relaxed, **sporty feel** of this garment.

The interesting combination of diagonal and vertical stripes is designed to give the impression that part of the garment is cut on the bias. This is achieved through **punch-card patterning** and partial knitting to create **directional striping**. Excess fabric is achieved by increasing then gathering the surplus to create drape at the front waist.

The underlying **sports vibe** of the black-and-orange, knee-length, V-neck T-shirt styling is juxtaposed with **printed scrolls and cherubs**. The use of tone within the print gives the impression of a raised surface.

Tank

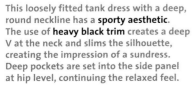

The tank is a sleeveless sweaterdress or jersey vest, and an extension in length of the tank top. Derived from the vest, the tank is normally a spring/summer item and is worn as an individual garment, though it can be layered over another garment with sleeves and worked as a pinafore dress.

Vivienne Westwood reshaped the T-shirt to create a tank dress, and the punk scene explored the adaption of garments by deconstruction through cutting, fraying, and utilizing the rolled raw edges of the jersey. Further exploration of the tank shape was made popular in the 1980s by Madonna, who layered tank over tank with deep armholes over exposed underwear or swimwear. The garment shape has since been refined and developed from sportswear references, using jersey fabrics that take on performance features originated in sportswear or dance wear, such as Airtex and spandex. The armholes are cut for design styling, such as racer, and, along with the neckline, finished with ribbed detail or facings, sometimes with invisible or integrated bra support.

This loosely fitted tank dress with a deep, round neckline has a **sporty aesthetic**. The use of **heavy black trim** creates a deep V at the neck and slims the silhouette, creating the impression of a sundress. Deep pockets are set into the side panel at hip level, continuing the relaxed feel.

Body-conscious, mid-thigh tank-inspired dress. The **geometric pattern** is achieved by reversing and tucking **double-faced bandages** down the center to create a three-dimensional, two-tone effect. Jacquard bandages complete the neckline, hem, and side seams.

KEY CHARACTERISTICS

☑ **Elongated vest**

☑ **Sleeveless**

☑ **Loose fitting or body conscious**

☑ **Can be layered over other garments**

1 The simple, oversized vest shape in foil-printed jersey is influenced by the 1920s flapper. The low-cut neckline and hemline have been laser cut. **2** This understated, simple tank style, in fine black-linen knit, has a lightweight, semitransparent appearance that skims the body. **3** Separately knitted bandages with houndstooth patterns are linked together with individually sewn hardware pieces. **4** Bandages in different colors are attached together to create an oversized geometric pattern. The neckline and shoulder straps are made from narrow bandages and hardware pieces. **5** Lace-knit halter-neck dress with a fitted empire-line bodice that has been adorned with a floral corsage. Fringing gives a variety of surface interest. **6** Individually knitted bandages are woven through hardware pieces, resulting in an all-over chainmail effect. **7** A drawstring cord at the waist gives shape to this loose dress and allows the bodice to blouson over the skirt. The cutaway shoulders create a vest effect. **8** Basketwoven knitted bandages in different colors create a one-of-a-kind piece with an intricate geometric pattern.

Tank (continued)

> Hand-knitted, heavy-gauge tank worn layered over a vest. The **ribbed hem** is knitted on smaller needles to create a tighter edge; however, the stitches get bigger toward the top to create a much looser, open fabric. Strips of woven fabric and heavy-slub yarn are used to create a **handmade**, artisan aesthetic.

Heavy-weight jersey mini-length tank dress with a scooped neckline. Two patched pockets, with long, **multicolored fringes** inset into the seams, decorate the hemline of the front of the dress.

1 The crisp, fabric belt contrasts with the languid drape of the wide, silk jersey hemline. 2 Versatile ankle-length tank dress in contrast-color, medium-weight jersey with side pockets. Lighter-weight jersey is gathered and inset into the zigzag bodice, then layered. 3 Lightweight, jersey tank dress cut on the bias and set into a high yoke with inset V panel at center front.

The embellishment cascades to the hem. 4 Tank dress with dropped waist and knitted bodice attached to a pleated silk skirt. The dress is extended and duplicated, then folded back, creating a multiple effect. 5 Knitted tank dress that grows into a mirrored duplicate. The second dress is left open at the side seams and worn over the first dress, folding back on itself at the hemline.

6 Gray, angora-mix tank dress with scooped neckline, deep armholes, and single breast pocket. 7 A patchwork of multicolored, textured scraps of knitting are stitched together in a random jigsaw of shapes to create a mini-length tank dress. 8 Nautical-inspired V-neck tank with horizontal stripes of crochet lace. The alternate patterns and widths are trimmed with stripes of knitted rib.

Polo

The polo dress originated from the machine-knitted Isis tennis shirt, which was first produced by British manufacturer John Smedley as early as the 1920s. Originally fully fashioned, like its shirt equivalent, the polo dress was defined by the three-buttoned placket, knitted-in one-piece opening at the front, attached to a shirt neck. The traditional, short sleeve is finished with a ribbed cuff with optional set-in sleeve or alternative saddle shoulder. The style was later worn for the sport polo, hence the name. The Lacoste polo shirt became a trademark synonymous with the preppy look and validated with a place in mainstream fashion in the late 1970s and early 1980s by labels such as Perry Ellis and Ralph Lauren. The polo styling has been adopted by brands that represent understated classic styling and that embrace the preppy look, such as Tommy Hilfiger, J. Crew, and Jack Wills.

The fabrics used reflect the sportswear styling, such as Airtex mesh jersey or knitted argyle patterned, ribbed, or cabled, often sporting a branded embroidered logo. Other styling options include an inset or patch breast pocket detail with ribbed trim. Sometimes pockets can be inset into the side seams of the dress.

The polo dress is rarely worn below knee length, because the style represents a sportswear aesthetic.

The oversized shift in heavy jersey knit with a **center-front zip** opening is belted to fit the waist. The polo collar, shoulder yoke panels, and pocket flaps are trimmed with contrasting fabric.

The **ribbed collar** and short rib-edged sleeves define this as a polo dress. The contrast print/solid color panels give a **body-conscious effect.**

KEY CHARACTERISTICS

☑ **Elongated polo shirt**

☑ **Buttoned placket, knitted in one piece, opening at the front, attached to shirt neck**

☑ **Sportswear styling and aesthetic**

1 Asymmetrical double-tiered, circular-cut frilled hem with graduating depth that complements the diagonal cut. Exposed zipper tape at center-front neck and a stand collar mimic the traditional polo shirt. **2** Contrast colors help to establish the sportswear feel. Despite the lack of a front placket opening, the ribbed collar is unmistakably polo inspired. **3** A subverted polo shirt with three-button placket and shirt neck with exaggerated proportions. The embellished fur gives it a whimsical twist. **4** Printed lightweight-jersey polo dress with short, capped sleeves and a flared skirt. The green rib collar and deep dropped waistband contrast with the print. **5** Ribbed-jersey bodice with collar, four-buttoned placket, and long sleeves, taking inspiration from the polo but creating a more feminine and formal version. **6** Bound with a contrast taping, the bib front extends to the curved hemline, crossing over the back at the hips to form the skirt of the dress. **7** Soft, mercerized-cotton, polo-inspired vest cut from large rectangles with ribbed collar, bound armholes, and hem. **8** Soft, feminine take on the polo dress, tapered to flare to the hemline.

Body conscious/tube/sheath

The body-conscious trend was fueled in the 1980s by a culture promoting the ideal body—a body that demanded appreciation in figure-hugging designs. Norma Kamali brought body-conscious garments out of the domain of dance- and sportswear and into mainstream fashion. Azzedine Alaïa was influential in introducing stretch and tubular-knitted garments into mainstream fashion, with a focus on clothes that enhanced the wearer's shape, creating curves in all the right places through the use of advanced knitted textiles, clever seaming, and perfect fit. Another popular technique, embraced by designers such as Pam Hogg, used color-blocked panels instead of seams. Hervé Léger showed his impressive "bandage" dress in 1989, a sleek dress that looked like it had been made from elasticized bandages wrapped around the body. British designer Julien Macdonald skimmed the body with gossamer knitted, complex, weblike lace structures, and, more recently, knitwear designer Mark Fast has taken the crown as king of knitted body-conscious fashion with his figure-enhancing statement pieces.

The body-conscious, and particularly sheath, styles are at their most dramatic when worn full length for evening wear. The body-conscious style can be practical and comfortable for day wear, working equally as well around the knee- or mini-length. When translated in jersey fabric, body-conscious seaming and color blocking can adopt a younger, sportier vibe. Sleeve lengths can vary from long and skinny to capped, sleeveless, and strapped. Necklines maintain the inherent simplicity of the shape, with scooped, horseshoe, and round necks being the most common.

Metallic-foiled quarter-inch bandages are braided together using the **macramé** technique. Each bandage is then secured by hand to a stretch-mesh base. The result is a body-conscious, one-of-a-kind couture dress.

Open-lace and laddering effects create design detailing and integrate the shaping. With a deep V neck and set-in armhole, the knit-stitch detailing on the sleeve head gives the effect of a **leg-of-mutton sleeve**. The stitch structure creates a scalloped effect at the hem and neckline.

KEY CHARACTERISTICS

- ☑ **Enhance body shape with advanced knitted construction**
- ☑ **Clever seaming and use of innovative technology for perfect fit**
- ☑ **New fibers and threads with inherent stretch qualities**

1 Knitted bandages are linked together to create this form-fitting style. Hardware pieces woven into the body of the dress add embellishment. **2** The drape of the cowl extends to waist level, with the drape continuing into the skirt, creating a soft, fluid silhouette. **3** Knitted-jersey tunic dress with contrast color blocking to create graphic impact. The turtleneck and capped sleeve trimmed in red, and the white yoke panel, create accents. **4** Vertically running bandages are inserted into the hip and thigh area to create an exaggerated hourglass shape. The surface of each bandage is flocked, adding a luxurious dimension. **5** Bandages in variegated widths are combined with hand-woven inserts that wrap over one shoulder and run down the side seam. **6** Nude-color rhinestone-embellished fabric stretches over the body to form a strapless dress. Ruching at the sides creates movement and a twist at the bust adds interest. **7** Bandage panels are blocked with metallic liquid-jersey and sheer stretch-mesh panels in this form-fitting dress. **8** Individual bandages are woven through hardware pieces at the side and rib cage.

Body conscious/tube/sheath (continued)

> Strapless dress with built-in bust support. Individually knitted bandages are linked together to follow and highlight the curves of the **female form**. The waist and center-front skirt detail is made from multiple narrow bandages held together with **hardware pieces**.

High-twist rayon yarn is knitted into individual bandages that are linked together to create this **form-fitting** dress that sculpts and enhances the body. The **tonal leather harness** worn on top defines the waistline and highlights the silhouette.

KNIT DRESS

Separately knitted and foiled bandages are **wrapped, linked, and woven** together to create this unique body-contouring dress. The **metallic finish** of the bandages adds definition and dimension to each detail.

Individual bandages are linked together to create this form-fitting dress. Contrasting bandages with a **three-dimensional rubberized print** are attached on top, highlighting the silhouette and accentuating the curves.

Constructed from signature Hervé Léger bandages, this form-fitting dress has **corsetry inspired** style lines that restrain and contour the body. Open-mesh, laddered **macramé panels** embellished with metal beads are inserted at the hip and shoulder.

1 The halter neckline of the sheath dress is gathered by shoestring straps that tie at the back. **2** The column shape is broken up by a diagonal seam with a draped frill from shoulder to waist, accentuated by contrast inverted coloring. **3** A simple column-shaped dress that is broken up by a revealing, deep slash to the hip. **4** Figure-clinging sheath dress with a high neckline and elongated sleeves. A diamond-shaped cutout makes the dress backless and breaks up the solid column silhouette. **5** Multicolored crochet circles create an artisan look. The simple tubular shape is an ideal vehicle for such a complex pattern. **6** The curved split of the dress gives a petal effect at the hemline. Fitted at the bodice to accentuate the contours of the body, the strapless effect reveals the cleavage, while a yoke attached at the underarm suggests a separate shrug. **7** A black sheath dress broken up by geometric color blocking at the hip and neck. The split to above the knee allows for ease of movement. **8** This multistrapped knit dress has a dramatic cutaway at the waist that is balanced visually by the feathered bottom-half of the skirt.

Body conscious/tube/sheath (continued)

KNIT DRESS

Use of full-fashioning creates contrasting horizontal and vertical striping that fit and complement the curves of the body. The column effect is accentuated with an **elongated silhouette,** from high neck to ankle length.

Alternative technique and bodice: Color blocking has been translated into rib texture with cutaway armholes and spaghetti straps

The illusion of multiple garments is created with the use of **varying gauges, yarns, and colors,** with rib, cable, and stockinette, and the use of full-fashioning. The color blocking helps to accentuate the body contours with waist and bodice definition.

An ankle-length sheath dress in **bronze Lurex.** The demure high, round neckline and elbow-length sleeves are contradicted by the **clingy, reflective fabric** that reveals every curve of the body.

Body conscious/tube/sheath (continued)

Separately knitted bandages in variegated widths and different shades of **gray ombré** are combined with hand-woven inserts inspired by the **lacing** on athletic footwear.

Panels in **varying colors and weights** contrast matte and shine. The jersey skirt in a heavier weight suggests **overalls** with a narrow bib front that is incorporated into the crew neck.

Alternative neckline: V neckline with narrow double straps merging into a wrestler back

Double-faced bandages are folded and woven through elastic cording down the side seam and at the center front of the dress. The result is a soft **geometric pattern** in a flattering, body-contouring silhouette.

Silver **sequin-embellished** knitted-mesh minidress with three-quarter-length sleeves and exaggerated shoulders. Fullness at the sleeve head helps to accentuate the **squared shoulders**.

< Fine-gauge **spandex-mix** jersey knitted dress with intarsia and printed mirror-image pattern. Typical **T-shirt silhouette** with a crew neck and short sleeves, the dress can be worn as a micro mini or teamed with separates.

KNIT DRESS

COATDRESS

Taking inspiration from outerwear, the coatdress is an essential consideration in many collections. The tailored dress style, traditionally translated in suiting or heavier-weight fabric, makes it a wardrobe staple and an ideal style for career dressing.

Button-front coatdress with 1920s flapper and 1960s Yves St Laurent influences, evident in the dropped waistline, buckled belt, bracelet-length sleeves, and over-proportioned decorative revers collar.

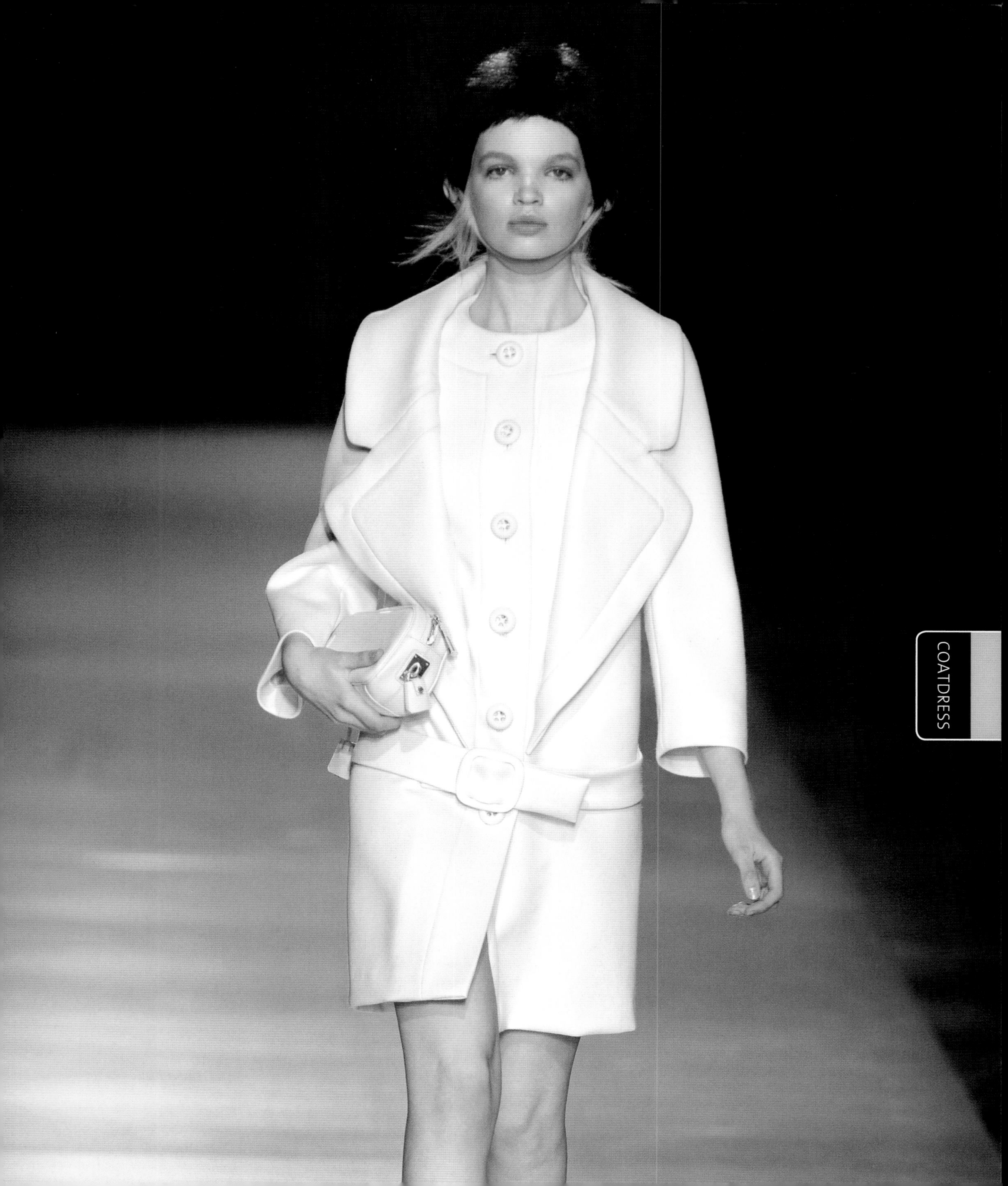

In context

From Armani's Fall 1983 ready-to-wear collection, the coatdress has obvious outerwear characteristics. The broad, padded shoulders with long set-in sleeves create a strong masculine silhouette typical of the power dressing of the 1980s. The heavy vertical stripe woven fabric gives weight to the pared-down rectangular form, and the patch pockets at hip level on each side of the front panel reinforces the coat styling.

The coatdress design references outerwear-garment details and often borrows stylistic accents from the classic trench coat and tailored suiting styles. Coatdresses can be double- or single-breasted, with leather or tie belts to add definition. The coatdress incorporates fastenings such as large button, toggle, and zipper closures that further reflect the outerwear style. It includes large patch, besom, and welt pockets.

Today, the coatdress will usually have a front fastening, although in the 1960s the center-back zipper fastening was a popular alternative, offered in contrasting black and white and pastel-colored cottons and wool. Designs were mainly collarless or included a Peter Pan collar with faux-front button fastening. Trims played an important part of the coatdress design, with embellished and contrast-color binding on necklines, collars, and pockets.

The popularity of the coatdress style continued into the 1970s, when it became the uniform for the strong, independent working woman. The style evolved through the decades, mirroring the silhouette of the time. In the 1980s, it became boxier in shape and less tailored, with oversized shoulder pads to accentuate the square silhouette of the time, typified by Donna Karan and Armani. The dress often had rolled-up sleeves with contrast fabric lining and was rarely worn cinched in at the waist. It was often teamed with leggings and ski pants. Rei Kawakubo subverted this less-formal approach in her 1983 collection, which included oversized coatdresses cut large and square with no definitive shape or silhouette. During the 1990s, the coatdress style was at the forefront of fashion and echoed more of a frock-coat style, with a fit-and-flare silhouette. Often sleeveless, with exaggerated wing collars, the coatdress became an ideal garment for spring/summer when translated in lighter-weight and sheer fabrics.

Today, with less distinction of silhouette and more choice in design than ever before, the coatdress emerges in a variety of styles and silhouettes.

Double-breasted coatdress in wool tweed by Dior in 1955. The oversized grown-on collar with revers open wide, touching the armhole. The side placket opening is buttoned from below the bust finishing at the hip, creating a figure-hugging silhouette to calf length. This creates a sheath style with a nipped waist accentuated by padded shoulders and full gathered sleeves.

Design considerations

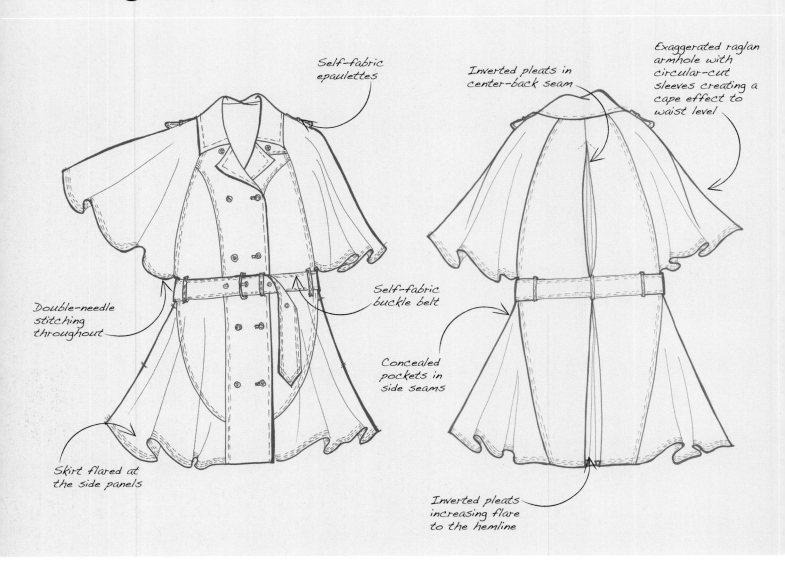

Self-fabric epaulettes

Inverted pleats in center-back seam

Exaggerated raglan armhole with circular-cut sleeves creating a cape effect to waist level

Double-needle stitching throughout

Self-fabric buckle belt

Concealed pockets in side seams

Skirt flared at the side panels

Inverted pleats increasing flare to the hemline

Silhouette Taking direction from outerwear and tailored garments, the coatdress silhouette is wide-ranging. From cocoon shapes inspired by generously cut winter wool coats (that is a rounded, soft form with little body definition), to semifitted silhouettes echoing the fit and structure of tailored jackets.

Shaping The coatdress can be loosely styled, semifitted, or fitted, with style lines that create the desired silhouette as well as reflect the shaping on coats and tailored garments. The shape must utilize the characteristics of outerwear in order to accomplish the coatdress style.

Hemlines If designed to be worn alone, the coatdress usually falls around the knee, either slightly above or below, with a deep felled hem replicating the substantial finishings of the coat. Often designed as part of an outfit, the coatdress can be maxi length with a fluid, wider hem width.

Fabric Although traditionally manufactured in heavier-weight fabrics, such as wools and suiting, and fully lined for the fall/winter season—to reflect its outerwear origins—the coatdress style can also be translated in lighter-weight fabrics, such as linen, georgette, and organdy, making it a perfect garment for spring/summer and special occasions.

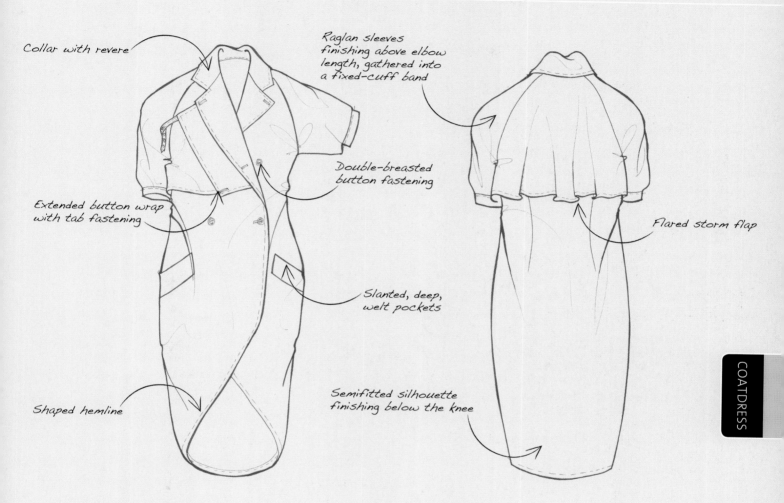

Collar with revere

Raglan sleeves finishing above elbow length, gathered into a fixed-cuff band

Double-breasted button fastening

Extended button wrap with tab fastening

Slanted, deep, welt pockets

Flared storm flap

Shaped hemline

Semifitted silhouette finishing below the knee

Fastenings Can be either front- or back-neck fastened with large button or zipper closures, depending on the design. Front-fastened coatdresses can be wrap, single-, or double-breasted with tied or fixed belts, concealed button or zipper plackets or toggles with rouleau loops.

Necklines and collars Usually round or V neck, though if designed with a collar, the collar and fastening type will dictate the neckline shape, width, and drop.

Styles can include tuxedo-inspired revers, and wing, mandarin, or Eton collars.

Sleeves The nature of the silhouette will inform the type of armhole and sleeve. Typically, a generously cut coatdress will have wide rounded shoulders and raglan, magyar, or dolman sleeves. A more fitted silhouette usually dictates narrower shoulders and skinnier sleeves, often a two-piece set-in sleeve.

Pockets Pockets are an important consideration in the design of the coat, a consideration that is also reflected in the design of the coatdress. As well as adding interest to the style, they also need to be functional and well positioned. Pockets can be welt, besom, oversized patch, or concealed in side seams, reflecting tailoring details.

Tailored

Traditionally a semiformal garment resembling a dress, the tailored coatdress utilizes many stylistic features of the tailored jacket and coat. Tailoring is synonymous with craftsmanship, resolute quality, and attention to detail, which the tailored coatdress aims to reflect in its design. The dress is front-fastened, button-through, and can be single- or double-breasted with collar and revers and two-piece sleeves.

Conventionally a fall/winter garment in suiting fabric and fully lined, the tailored coatdress is now commonly translated in lighter-weight fabrics and can be worn as a dress or coat. Ranging from sleeveless to short sleeved and long sleeved, the tailored coatdress can be fitted and body conscious or maxi length and flared, reminiscent of the frock-coat style. Bodice seams and style lines reflect those found on tailored jackets and often include a center-back vent for ease of movement. In contrast to the wrap coatdress style, the tailored coatdress relies on balance or symmetry. This is achieved by including identical design details placed either side of the center front, such as pockets, tabs, or stitching. The pockets on the tailored coatdress are often angled and can be besom with pocket flaps or welt. Repetition is also an important design consideration and happens when a particular feature or trim is repeated throughout the garment to create a well-balanced design.

These attributes all make the tailored coatdress an ideal garment for career dressing.

KEY CHARACTERISTICS

☑ Stylistic features of tailored jacket and coat

☑ Front fastened, button through, single or double breasted, with collar and revers and two-piece sleeves

☑ Balance and symmetry

Tailored coatdress with a wrap that crosses center front with a **curved detail** at bodice front, reinforced by a curve at the front hem opening.

Alternative fastening and collar: Straight cut, displaced button wrap with asymmetric collar

The leather bodice is cut and fastened edge to edge with a collarless neckline. The bodice is fitted and formed, defining the bust and creating a **structured** look. This is contrasted by the soft fake-fur skirt, which creates **softness and volume**.

COATDRESS

1 A deep collarless V opening is wrapped at the waist, revealing a contrast band of black. Fastenings are hidden, maintaining an architectural, minimal structure. 2 Trapeze-style coatdress with a high V neck. Color-blocked side panels and sleeves create an optical illusion. 3 Tuxedo-style coatdress with an asymmetrical wrap fastened on the left. The placket and collar revers change in scale and shape. The placket opening ends at the hip but visually continues. 4 Double-breasted sharp tailored coatdress with a four-button fastening and four decoy buttons, giving a military effect. The caped shoulders form a short draped sleeve. 5 This four-button, knee-length, double-breasted sleeveless coatdress has a wide shawl collar and deep pockets with flaps. 6 Oversized trench coatdress. Silk softly blousons into the belted waist and cuffs. 7 A slim, fitted trench coatdress with traditional details, such as the tie belt through belt tabs and vertical side-slash pockets with stand. 8 Single-breasted and buttoned up the front to the neck, with a high funnel collar, this fitted dress has contrast paneling in cotton sateen, giving a bibbed tuxedo effect.

Tailored (continued)

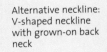

The mock coat effect is accentuated by **decorative revers** and draped pockets with black lining, contrasted against the gray mélange. Short sleeves and **shoulder-buttoned** fastenings redefine the traditions of the coat shape.

Heavy wool coatdress fitted to the waist and flared to below the knee hemline. The **diagonal darts** to the waistband create shaping and open out as boxed pleats, giving volume to the skirt. A concealed-button placket within the facing at center front perpetuates the **uncomplicated** silhouette.

Alternative neckline: V-shaped neckline with grown-on back neck

Graphic monochromatic dress with contrast **single breast welt pocket** that continues in a sweeping curlicue to form a double-breasted, concealed-button opening. The high break point of the neckline juxtaposes with the **deep hem opening**, providing visual contrast.

< The deep, wrap-over stand collar with button-strap fastening, deep raglan armhole, epaulettes at the shoulder, and buttoned cuffs give a **military feel**.

COATDRESS

Wool coatdress with military references. It has a curved edge and a **distinctive buttoned flap** stitched into the side seam. Wide three-quarter-length sleeves are trimmed with buttoned flaps at the cuffs.

Alternative neckline, armhole, and sleeves: Double-breasted V neck with raglan armhole and extended shoulder seam

Tailored (continued)

> A column silhouette is created with the positioning **vertical darts** that create definition of the bodice, then open to create pleats each side of the back and front panels. The deep round neckline has an elongated **funnel neck**. The deep silver leather belt breaks up the column and defines the waist.

Double-breasted coatdress with shirt neck-stand collar. **Military influences** are expressed by self-fabric epaulettes. Vertical seaming, left and right of front panels, reinforces the straight-column silhouette.

Alternative shoulder detail: The double fabric front and back yoke is left unattached at the sleeve head, allowing the set-in sleeve to be inserted into the recess

With strong references to coat styling, this dress suggests a front opening with a **deep box pleat** running down the center front. Pleats again define the shoulder, running from front to back, and continue in a vertical line outlining the **side panels.** Set-in sleeves complete the elongated column effect and center-back fastenings allow the streamlined front to remain uncluttered.

Understated simple coatdress with no evidence of trim or embellishment. **A concealed-button front** is disguised in the placket facing with center-front opening.

Alternative sleeves and neckline: Short sleeves with a round neckline

Colorful, kaleidoscope-inspired florals decorate this otherwise simple straight coatdress. The plain black collar and **deep placket** break the pattern at center front. Straight, long, set-in sleeves contribute to the **simple silhouette.** The dress has a sense of cultural reference, defined by the ornate pattern.

Housecoat

With its origins in the 1940s and '50s, and sometimes referred to as a duster coat, the housecoat was worn to protect the day's outfit while performing the household chores. Varying in style, though usually knee length or longer to conceal any undergarments, the housecoat developed during the 1950s into a more elegant and sophisticated garment for entertaining at home.

Originally in lightweight fabric and sometimes quilted for warmth, the housecoat had a loose and easy cut with little waist definition to allow for ease of movement. Often designed with a front and back yoke, the housecoat of the 1940s hung from the shoulders with soft gathering at the yoke seams. Front fastened with buttons or zipper and with a round neck and collar, the 1940s housecoat was either long- or short-sleeved.

Over time, the housecoat silhouette evolved to reflect Dior's New Look. The waist was defined and sometimes accentuated with a tie belt, the bodice was fitted, and the skirts long and full. Styles were single- and double-breasted with more variety of collars, such as revers and shawl. Sleeves were often dolman with turn-back cuffs and could be short, long, or three-quarter length. With its roots as a functional, practical garment, all housecoats had pockets, usually in the form of patch pockets, though during the 1950s the pocket designs were more varied and elaborate.

The floor-length housecoat with long sleeves has a **monastical** appearance. The high stand-up collar dips to a V-neck opening, and strategic darts help to create the stand. Fitted to the waist seam, the dress has a slight **A-line shaping** to skim the floor. The cut edges of the felted fabric are left unfinished.

The rectangular shapes, straight front placket, and tie belt demonstrate a nod to the **kimono**. The contrast of matte and shine fabrics forms the main surface interest.

Alternative belt detail: Belt loops have been integrated into the main body of the design

1 Oversized geometric shapes form a loose dress. The deep V neck meets a center-front seam that runs to a low waistband. The skirt has a center-front seam with a turn-back mock opening.
2 A deep funnel-neck collar falls softly to create an unstructured effect, framing the neckline. 3 Deep V-neck jersey dress with a wide self-fabric belt tied at the waist with references to the bathrobe.

Sleeves are fitted to the elbow, where a a bell-shaped lower sleeve attaches. 4 Bold, geometric-printed taffeta trapeze dress. Wide elbow-length sleeves have a deep turned-back cuff. The zippered front opens to a revers collar. 5 Maxi-length, shirt-style housecoat with placket front opening buttoned to thigh. The striped fabric is cut directionally to contrast and define the different

panels. 6 Wrap housecoatdress with deep shawl collar. Cuffs are edged with narrow satin ribbon, which is also used to tie the waist. 7 Contrast panels of sheer and solid patterned chiffon are left to hang loosely from the waistline. The overlay on the right-hand bodice is looped and anchored to create a three-dimensional effect. 8 Bold-floral A-line housecoat-style dress inspired by 1950s vintage.

Wrap

The wrap coatdress has a front closure created by wrapping one side of the garment over the other and securing with a self-fabric tie or separate leather belt. The easygoing lines of the wrap create an informal balance or asymmetry to the design. The wrap closure invites the eye to travel without interruption over the entire garment. This loose-fitting, casual shape shows similarities to the menswear polo coat or camel's hair coat popularized in the 1920s, worn by polo players after their games. This gentle silhouette was modified with a dropped waistline on a shift shape for womenswear in the 1920s. Eventually, the polo-coat influence was surpassed by the emergence of the trench coat. The current wrap coatdress takes direction from both these design classics.

The traditional trench coat is a windbreaker and raincoat, with its origins in military use. Styling details, such as raglan sleeves, epaulettes, and deep patch pockets with flaps, are common qualities of the wrap coatdress, particularly popular during the 1980s and the power-dressing 1990s. Although masculine in its foundation, the wrap front closure accentuates the female body and forms a flattering V neckline, personifying the silhouette of the 1950s. At this time, the wrap coatdress was very feminine in its translation, often in taffeta, with dolman sleeves and a very full skirt, indicating little acknowledgment of its mannish heritage.

Silk gazar fabric holds its shape to achieve a strong silhouette within this dramatic coatdress. The **extended draped collar** breaks at the waist, exposing a plunging neckline. The wrap front is shaped and curved at the hemline, reinforcing the **rounded shapes**.

The **curved wrap front is** attached at the side seams. Short, puff, set-in sleeves are trimmed with a single button cuff. The **contrast color blocking** emphasizes the collar cuff and pocket details and defines the front placket opening.

KEY CHARACTERISTICS

- ☑ **Front, wrap closing**
- ☑ **Menswear polo-coat and trench-coat influences**
- ☑ **Double-breasted and tie-front fastenings**

1 A round neck and softly curved shoulders of magyar sleeves create the cocoon shapes of this wrap dress. **2** Two-tone matte-and-shine woven fabrics give a contemporary edge to a traditional shape. **3** The wrap on this coatdress is deceptive, seemingly crossing in opposite directions at the bodice and the skirt. The lack of symmetry is accentuated by the shawl collar on the right and the single pocket at the left hip. **4** With caftan references, this wrap-front dress has dropped shoulders, wide kimono sleeves, a simple round neckline, and a deep sash at the waistline. **5** Coatdress with a diagonal wrap styling in quilt-effect satin. **6** Sleeveless silk coatdress with a stand collar that extends at the neck opening to form a tie. **7** The print is engineered to take into consideration the asymmetry of the garment's cut while maintaining the symmetry of the print at center front. The A-line of the skirt is echoed in the V neckline and emphasized by the placement of the border print. **8** Stone linen wrap coatdress with contrasting gray silk sleeves, grown-on collar and revers, and shoulder yoke.

Cape

Based on a sleeveless outerwear garment, the cape coatdress takes inspiration from ponchos, cloaks, capes, and opera coats. Frequently used as a fashion statement, the cape shape reflects the origins of the cape as a rainwear garment, or its function to protect the fine fabrics of evening-wear garments that may be crushed by more traditional coats with set-in sleeves.

The cape is derived from a simple garment, the cloak being the longer version. Based on a circular shape, ranging from a half circle to a full circle, though rarely translated in this simple form, the cape shape nowadays requires fit and tailoring around the shoulder. The sleeveless, circular cape shape can be used to inform the entire coatdress silhouette, cut long, like a cloak, with openings in the front panels to allow easy movement of the arms without the garment's riding up. This shape can be belted at the front to define the waist and keep the fabric close to the body while hanging loose, voluminous, and away from the body at the back, creating a striking side view. The shorter-length shape can often add interest to the shoulder area in the form of a tier inserted into the neckline over a fitted dress, to contrast the fullness of the circular cape. The exaggerated collar, shawl, and traditional cape styles can be traced from Paul Poiret to Rei Kawakubo for Commes des Garçon.

Fitted mini-length dress with a **multicolored basket-weave** pattern. The sleeve head is set into the shoulder at the top, leaving the underarm as sleeveless. The sleeves fall over the bare arms, increasing in volume to the cuff to achieve a **cape effect.** The round neckline and patch pockets complete the look.

The asymmetrical cape detail across the **left shoulder** is attached at the waistband at front and back, and the coat style is further emphasized by the use of epaulettes.

Alternative neckline and sleeves: Round neckline with button front fastening and short, flared sleeves

KEY CHARACTERISTICS

☑ Derived from ponchos, cloaks, capes, and opera coats

☑ Based on a circular shape

☑ Openings in the front panels to allow easy movement of arms

1 Oversized sleeves wrap across the body to mimic a cape. The saddle shoulder leads to a dropped sleeve that has a vent opening at underarm for practicality. 2 The storm cape with buttoned epaulettes is attached to a collar that buttons at the neck and fastens with buttons to the bodice. 3 Rectangular and structured, the envelope effect is created by a pleat with a deep return that folds back vertically from the extended square shoulder line, giving the cape effect. 4 The exaggerated trapeze shape and wide, bell-shaped, three-quarter-length sleeves give the impression of a cape. 5 Heavily embellished dress with exaggerated shoulders and slash V front that forms the focal point of the design. 6 Fitted wool dress that gently flares to the knee. The oversized bell-shaped collar turns back, falling below armhole level to form a cape. 7 Fluted gathers are cut from a circle and gathered into a flat bib-front bodice; they extend over the armhole and shoulder, giving a cape effect. 8 Sleeves integrated into a voluminous floor-length cape. The round neck and circular armhole, cut from the cape, continue the curved lines.

CULTURAL INFLUENCES

The wealth of the world's cultural heritage has been a source of inspiration for designers throughout the ages, providing references for ideas that inform silhouette, pattern, detail, color, and textiles.

A substantial quantity of fabric is softly gathered at the waistline, cinched with a feature metal-buckle belt. The sleeve and bodice are integrated, cut from one piece and draped diagonally across the body into the skirt. The contrasting skintight jersey body on the left side creates a plunging V neckline to the waist.

In context

Laura Ashley captured the romantic 1970s ideals of pastoralism most often seen as British country or American prairie aesthetic. Particularly important were the ditsy floral prints, puff sleeves, and sweet ruffles that decorate this dress of 1974. The dress is girlish, suggesting an innocence or absence of the cares of the world.

Throughout history, historical and cultural costume and textiles have been cross-fertilized as design references. The conquests and subsequent spoils of war have meant that exotic and valuable merchandise has been transported across the world and adopted by various civilizations. International trading throughout continents, promoting cultural exchanges, has also resulted in the cross-fertilization of ideas. With the migration of pioneers looking for new lands to create a better life, traditions and skills have transferred overseas and mingled with other cultures, inseminating knowledge, ideas, values, and philosophies, and embracing new ways of looking.

The human desire to collect and interpret has led to the establishment of museums, exhibiting rich and varied collections that allowed ordinary people, without the means to travel, to view interesting relics and works of art from foreign lands.

Immigration has always been a catalyst for cultural exchange, and the melting pot of ethnicity, particularly within larger cities, has provided a rich and exciting mix of multicultural inspiration. With budget travel making the world accessible to many, and the Internet giving access to a wealth of information, international cultural influences pervade our lives.

Designers have always taken advantage of the treasure trove of resources available. Kenzo, Anna Sui, and Betsey Johnson, among others, focus not only on the cultural heritage of fashion and textiles, but more widely investigate art, decorative arts, architecture, and historical and popular culture. Process and techniques have also crossed nations, resulting in changes in influence on fashion houses. Design directors, crossing continents, shape changes in direction of labels such as Missoni, Chanel, Givenchy, Saint Laurent, and Balenciaga.

The languid beauty of Greek sculpture influenced Madame Grès, who created stunningly modern gowns. Throughout the 1930s and 1940s Madame Grès used incredible amounts of fabric to create these pleated dresses, constructing them by hand. The inset, horizontally pleated panels create the visual effect of a small waist, while the vertical pleats elongate the figure.

Design considerations

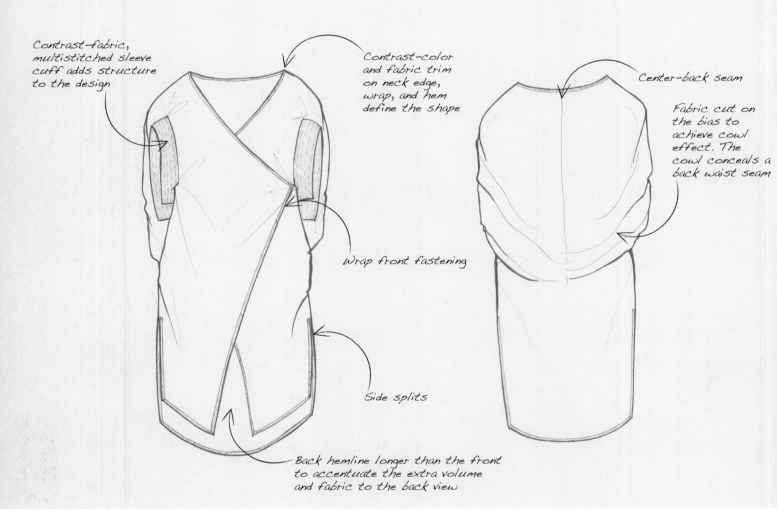

Contrast-fabric, multistitched sleeve cuff adds structure to the design

Contrast-color and fabric trim on neck edge, wrap, and hem define the shape

Center-back seam

Fabric cut on the bias to achieve cowl effect. The cowl conceals a back waist seam

Wrap front fastening

Side splits

Back hemline longer than the front to accentuate the extra volume and fabric to the back view

Silhouette The silhouette is dictated by the point of reference and can be oversized and voluminous, enveloping the body and disguising its contours, or long, lean, and sheath-like. From loosely fitting, comfortable to wear, and one-size-fits-all, through to semifitted or body defining, the silhouette is dictated by the cultural theme.

Length Short and sassy, long and languid—the variations of length reflect the cultural inspiration. Layering is a common trend, and asymmetrical hemlines can blur the definition of length and silhouette.

Fabrics The cultural origins of the style can be translated through richly ornate textiles: fine chiffon and sunray-pleated silks; jerseys appropriate for draping and gathering; cotton lawns, fine wools, silk habotai, terry voile, seersucker, cheesecloth, muslin, linen, slubs, and sanded silks; woven silk brocades, jacquards, ginghams, ikats, lace and embroidered lengths, floral and geometric prints, dip-dyeing, batik and shibori, broderie anglaise, distressed rayon, and other manmade fabrics, and many alternative fabrics that suit the particular theme.

Embellishment Lace, braiding, smocking, embroidery, beading, fagoting, pin tucks, rouleaus, shirring, frogging, quilting, appliqué, and patchwork are among the numerous options available.

Empire-line bodice with underbust seam accentuated with piping

Straight sweetheart neckline

Front panel heavily embellished with embroidery and sequins

Knife-pleated side panels

The ornate embellishment creates interest and complements the seaming and style lines

Center-back invisible zip

Bracelet-length set-in sleeves

Semifitted silhouette finishing at midi length

Necklines The design of the neckline is a strong feature because it often shows a seductive flash of cleavage or a flaunt of shoulder with a slash neck. The neckline can be a V, round and scooped, boatneck, or shaped into a decorative front yoke. Cultural references can inform neckline styling, collars, and yokes, creating a focal point and design statement.

Sleeves Sleeves can make a dramatic statement and define a look and theme. The sleeve may be integrated into the body if the garment is a large rectangular shape, like a caftan. Drop shoulders are commonly used to mimic kimono sleeves, or for a Westernized version of the caftan. More elaborate statement sleeves can be set in with gathered sleeve heads and cuffs. Spaghetti straps and capped or short puffed sleeves can provide a softer, more feminine aesthetic, particularly evident in boho and prairie styles.

Boho

The word *bohemian* describes a multicultural, gypsy traveler with artistic and romantic tendencies and exemplifies a nomadic and spirited lifestyle unconstrained by the rules of society. Boho chic reflects this spirit, and looks to the hippies of the 1970s for inspiration. The style mismatches an eclectic mix of ethnic sources, as if the wearer has traveled around the world and picked up decorative textiles and authentic garments along the way and put them back together in a melting pot of styles, patterns, and colors.

Soft, unstructured cutting and draping, mixing fabric qualities, and not being afraid to mix scales of print and fabric textures are characteristics of this style. Decorative embellishments that take advantage of handicraft techniques can be added; as can braids and ribbons, ties and leather thongs, and trims, fleece, and fur. Gathers, dirndls, pleats, and tiered layers may be used to add volume and create a feminine aesthetic. Tie-dye and batik, discharge- and dip-dyeing, and overdyeing prints with shibori techniques can all add to the ethnic quality.

Loosely fitted silhouettes with an emphasis on layering implement a variety of lengths from mini, midi, to maxi. Hemlines can be asymmetrical, using handkerchief shapes, or layered with petticoats. Dresses may be sleeveless or feature big, billowing sleeve shapes with gathered sleeve heads and cuffs.

This **geometric, Aztec-inspired** sundress has a deep printed border at the hem that complements the embroidered front bodice bib. The scalloped hem of the bib is reflected in the design of the **embroidery,** and is mirrored either side of the center-front button placket that ends just above the top-hip level.

This printed sundress has a high round neck that complements the cutaway armholes, reflecting a **sportswear cut. The voluminous skirt** is paneled to achieve more flare.

Alternative neckline: Deep V neckline with drawstring under-bust tie

KEY CHARACTERISTICS

- ☑ **Eclectic mix of ethnic sources, prints, and textures**
- ☑ **Loosely fitted silhouette**
- ☑ **Decorative embellishments that take advantage of handicraft techniques**

1 This mini shift shape has a crochet neck trim that continues down to create a detailed center front. The skirt has deep embroidered side panels and a wide lace border at the hem. **2** The full-length skirt is gathered into the empire line to achieve volume. The horizontal bands give structure and interest to the skirt. **3** Simple A-line shaped silk dress with ornate embellishment on the chest and sheer sleeves. **4** The contrasting floral prints on the yoke, the long sleeves, and the shirt-dress panels evoke a folksy boho look. **5** The use of multiple complementary prints in one design emphasizes the garment details and features. **6** This Navaho-inspired dress is mini length, with a wide and scooped neckline, a deep feather border at the hem, and a heavily embroidered and appliquéd front-placement design. **7** High-waisted, peasant-style midi dress in black muslin cotton. Brightly colored embroidered florals decorate the bodice and are scattered across the skirt. **8** A loosely fitted, georgette dress with a self-fabric drawstring neckline and waist. Frills at the cuffs and hemline reflect the gathered waist.

Boho (continued)

> This velvet dress and jacket give the impression of **patchwork** construction. The silhouette, proportions, rope binding, and tassels reference the 1960s and 1970s counter-culture's fascination with **alternative** craft and sources of fashion.

This cotton dress has a **wide scooped neckline**, the curve of which is reflected in the shape of the sleeves and fullness of the skirt. The folkloric-inspired **floral appliqué**, placed around the skirt border and waistline, defines the silhouette.

Alternative neckline and sleeves: Square neckline with flared, short sleeves

This garment has been designed to complement the **chiffon allover-print pattern** while accentuating the garment's style lines and silhouette. The bias-cut skirt and godet inserts exploit the characteristics of the lightweight chiffon fabric. The full, **bell-shaped long sleeves** gathered into a traditional cuff and oversized, self-fabric bow give a thrift-store appeal.

Traditional **scarf designs** have been reworked in a contemporary way to create this modern **patchwork** print. The print's colorway and the relaxed, draped silhouette achieve a boho aesthetic.

A **contemporary interpretation** of folklore-inspired lace that has been translated into a **simple caftan shape** to maximize the fabric's design. The lace design is used instead of style lines to define the body and give proportion to the style.

CULTURAL INFLUENCES

Prairie

Prairie styling originates from images of the American Midwest, with design references to the idealized sentimentality and wholesome values of the pioneers of the new frontiers. Calamity Jane meets The Waltons meets Little House on the Prairie and Anne of Green Gables.

Textiles feature Navajo Indian geometric patterns, ikats, cowgirl ginghams, broderie anglaise, embroidery, lace trims, pin tucks, patchwork, checks, denim, and suede-leather fringes. Silhouettes include calf- or full-length gathered skirts, high-waisted or waisted, sometimes tiered or worn over lace petticoats, as well as poncho-style caftan shapes with fringes. Dresses vary from smocks, knitted, Fair Isle sweaterdresses, dungaree dresses, and full-length riding-coat dresses to oversized shirt dresses. Trims derive from fringed Indian-inspired yokes, hemlines, and sleeves, to handcrafted folk art, Indian beadwork, saddlery hardware, and leather strapping. Looks can be accessorized with cowgirl boots, leather belts, and saddlebags.

The prairie style is the trademark look of American designer Ralph Lauren. Natural kei is also a trend that evolved in Japan in the 1970s, reflecting period and pastoral life. Laura Ashley popularized the prairie look in the 1970s and 1980s, with tiered cotton printed dresses. The trend can be seen in Marc Jacobs' spring/summer 2009 collection; Rodarte's rustic, full-length coats with patchwork and wheat prints for fall/winter 2011; and Isabel Marant's fall/winter 2011 collection.

This dress has a simple slashed neckline with grown-on capped sleeves in a busy allover print. The relaxed, **loosely fitted bodice**, full maxi-length gathered skirt, and **ethnic-inspired woven waistband** detail add a feminine and sophisticated hippie feel to this style.

The **oversized cut** creates a relaxed, easy-to-wear garment. The raglan sleeves are voluminous and the wide, **elasticated neckline** could be worn on or off the shoulder. A striped belt defines the waistline and breaks up the bold print, while the tucks on the skirt generate additional volume.

KEY CHARACTERISTICS

- ☑ Sentimentalized American Midwest aesthetic
- ☑ Broderie anglaise, gingham, and denim
- ☑ Embroidery, lace, pin tucks, and hardware trims
- ☑ Layers and petticoats

1 The dress consists of two layers, with the overlayer tucked and secured at the center-front hip level, creating a bustle effect on the back view. **2** Shirt-style dress with a gathered waist and dirndl skirt with frilled hem. The front bodice has pin-tucked and frilled panels that epitomize the prairie style. **3** Floor-length dress with full multilayered chiffon skirt and gathered frill hem.

4 The full, ankle-length skirt and long sleeves gathered into deep cuffs accentuate the beautiful drape of the fabric. The shirring detail on the shoulders, cuffs, and waistline create and balance the subtle drapery. **5** Semifitted sundress with a fitted bodice and A-line skirt. The large bertha-style collar, curved front yoke, and puff sleeves feature self-fabric frills. **6** The large waist tie

dominates this silhouette. The wide, round neckline has an inverted V-shaped cutout. The short raglan cap sleeves create a 1950s feel. **7** A traditional semifitted shirt bodice and short dirndl skirt, with a border detail that emphasizes the fullness of the skirt. **8** The border detail emphasizes the neckline, dropped waist, and skirt border and gives a contemporary peasant feel.

Grecian

With its heritage in Greek classical dress—and taking inspiration from wet drapery evident in Greek sculpture, where the fabric appears to cling to the body—the Grecian style reveals and disguises the contours of the figure, allowing scope for the designer to enhance and conceal different parts of the female form. To achieve the fluid classical forms of the Grecian aesthetic, fabric is draped on the body rather than cut flat, to create sumptuous, flowing folds and pleats and body-revealing drape. This technique was pioneered in the 1930s by Madame Grès, with her skillful securing of vertical pleats on jersey gowns. Precursors to Madame Grès include Mariano Fortuny, Raymond Duncan, and Madeleine Vionnet, all passionate advocates of classical dress. Fortuny was well versed in Greek art and costume, with an appreciation of a wide variety of cultures and ethnic dress. These combined influences inspired his rich color palettes and beautiful textiles, and initiated the groundbreaking pleated silk Delphos dresses, reminiscent of fluted Greek columns, are still worn today. The Pleats Please brand, launched by Issey Miyake in the 1990s, took the essence of Fortuny's easy-to-wear and comfortable aesthetic and translated it into machine-washable, lightweight polyester pleats.

The Grecian influence on fashion can transpire in a variety of ways, from fluid, draped asymmetric dresses and floor-length tunics to narrow-pleated sheath-like columns. Many contemporary designers reference this classical mode of dress and acknowledge the timeless beauty encapsulated in this aesthetic.

Sunray seaming and diagonal panels accentuate the deep V. Long, **batwing sleeves** complete the look.

Alternative neckline: Straight, slashed neckline with shaped waistband

Sarong-style wrap-over, **strapless**, long, tent-shaped dress. Although simple in appearance, the dress is built onto a structured foundation, giving hidden support.

KEY CHARACTERISTICS

- ☑ **Inspiration from wet drapery of Greek sculpture**
- ☑ **Reveals and disguises the contours of the figure**
- ☑ **Fabric draped rather than cut in flowing folds and pleats**

1 Dramatic floor-length red evening dress. The drape across the left shoulder is mirrored with an overskirt that drapes at the left hip. 2 Circular bias cutting, shirring, and asymmetrical draping create a look of classical Greek styling. 3 Geometric, rectangular shapes are shirred and gathered to create soft draping. Asymmetric draping blocks one shoulder while revealing the other. 4 Over a simple minidress foundation, tonal-colored fabrics are draped from leather straps to create an asymmetric design. 5 Mixing Grecian and sari styling, the single long sleeve and contrasting bare arm give irregularity to this cocktail dress. 6 A bodice gives fit and shape to the bustline and creates a foundation from which to overlay the chiffon draping, which continues over the sleeves and the shoulder line, then wraps and knots at the waist. Fine gathered pleating creates volume and layering to the floor-length skirt. 7 A structured high-round neckpiece is the focal point of this design and contrasts well with the sumptuous fabric of the dress. 8 Ombré-printed layers of solid and transparent fabrics give a soft, unstructured appearance to a sarong-style evening dress.

1 Short, silk satin, sleeveless skater-style dress. The contrast black V-neck insert is matched by black binding set into raglan shaping. 2 Loose-fitting, silk satin asymmetric-hem dress. The skirt is draped to create a long cowl effect on the right side. 3 Translucent organza forms a statuesque floor-length dress. Gold foiling gives the visual effect of a strapless bodice and shimmers beautifully. 4 The box shape of this dress is accentuated by the square of the slash neckline. 5 An elegant, asymmetric, single-shouldered jersey column dress. The sleeve and body are cut in one, with the wide sleeves maximizing the drape. 6 Concertina pleats are fixed to the waistband, giving definition to the body. The sleeveless armholes have been cut wide, continuing the squareness of the pattern pieces. 7 Fabric is softly draped across one shoulder, forming a wide single sleeve. The embellished border emphasizes the asymmetric neckline and adds interest to the expanse of chiffon. 8 A contrast-color, deep border drapes from the left shoulder, around the hem, and up into the back view, creating folds and a cowl effect at the side hem.

9

10

11

12

13

14

15

16

CULTURAL INFLUENCES

9 Silk dress with wide, plunging V neckline that leads to a curve-shaped waist seam. The flared skirt has sunray-pleated side panels enhancing the volume. **10** The bodice is cut and constructed to appear twisted at the center front. The circular-cut, sunray-pleated skirt is reminiscent of classical columns. **11** Multilayered chiffon strapless dress with varying-length tiered hem. **12** The diagonal of the fabric forms the neckline of this one-shouldered dress. A simple strap on the alternate side prevents the dress from slipping. **13** Toga, kimono, sari, and caftan references are all evident within this maxi dress. **14** Simple, oversized rectangular shapes form a tabard style with very little shaping. Additional fabric cut into the front panel of the dress forms the drape at the slash neckline. **15** The continuity of a length of fabric knotted and draped around the body is suggested here. In fact, clever draping builds an innovative silhouette. **16** Sheer chiffon has been draped from the shoulders and secured at the waistline by a structured, contrast-color belt. Straps define the plunging square neckline.

Grecian (continued)

A washed-silk dress that is tucked and draped from the left shoulder and over the bustline to create an empire-line effect. The excess fabric from the drape is left open and fluid to accentuate the Grecian style. Fullness is added throughout the skirt, leading to an **asymmetric hemline** that finishes just below the knee at the shortest side. The clever **print placement** accentuates the shape of the dress.

A floor-length, chiffon evening dress with **thigh-high front split** in the skirt and unusual **twisted self-fabric straps**, which act as a bold finish for the neck edge as well as informing the double-strap detail. The expanse of color and voluminous skirt, with multiple chiffon layers, create a dramatic effect.

This Lurex jersey **halter-neck** dress has a plunging, generously draped cowl neckline to the waist. The bodice blousons over the **dropped waistline** and into a draped skirt, with tucks engineered into the side seams, creating a cowl effect to the skirt and concealing pockets in the side seams.

Alternative sleeves: Extended shoulder with gathered seams creating draped cap sleeves

This fluid, empire-line, floor-length dress has a generous amount of fabric gathered into the shoulder seams, forming the **batwing sleeves** and creating a deep V neckline. The bodice is softly gathered into an **underbust seam**, leading to a dramatic expanse of fabric for the skirt.

< Asymmetric, V-neckline dress with extended shoulder seams and **deep armhole openings** that complement the loose and draped design. The **off-centered V-neck** shape reflects the draped and tucked left-side detailing.

CULTURAL INFLUENCES

Grecian (continued)

Silk satin, one-shouldered, floor-length dress with **train**. The bias-cut fabric enables the dress to skim the contours of the body with **minimal darting**. The dramatic dress length and ostrich-feather shawl add glamour.

Alternative neckline and sleeves: V neckline with extended shoulder line and asymmetric overlayer sash to side seam

Flared, bias-cut, floor-length evening dress with a **crossover front bodice** extended to create the grown-on, self-fabric wide straps. The bias-cut fabric contours the body to the lower hip, in contrast to the acutely **flared skirt** that reflects the diagonal strap detail.

This dramatic evening dress has a wide, plunging V neckline created from **fringing** layered over the bust cups and secured into metal clips at the underbust level to the waist, where it is left to hang over the skirt to achieve more movement when walking. The fringing is also tiered over the hip. The underskirt is floor length with a train and has two **thigh-high splits** either side of the center front.

1 The chiffon skirt is made up of several layers of fabric, creating a billowing silhouette. The bodice has a twisted, self-fabric neck edge that continues into the shoulder straps. **2** A butterfly-effect sleeve on the left side contrasts with the sleeveless right side. The drape across the bodice is gathered into a sequined motif on the right side of the waist. Drapery continues down the right side of the skirt. **3** Silk habotai maxi dress with deep V neckline. A sequined and embroidered waistband reflects the shape of the neckline. **4** Fine sunray pleats in an abstract floral print, with gathers at the boatneck and knot-gathered waistband that add structure and drape to simple rectangular shapes. **5** Sleeveless mini-length dress with fringing tiered over the foundation garment.

6 Asymmetric wrap-over dress with an intricately draped skirt that complements the ombré fabric treatment. **7** A fitted bodice with a fringing overlay that forms a double-strap detail. The mini-length skirt is tiered with the fringing left loose. **8** Wrap-front dress with batwing sleeves. The loose-fitting bodice blousons over the belted waistline and into a draped skirt with a twisted hemline.

Caftan

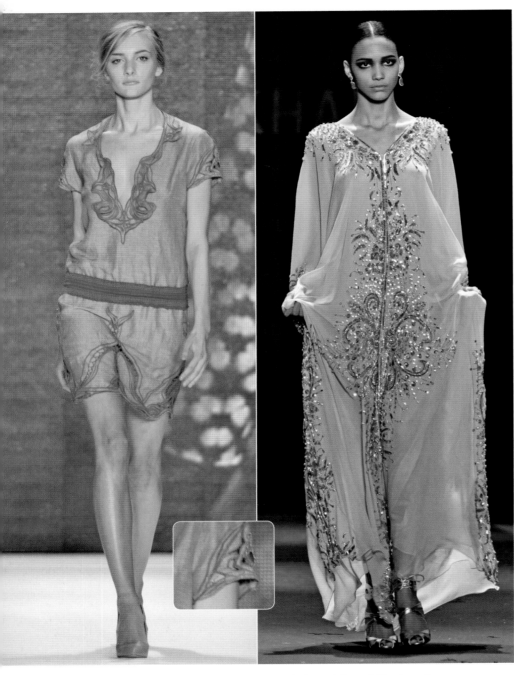

Originating in the East, the caftan has been adapted and worn as a long, loose dress, usually belted, with long, wide sleeves, sometimes integrated into the main garment. Persian, Moroccan, and African in origin, the caftan is often colorful and heavily embellished. It is no surprise, therefore, that hippies of the late 1960s and early 1970s adopted the ethnic caftan as part of their fashion statement.

Although the shape is designed not to hug the curves of the body, the caftan is a sensual garment, often showing a flash of cleavage or shoulder, while soft and floaty fabrics drape and billow. Some body shaping can be achieved by fitting a sash across the front of the body and into side vents, and around the body inside the tented back of the dress, tied at the front or back. Any embellishment would generally focus on the neckline, yoke, edge of sleeves, hemline, or sash. This is a good shape to dress with costume jewelry, so keeping embellishment to a minimum may be a consideration. The cultural origins of the style can be translated through richly ornate textiles, bold print treatment, and strong colors.

Talitha Getty and Diana Vreeland are famous caftan aficionados, and Emilio Pucci, Roberto Cavalli, and Dior have included the caftan in their collections. Caftans are often used in summer collections because the loose-fitting, wide sleeves offer a cool solution in hot weather, and it is ideal as a beach cover-up. The body-enveloping proportions also make the caftan perfect maternity wear.

Tape-embroidered **cutwork lace** detailing forms the main focus of this mini-length caftan style. The lace is translated in a color that is darker and slightly contrasting to the main fabric, complementing the dropped-waist elasticized band to create a somewhat **sporty aesthetic**.

Applied to a delicate chiffon base, the **sequined, ethnic-inspired embroidery** defines the V neckline, framing the face and leading the eye to an elaborate motif on the torso. The **vertical design** helps to elongate the silhouette, offsetting the generous width of the cut.

KEY CHARACTERISTICS

☑ Long, loose dress with long, wide sleeves

☑ Soft, floaty fabrics allow the dress to drape and billow

☑ Colorful and decorative

☑ Heavily embellished around neckline, yoke, cuff, and hemline

1 The wide, round neckline has a center-front seam, left open over the bust area and fastened at the neck edge. The body and sleeves are cut in one piece. **2** Maxi-length chiffon dress, cut full and circular. The fabric is drawn in at the waistline with a contrast-color patterned waistband. **3** The boatneck and kimono-style sleeves of this simple caftan allow the dramatic print to be viewed uninterrupted and remain the focal point. **4** The graphic color blocking of this minidress is an ideal backdrop for the soft silhouette. The straight lines formed by the slash neck are reflected in the paneling, and create a contrast to the draped sleeves. **5** This oversized placement print is engineered to work with the garment shape and is carefully positioned in relation to the body. **6** The plunging, slashed-neck opening of this long-sleeved dress has a self-fabric trim on either side to add interest to the overall simple aesthetic. **7** A simple caftan shape that uses print to suggest yoke and front-bodice paneling. **8** The draping from the neck creates rounded shapes that contrast with the handkerchief points at the hemline.

Caftan (continued)

This contrasting **color-blocked** caftan-style dress is cut generously to maximize impact and create a fluid, **billowing effect**. The placement of the diagonal paneling has been considered to work perfectly with the neckline and sleeve shape, as well as to incorporate the volume of fabric needed to achieve the silhouette.

Vertical color blocking with **Mondrian influence** reinforces the geometric shapes of the caftan styling of this day dress. The dropped shoulder line and wide armholes, deep placket opening, and round collarless neckline are all trademarks of **the traditional caftan** shape.

Alternative color blocking: V-shaped color blocking

This maxi-length column dress has a Greek-mythological mosaic-inspired **placement print** with fresco border that defines the **boatneck**, shape, and hem. The relaxed, easy-fit silhouette is complemented with loose kimono-style sleeves and draped side pockets.

1 A subtle asymmetric design with a soft V neckline and draped right-hand side that creates a grown-on armhole with a deep opening. **2** Fullness is achieved through the softly gathered fabric controlled within a structured self-fabric band that forms the neck edge of this caftan. **3** Square-neck caftan with rectangular-shaped sleeves set into a square, low armhole. **4** Silk chiffon maxi dress that completely swathes the body in fabric. The neckline is a grown-on funnel, cut close to the neck to contrast with the very full, flared skirt. **5** Voluminous, floor-length caftan with a clever use of color blocking to define the square neckline and displaced side seams. The back panel has been brought forward to create a cocoon effect. **6** Round-neck dress with plunging slash-front opening. The deep, patterned hip band defines the body shape and adds interest to the solid-block color. **7** Color blocking creates a strong, graphic design that contrasts with the flowing fabric. Generous side splits reinforce the garment's fluidity. **8** The pleating forms a concertina effect, particularly at the hemline, which rises and dips with the movement of the body.

Kimono

The traditional kimono is made from a bolt of cloth 13 yards (12 m) long and consists of rectangular pieces of cloth that form a T without darts or shaping. The sleeves are also geometric and square, with an underarm opening. The kimono has a placket that runs up the front opening around the neck and back down the other side, which sometimes falls short of the full length of the garment. The kimono is often lined with beautiful fabrics. The traditional garment is worn as a wrap with an obi belt as a kind of sash. Western versions are usually belted with a tie.

A traditional Japanese costume, the customary kimono is still worn today by the geisha and for special occasions. It is an indication of wealth and status, and elaborate, woven, hand-painted fabrics are still being produced using ancient methods. The kimono shape has been embraced within Western dress and, like the caftan, is a comfortable and easy shape to wear, accommodating a variety of body shapes. Elements of the kimono, such as the sleeves, are often applied to a dress with no front opening.

Designers often take elements of the kimono as inspiration, not necessarily copying it literally. Emilio Pucci, Dries Van Noten, Haider Ackermann, Hermès, Fausto Puglisi, Lanvin, Aquilano.Rimondi, Bill Gaytten for John Galliano, Mugler, and Uniqueness have translated the kimono into dresses using volume and proportion as the key, while Prada and Etro have included elements of Japanese kimono styling in dresses for Spring 2013.

Cut from **rectangles** on the bias, the bold color-blocked stripes resembling a nautical flag emphasize the diagonal running across the body and falling in a **handkerchief hemline**. Kimono sleeves are integrated into the dress and the rectangular pieces emphasize the kimono aesthetic.

Oversized mini-length shift dress with **dropped shoulders**. The wide, bound, deep V neckline suggests a kimono placket, which is echoed in the border at the hem. The bold, **monochrome digital print**, with contrasting appliqué floral motifs, suggests kimono patterns.

KEY CHARACTERISTICS

- ☑ Rectangular pieces of cloth, without darts or shaping, forming a T
- ☑ Geometric, square sleeves
- ☑ Worn as a wrap, sometimes with an obi belt
- ☑ Luxurious, elaborate fabrics

1 Wrap kimono-inspired minidress embellished with elaborately embroidered motifs in a traditional oriental style. 2 The velvet skirt is attached to a brocaded silk bandeau that cuts straight across the bustline. The kimono sleeves in ombré chiffon fall to the fingertips. 3 The wide slash neck and kimono sleeves emphasize the simple rectangular cut. The placement of the wide black stripe within the brightly colored, abstract-geometric print visually suggests a high waistline. 4 The geometry of the kimono sleeves contrasts with the long, fitted dress. The uneven hemline dips toward the back and reveals a flash of lining. 5 Exaggerated, bold scarf print, engineered so that the corner is curved to form the hemline. Kimono sleeve on the right and sleeveless on the left.

6 The square neckline, kimono sleeves, and dropped shoulder line are counterbalanced by the soft drape of the fluid skirt. 7 Square lines are softened by bias cutting, allowing for drape at the neckline and at the deep armholes. 8 Authentic kimono references inform the shape of the wrap dress. Embroidery on the cuffs and at the back of the dress maintain the geisha influence.

Kimono (continued)

> The kimono is deconstructed and subverted in this dress. Combining **rectangles and circles**, and mixing the strapping of the kimono with bias-cut rounded shapes, forms a draped skirt onto a straight hemline. **Matte and shine** fabrics help to define the cut. The diagonal bodice reveals one shoulder.

The combination of contrasting **geometric prints** in soft silk satin provides interest to an otherwise simple silhouette. With a slash neck and kimono sleeves, the dress is cut from **one piece of fabric**, taking design references from both the kimono and caftan.

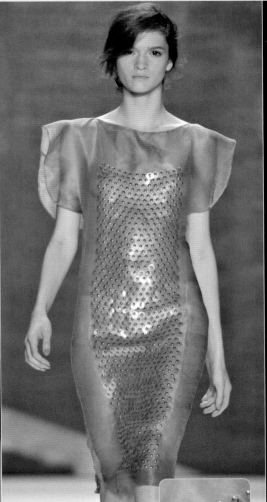

This kimono-inspired minidress uses the **scarf-inspired print** to maximum effect, considering the print border placement in relation to the center front, hemline, and sleeve shape. The nature of the print enforces a **strong symmetry and outline** to the design.

The body and sleeves of the dress are cut as one piece. Crisp organza helps to keep the sharpness of the kimono sleeves, which form a cap style. The skin-tone color and transparency of the fabric gives the impression of a **second skin**. A vertical **panel of studs** is strategically placed down the center-front and back panels to provide some concealment to an otherwise transparent dress.

This garment is constructed to seem like two scarves are joined together. The **large bold print** dominates the center of the front and back panels, and the borders of the scarf trace the hemline, slash neckline, shoulder, and perimeter of the armhole. The edges are finished with a **rolled hem**, keeping to the traditions of the scarf.

1 Wide kimono-inspired sleeves extend from the neckline and form the neck shape. The wide, open neckline frames the face. 2 Kimono references can be traced in the stand-collar neckline and the bold floral print with a contrast geometric flower at the front-yoke panel. 3 Asymmetrically cut panels combine print with color blocking. The wrapped placket around the neck and the wide sleeves contribute to the kimono-inspired aesthetic. 4 Charleston-inspired, dropped-waist shift dress finishing just above the knee. The tiered fringing wraps around the dress from hip level to hem. 5 The unstitched underarm seam of the sleeve mimics the kimono. The contrast color and the overlapping bodice give the impression of two separate garments. 6 The simple shift shape and high, round neckline are in contrast to the full circular-cut, kimono-inspired sleeve. 7 Asymmetric wrapping and layering juxtaposing varying lengths creates an abstract garment with underlying kimono features. 8 The shaping of the dress can be attributed to Ottoman and Eastern European references, but the kimono sleeves suggest a diverse mix of multicultural inspiration.

Kimono (continued)

Floor-length, silk jersey dress with **plunging V neckline** to waist level. The bodice and elbow-length, kimono-inspired sleeves are cut in one piece, maximizing the inherent drape in the fabric. The **deep waistband** defines the shape and separates the slender, gradually flared skirt. A thigh-high center-front split reflects the low neckline.

Loosely fitting, wrap-front, floor-length dress with main body and sleeves cut in one piece and secured at the waistline to achieve definition at the waist. This **uncomplicated shape** is an ideal vehicle for **bold prints**.

The bold, **Japanese-inspired** floral placement print immediately evokes the kimono. The references are continued in the shape of the wrap bodice, with the V neckline and **high waist** suggesting the obi.

CULTURAL INFLUENCES

Chinoiserie

The high neckline of the **mandarin collar** and frog fastenings contribute to the oriental aesthetic of this floor-length coatdress. Long fitted sleeves are set into a decorative yoke shaped and curved like a **Chinese pagoda**. Embroidered fans, florals, fruit, and butterflies decorate the dress.

Body-conscious dress fitted to the knee with an abstract **textured print** in a cotton sateen fabric. The dress has a round neckline and straight capped sleeves forming epaulettes at the shoulder, with kimono references.

Derived from the French word for *China*, this style of dress is inspired by Asian art, design, and crafts. The obsession with orientalism in the 1920s manifested in the decadent work of Paul Poiret. The typical cheongsam dress features a mandarin collar with a diagonal front opening to the underarm. The fitted dress has a side split, revealing the leg, and can be knee-to ankle length. Exotic woven silks, embroideries of florals and dragons, prints inspired by hand-painted birds and bamboo, or blue and white porcelain-inspired patterns, are all trademarks of chinoiserie.

In 2004, Tom Ford embraced chinoiserie in his collection for Yves Saint Laurent, introducing the pagoda shoulder and referring back to the YSL imagery for the launch of the perfume Opium in 1977. Rodarte's fall/winter 2010/11 and Louis Vuitton's spring/summer 2011 collections demonstrate a chinoiserie influence. Paul Smith's fall/winter 2011 and Givenchy's spring/summer 2011 collections are also good examples of how the theme has informed shape and fabrication.

Designers hoping to attract favor with the ever-growing Chinese market by reworking Chinese cultural references and marketing these back to a Chinese customer may be in for a shock. Modern Chinese women would rather buy Western luxury brands than recycled versions of their own cultural heritage. This does not detract, however, from the continued Western obsession with the mysticism, exoticism, and romanticism of the orient, and therefore chinoiserie will persist.

KEY CHARACTERISTICS

- ☑ Inspired by Asian art, design, and crafts
- ☑ Mandarin collar with diagonal front opening to the underarm
- ☑ Exotic, luxurious fabrics and prints

1 Dramatic pinafore dress with capped sleeves worn over matching oriental floral-print blouse. 2 Vertical and horizontal border print that frames images of fans and dragons. The short shift dress has a dropped shoulder and kimono sleeve to elbow length. 3 Full-length empire-line dress with long sleeves. Enlarged printed jewelry decorates the dress to give a trompe l'oeil effect. 4 The

turtleneck and mini length of this dress balance the detailed, textural fabric treatment. 5 This dress has a silhouette that resembles a Chinese cheongsam. Metallic gold-on-gold brocade creates a feeling of opulence. The wrap opening of the skirt is curved in a tulip shape, giving the appearance of a sarong. 6 Pagoda references are evident in the shaped front bodice and paneled

skirt. The contrast print of the sleeves, yoke, and high neckline reinforces the oriental references. 7 The trailing, graduated embroidery from shoulder to hip level balances the A-line shift shape and leads the eye to a flirty, fringed skirt. 8 Chiffon maxi dress with a paneled fishtail hem. The sheer fabric creates a nearly nude aesthetic, enabling the trailing embroidery design to take precedence.

Chinoiserie (continued)

> A simple, sleeveless shift shape with a soft V neck and dropped waistline. The dramatic, **contrast-color** trailing embroidery has been engineered to complement the dress shape, and the **ostrich-feather skirt** gives a lighthearted and flirtatious feel to the design.

This pretty chiffon dress has been heavily **embroidered and embellished** with bold peonies that contrast with the delicate characteristics of the fabric. The garment design takes inspiration from **romantic petticoats**, with horizontal, ruched trim and scalloped, dropped waistline.

This maxi-length dress is **tiered** down its entire length, incorporating and concealing the shape needed to achieve a **perfect fit.** The embroidered floral pattern wraps around the body, complementing the design. The feather neckpiece balances the overall silhouette.

The contrasting black-and-white print placement has been engineered to work with the garment design for maximum impact. The **sweetheart neckline** frames the face, and the bias cutting enables the fabric to follow the contours of the body without interrupting the **print design.**

A bold floral print, enlarged in size to huge proportions, is an ideal choice for this simple chiffon bias-cut dress. The delicate **rouleau straps** and sheer, floaty fabric contrast with the **daring print.**

Chinoiserie (continued)

A contemporary version of a traditional **toile de Jouy pattern**. This bias-cut, maxi-length column dress has a deep **cowl neckline** that softly merges into the bodice. The bias cutting enables the dress to skim the body contours.

A chiffon wrap-over maxi-length dress with kimono style references. The full, long sleeves are gathered into cuffs, allowing the fabric to **billow** over. The neckline is finished with a wide solid border to create shape and contrast between the **sheer and matte** detail in the design. The chinoiserie-style print works well with the kimono-inspired design.

This **simple foundation**—bias cut to hug the body with delicate rouleau straps in silk chiffon—is an ideal canvas for the elaborate allover embellishment. The bold, bright embroidery and appliqué **pops** on the black background and is allowed to shine on this effortless shape.

A dramatic devoré-printed, bias-cut dress that skims the contours of the body but also maintains a fluid and flirty hemline. **The matte and sheer** characteristics of the fabric add to the **drama of the design**.

< Chinoiserie-inspired **brocade** sleeveless minidress with boatneck. The **semifitted shape** is strong and simple, making it the perfect vehicle for such an ornate fabric. The embroidered body stocking is an ideal accessory.

SPECIAL OCCASION

Special-occasion wear encapsulates all that is exhilarating and spectacular in the world of fashion. From the stuff of fairy tales and storybooks, romance and nostalgia, to elegance and sophistication, the dress is worn to impress.

This highly constructed yet fluid gown recalls the looks created for Hollywood bombshells of the 1950s. A cowl hung from the neck mirrors the triple tucks at the knee to create the classic mermaid-shaped dress. The diagonal swath of fabric emphasizes the smallness of the waist and voluptuous hips.

In context

This look, created by the House of Dior in 1960, would go on to typify the 1960s cocktail dress. The slip dress in gold brocade has a simple yet elegant thin, bowed sash slightly below the waist. It is paired with a matching evening cape, pillbox hat, and elbow-length gloves. Similar dresses would be photographed on style icons, such as Audrey Hepburn and Jackie Kennedy, cementing this iconic look.

After World War II, the return of "the season" re-established the importance of appropriate attire. Debutantes—young women from aristocratic backgrounds—were introduced into society in order to meet suitable husbands. The season consisted of a round of extravagant social events that took place throughout the summer months, which demanded fitting attire and were a good source of business for the couture fashion houses and private dressmakers of the time. The traditional evening wear attire was rapidly seen as outdated by young debutantes, who no longer wanted to dress like their mothers. As a consequence, by the late 1950s, couturiers found it increasingly difficult to attract a young clientele and embarked on new ready-to-wear boutiques that guaranteed a high standard of finish, close to couture, but which only required minimal fit sessions.

The charity ball gradually replaced the private ball. Accessible by purchasing a ticket, the charity ball by the late 1970s attracted a more diverse patron. Actors, musicians, and writers mixed with the aristocracy and helped pave the way for a new generation of designers, such as Ossie Clark and Zandra Rhodes, who imparted a more natural and fluid way of dressing for these formal occasions.

By the 1990s, fueled by a growing celebrity culture, there was a new context for these formal dresses in the form of the red carpet. These glamorous dresses continue to make appearances at entertainment-industry award ceremonies, such as the Oscars, in the form of red-carpet dresses by designers, such as Elie Saab, Versace, and Valentino.

Special occasion dresses are typically worn for only a few hours, and comfort is not always a priority. Women want a fantasy and an experience that can transport them to that special event like a charity function, fund-raising ball, or wedding. Even the act of dressing, such as lacing the corset and complicated buttons, becomes a ritual.

Jacques Fath was an influential French designer that attracted a young, international clientele. This dress epitomizes the cocktail dresses of the 1950s, with the idealization of extreme beauty and the pursuit for ultimate perfection through precision cutting and proportion. The nipped in waistline, tight bodice, and full skirt accentuate the female form, while the slashed neck elongates the shoulder line, leading the eye to the exaggerated balloon sleeves.

SPECIAL OCCASION

Design considerations

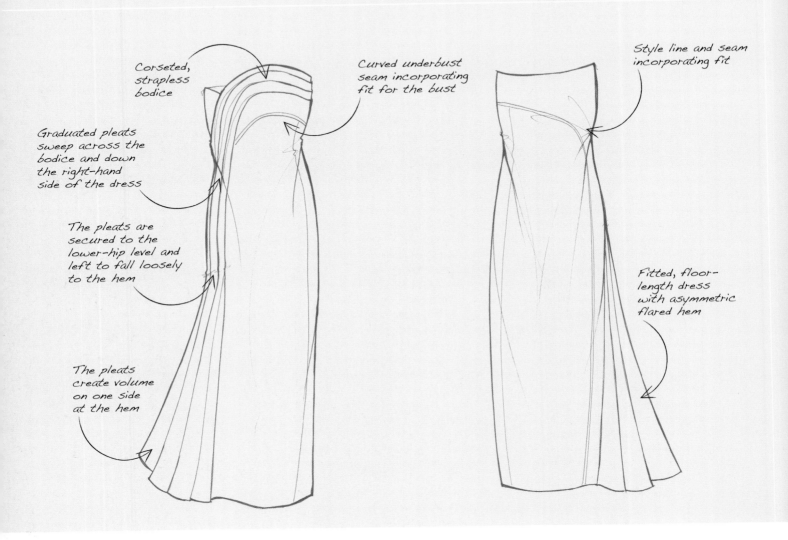

Corseted, strapless bodice

Curved underbust seam incorporating fit for the bust

Style line and seam incorporating fit

Graduated pleats sweep across the bodice and down the right-hand side of the dress

The pleats are secured to the lower-hip level and left to fall loosely to the hem

Fitted, floor-length dress with asymmetric flared hem

The pleats create volume on one side at the hem

Silhouette Special-occasion dresses are often slim fitting, either skimming the contours of the body for evening wear, or more structured and waist defining for day wear. Foundation garments are commonly used to help create the desired silhouette, particularly popular in bridal wear and ball gowns.

Length Dress lengths will fluctuate depending on the event, and range from mini for cocktail and prom dresses, to floor length and trailing for bridal wear and ball gowns. Usually dresses worn for special occasions in the daytime, such as weddings and funerals, finish around knee length to achieve a smart, polished look.

Sleeves Depending on the occasion and climate, special-occasion dresses can be strapless, sleeveless, short sleeved, three-quarter, or long sleeved. Any possible permutation of sleeve and armhole design can be utilized, as long as it is appropriate to the event and works in the fabric chosen.

Necklines and collars Necklines can vary from the demure to the seductive. When designing ball gowns and bridal wear the emphasis is on exposing the décolletage. Taking inspiration from historical and cultural garments offers the designer endless styling choices where drama and extravagance is the prime consideration. Dresses worn to christenings, weddings, and funerals adopt a more restrained choice of neckline.

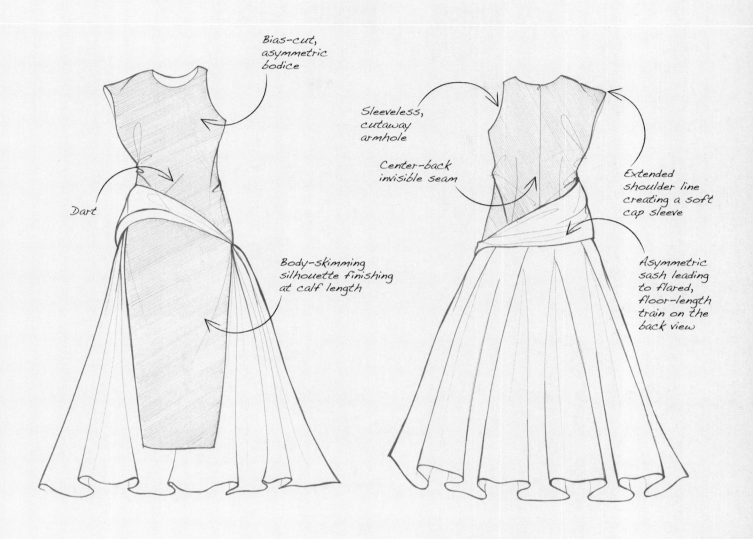

Bias-cut, asymmetric bodice

Sleeveless, cutaway armhole

Center-back invisible seam

Dart

Body-skimming silhouette finishing at calf length

Extended shoulder line creating a soft cap sleeve

Asymmetric sash leading to flared, floor-length train on the back view

Fastenings Fastenings intended not to interrupt the flow of the design may take the form of invisible zippers concealed in the seams or, in contrast, be part of the decoration, such as rouleau loops and covered buttons. Lacing and eyelets are a decorative feature but can also help define the waist, creating the desired shape.

Details Fine detailing, such as pin tucks and shirring, are all commonly used on special-occasion dresses to add decorative interest to the silhouette while also creating shaping and fit. Frills, flounces, ruffles, lace trims, and inserts can soften and feminize the look. On ball gowns and wedding dresses, design interest or detailing may be a feature on the back, the angle at which these dresses are often viewed. Dress seams and hems must reflect the quality of the fabric and should be French-seamed if lightweight and sheer, with fine-rolled hems.

Fabric The infrequent use of a special-occasion dress can inform the fabric selection. Often delicate and needing special laundry care, the fabrics can be heavily embellished. The fabric choice is instrumental in the development of the garment design, and its weight, drape, and handle should be considered. Copious amounts of luxurious fabrics, such as silk habotai, taffeta, and chiffon are often used to create bridal wear, ball gowns, and cocktail dresses, with more structured, medium- to heavyweight fabrics used for christenings and funerals.

SPECIAL OCCASION

Formal

The formal special-occasion dress encompasses an extensive variety of styles that reflect the traditions, protocols, and etiquette of each individual event. Worn for occasions such as christenings, weddings, and funerals, the formal special-occasion dress can vary from body conscious to oversized and billowing, structured to draped and fluid, and just above knee length to maxi length, though very rarely mini length. For weddings the formal dress is often in a lined lightweight woven fabric, such as georgette or chiffon, and can be brightly colored with floral or bold geometric prints. The silhouette can be semifitted in a structured woven fabric or more voluminous in a soft woven fabric. In contrast, the formal dress for funerals is traditionally black and tailored, and accessorized with jackets and hats to cover the shoulders, arms, and head.

Fabrics often reflect men's tailoring, with suiting fabrics commonly used, and silhouettes are usually semifitted, with lengths finishing around knee level. A similar style of formal dress is worn for christenings and weddings. The color palette is cheerful, and silhouettes are often body conscious or semifitted in medium- to heavier-weight woven fabrics, depending on the season.

The influence of the **Chinese cheongsam** is suggested in the mandarin collar and capped sleeves of this elegant dress. The yolk panel is curved to front and side seam points. The soft matte skin-blushed silk falls to just below the knee, creating a relaxed, **lingerie feel**.

Grecian-style dress with dirndl **elasticized front panel** giving fit-and-flare shaping and a definition to the waist. The soft folds gather above the bustline to form a **boatneck** with a contrast shoulder-strap detail that echoes the Hellenist features.

KEY CHARACTERISTICS

☑ **Fabrics can reflect men's tailoring**

☑ **Fitted or semifitted silhouette**

☑ **Feminine, fluid drape, gathers and pleats**

☑ **Matte and shine fabrics**

1 Staggered asymmetrical features of the off-the-shoulder dress draw the eye to bare shoulders. The body-conscious silhouette is slashed at the front side. 2 Deep V-necked, sleeveless, tabard-style pinafore over cream silk underpetticoat. 3 The black strapping and panels against the floral print suggest a window frame looking onto a garden. Vertical panels elongate the body, giving a column silhouette with shaping integrated into the panels. 4 A 1950s-inspired fit-and-flare belt-waisted dress. The scooped round neck reflects the simplicity of the cut. 5 Deconstructed details, such as exposed seams, unfinished edges, and a broken side zipper, give a modern twist and questions the correctness of formal wear. 6 Clean parallel lines, at the center pleat-pocket vents, waistband, and yoke, cut through the proportions of the dress. Contrast fabric gives the effect of a T-shirt under a pinafore. 7 The wrap-over at the front of this asymmetric dress gives way to a lower length on the left-hand side. The sloping neckline runs parallel to the hemline. 8 Slash-neck dress with a fitted bodice and wrap circular skirt. The metallic woven fabric creates a low luster.

Formal (continued)

The graphic-print and **laser-cut** pattern creates the illusion of a **three-dimensional fabric**, while the modern silhouette with clean lines complements the nature of the print. The subtly curved skirt and solid-color border, shoulder, and waist cleverly soften the design.

High-luster silk satin, empire-line dress with **fur high-muff neck collar**. The soft, full skirt falls below the knee and is gathered below the bust to a **darted, fitted bodice**. Long set-in sleeves are fitted to below the elbow, where a full gathered bell shape spills over the tight cuff.

Color-blocked panels give an asymmetrical, Mondrian-inspired look to the **loose-fitting shift** dress. A simple round neck and kimono dropped-shoulder sleeves emphasize the **geometric shapes**. The positioning of color panels emphasizes the waist in order to give the illusion of shaping.

1 Vertical stripes are offset by the narrow horizontal waistband and softened by the side splits in the hemline. **2** A conservative knee-length dress with elbow-length sleeves and over bodice. Long gloves and boots ensure no flesh is revealed. Yet the color gives a vibrant twist. **3** Midi-length dress with sheer chiffon sleeves and front yoke. Shoulders and side panels are solid color and

offset by a contrasting, graduated-stripe front panel that blends into a sheer striped skirt. **4** Hexagonal shapes are pieced together with fagoting embroidery to form the sleeves, neck, and hemline. A printed version of the pattern is used as an underlayer. **5** Embroidered minidress with demure neckline. Black cuffs and a half-belt add to the formal aesthetic. **6** Raglan-sleeved dress

with a solid-black lining and a sheer overlayer, embellished with a corded stand collar leading to a center-front panel with a deep waist-defining band. **7** Simple silhouette with a modern aesthetic, a concealed-button placket, and horizontal half-belt that contrasts with vertical stripes. **8** The severe aesthetic of this high-necked dress is balanced by the circular-cut peplum at the waist.

Body conscious

The special-occasion interpretation of the body-conscious style is often based on today's ideas of classical dress, with the fabric draped rather than cut to fit the shape of the body.

In the 1920s, this free-flowing approach was a reaction against the style lines of the period, as epitomized by Fortuny's fine-silk pleated Delphos column dresses and the bias-cut clinging dresses of Madeleine Vionnet. In the 1930s, Hollywood became a strong inspiration for this look, where dresses were bias cut to create a slinky, body-defining silhouette. Flattering a slim figure, the bias-cut fabric subtly reveals the body underneath, which is accentuated with every move. Madame Grès's gowns of the 1930s pioneered this style and were notable for their innovative seaming and pleating that created body-conscious drapes. In contrast to this organic approach, during the 1950s, Madame Grès developed a technique that married her love of fluid classical shapes with the fashion for an extreme structured body, as popularized by Dior's New Look. Her pleated jersey gowns at this time incorporated a skillful securing of the carefully manipulated jersey onto a boned corset.

Evolving through the decades, the body-conscious dress was suited to the dance floors of the 1970s. Pioneering American designers, such as Halston and Geoffrey Beene, reworked a new aesthetic for fluid jersey and fasten-free dresses that were perfect for dancing.

The **tonal stripes** help to define the bandage effect of the paneling on this dress. The combination of vertical, horizontal, and diagonal seams helps to create a slimming effect to the body-conscious silhouette. Architectural influences include **Grecian references** and column effect.

This silk jersey dress naturally clings to the body, defining its contours. The high, round neckline, square shoulders, long, fitted sleeves, and maxi length create a **slinky, column effect**. The gathered shoulders and elasticized **blouson waist** maximize the inherent drape in the fine-gauge jersey.

KEY CHARACTERISTICS

- ☑ Slinky, body-defining silhouette
- ☑ Innovative seaming and pleating
- ☑ Often structured with integrated foundation garments to enhance the body contours

1

2

3

4

5

6

7

8

SPECIAL OCCASION

1 Stretch knitted fabric underlayer with horizontal bands of self fabric wrapped around the body, forming a diagonal shoulder strap. Corded bands create a vertical stripe at the left-front side.
2 This organdy dress gives the illusion of a body-conscious design with a contrast color print delineating the shape of the body. **3** Lurex fitted dress with a high luster that accentuates the body-conscious shape. Darts from armhole to hip define the slimline silhouette. **4** Metallic-effect silk satin helps to define the contours of the body. Darted and seamed for maximum fit, the folded tucks above the bustline are mirrored in the turn-back sleeves. **5** Trapunto stitching follows the body contours, giving subtle surface decoration. **6** The curved yoke seam above the bust flattens and streamlines. Snakeskin foil-effect panel gives an optically slimming effect. **7** Armadillo layering and body paneling give a sculpted look. Contour-defining directional seaming and flesh color suggests a 1950s corset influence. **8** A sweetheart-shaped bodice is accentuated by a keyhole cutout at the midriff, as well as above the curved bodice, to give a strapless look.

Tea dress

Although traditionally English, the tea dress has become a universal staple, worn to charity events, weddings, and other special occasions. The tea dress started life as a garment made solely for informal entertaining within the home, but over time has been adapted to be a more formal occasional garment.

After the turn of the twentieth century, the formal tea dress was no longer worn with corsets and became more liberating and individual, the start of a slightly more relaxed style of women's clothing. Tea dresses have taken inspiration from the Orient and Asian clothing, with the kimono and chinoiserie a primary source for design. The main characteristic of the tea dress is its soft, feminine style lines with a semifitted bodice and flared hemline, accentuating the waist. The tea dress has survived every runway trend, with its longevity as a style rooted in its timeless vintage elegance. Bright colors and delicate prints highlight the girly, flowing silhouette. Lighter-weight fabrics create a comfortable dress that is easy to wear and transcends different occasions. Collars and necklines can vary, from scoop necks to V, Peter Pan to sweetheart. In addition to the classic cut, ending at the calf, variations in length can be below knee and maxi length.

The tea dress can be adapted for evening wear with sleeveless styling—though more traditionally it has puff sleeves—but sleeves are generally cut short, or occasionally three-quarter length. Depending on the occasion, the tea dress can be translated in finer, more luxurious fabrics and accessorized with corsages, gloves, and hats to complete the look.

Fitted to the waist and flared to below the knee, this is a **typical 1950s style** but with a twist. The second of a double-layered bodice is drawn from the armholes to the waistband, where it is pulled together with the skirt and draped and gathered to give a **waterfall effect,** raising the hem at the left-hand side.

Buttoned down the front and falling demurely just below the knee. The suggestion of a halter neckline is created by a raglan-cut yoke at the front.

Alternative neckline and sleeves: Deep V neckline with batwing, three-quarter length sleeves

KEY CHARACTERISTICS

☑ **Semifitted bodice and flared hemline, accentuating waist**

☑ **Lighter-weight fabrics**

☑ **Classic cut, ending at calf**

☑ **Vintage elegance**

1 2 3 4

5 6 7 8

1 This sumptuous silk-velvet drop-waisted dress has a simple vest-shaped bodice, softly gathered flared skirt, and self-fabric waterfall-frill trims. **2** The sleeveless raglan-shaped armhole gives a halter-neck appearance. A tie-feature stand collar is attached to a V neckline. **3** Reminiscent of a 1930s cocktail dress, the full transparent skirt and sleeve details are contrasted with the waist cummerbund and deep V neck. **4** Fitted, elegant little black dress with a sweetheart neckline and wide shoulder straps decorated with self-fabric roses. **5** A fitted bodice and dirndl below-the-knee skirt give a 1950s feel. Contrast-fabric solid-color collar, turn-back cuffs, and waistband complement the busy floral. **6** A simple, petticoat-style dress with rows of horizontal tucks detailing the hipline. The lace detailing edging the V neck reinforces the lingerie references. **7** This 1960s-inspired silver sheath dress is at once youthful, with banded shoulder straps, and classic, with a traditional rose floral. **8** The A-line dress is loosely waisted with a self-fabric tie that is left to hang loose, echoing the grown-on fluted cap sleeves and longer-length back panels.

Tea dress (continued)

> Floral-print dress with contrasting chiffon beaded **underlayer**.

The bust suppression has been incorporated into the soft gathers at the neck edge, which are reflected in the elasticated waist.

The skirt is cut longer at the left side with more flare at the hem, maximizing the drape of the **bias-cut** fabric.

Pretty, floral, drop-waisted dress with a **handkerchief hemline** over a black net underskirt. The large cabbage-rose print on the skirt is combined with an art deco-inspired print on the bodice. Deep contrast tucks with a metallic floral clasp trim the waist. **Silver petals** scatter across the neckline, covering one shoulder.

A modern interpretation of a tea dress style, translated in **bold graduated stripes.** The stripes are used to accentuate the shape, with a vertical-striped fitted bodice that disguises the bust and waist suppression. In contrast, the skirt print has been engineered to work with the **circular shape** and is finely gathered into the waist seam. A prominent, contrasting belt and matching striped scarf complete the look.

A classic sleeveless **shift style** with quirky, oversized costume-jewelry print. Beading embellishment on selected areas of the print, creating a brooch effect, brings **humor** to the design.

Alternative neckline and bodice: Boatneck with V-shape bodice panels incorporating fit

Digitally printed fit-and-flare dress with symmetrical panels and inserts that bring a formality to the abstract imagery of the print. The **V-strap** neck detail reflects the shape of the paneling, ensuring a coherent design. The flared, **fluid hemline,** cut shorter at the front, is in keeping with the nature of the print.

Tea dress (continued)

This refined fit-and-flare silhouette is an ideal backdrop for the lightly **quilted**, intricately patterned fabric. The **organdy overlayer** has been extended over the sleeve hem and skirt hem to create a sheer border detail.

Sleeveless, ornately embroidered maxi dress with **fringed hem** detailing. The main body of fabric has been fringed at various heights, ranging from the lower hip to mid-thigh, to highlight the fact that it is not an attached trim but **integral to the garment.**

A-line slash-neck minidress with a wide self-fabric **bow belt** that softly defines the waistline. The shell-pink color characterizes this style, creating a young and fresh appeal.

1

2

3

4

5

6

7

8

1 Bias-cut, body-skimming, scooped-neck dress with double-layer, fluted short sleeves, and complementary flared, full hem. The bust suppression and skirt flare have been incorporated into the diagonal style lines. **2** Cap-sleeved, fit-and-flare dress with deep square neckline. The dress is bias cut with a wrap-front skirt that scoops up at the front. **3** Deep V-neck sleeveless flapper-style dress with bias-cut bodice. **4** This simple tubular silhouette disguises the body's contours and is an ideal template for the flirty, asymmetric fringing that creates surface interest and movement.

5 A softly shirred neckline creates a loose-fitting bodice, complemented with short, tiered puff sleeves. Tiers continue at hip level, cut circular and gathered onto the skirt. **6** This calf-length, deep V-necked lace dress is transparent and worn over a spaghetti-strapped solid black petticoat dress. **7** This soft slash-neck floral dress is draped to emphasize the soft and delicate fabric. **8** Cheongsam-influenced fitted dress. The demure stand collar, extended shoulder line, and body-defining silhouette are ideal for such a bold print.

Tea dress (continued)

> Soft, **layered** printed georgette is gathered into the waistband of this pretty tea dress, which opens at the front to expose a contrasting petticoat. The **strapless effect** of the bodice is finished by a transparent panel at the shoulder.

A pretty floral, vintage-style dress with **long gathered sleeves** and a Peter-Pan collar. A deep waistband is shaped under the bustline, where the gathered yoke gives shaping. The feminine print is **scaled down** for hemline border, waistband, sleeves, and collar. With a hemline above the knee, the dress is feminine and flirty—a typical example of the tea dress.

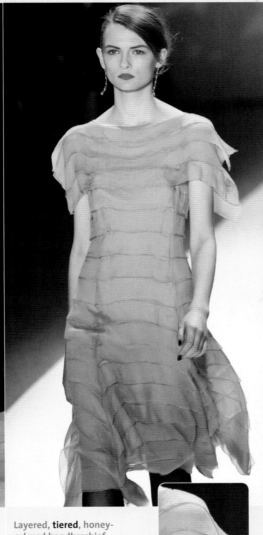

This short-sleeved raglan tea dress has a **boho aesthetic**. The look is highlighted by the skillful use of the border print, which plays on the proportion of color and placement of the floral and defines the style, complementing the draped fluidity of the silhouette. Deliberate creasing of the fabric enhances these elements, blurring the edges of the **border print** as well as accentuating the design.

Layered, **tiered**, honey-colored handkerchief dress with a 1920s **flapper influence**. The boatneck and squared collar drapes over the armhole, imitating a capped sleeve.

Three-quarter sleeved chiffon minidress with deep V neckline that is accentuated by a self-fabric placket, leading into the **full circular skirt.** The placket, waist seam, and sleeve cuff are highlighted by a solid-color **piping** insert that helps to accentuate the style details.

1 Boatneck, sleeveless dress with tiered, gathered skirt in various widths. The waist is defined by a belt. **2** Ombré-dyed pleated georgette, layered and fluted to give soft draping with Grecian overtones. **3** Multilayered dress constructed with contrasting fabrics to add depth. The cutaway layers and curved front hems, left to hang long on the back view, accentuate the drape of the fabrics.

4 Off-the-shoulder dress supported by fine spaghetti straps. The fitted bodice has a slashed neckline that is extended over the upper arms to fashion small sleeves. **5** A deep waistband is the main focus of this design, separating the dolman-sleeved bodice with plunging V neckline and the gathered miniskirt. **6** V-neck dress with extended shoulders creating a cap-sleeve effect. Appliqué in

a contrasting color on the neckline and front bodice leads into a delicate gathered chiffon skirt. **7** The cultural and historical influences are evident in the styling, fabrics, and silhouette of this dress. The triangular inset, revealed by the deep V neckline, is tipped by a pretty lace border. **8** Scoop-neck, sleeveless dress with fitted bodice and double-fabric tiered circular skirt.

Tea dress (continued)

Sleeveless fitted bodice with **demure** round neckline that creates an ideal balance for the asymmetric **origami-inspired** fold-detail skirt. The uncomplicated bodice, solid-color fabric, and simple silhouette make an ideal backdrop for the complex pattern-cut skirt.

Bias-cut wrap-over dress with a 1920s feel. The **high shine** of the fabric accentuates its inherent drape, and the uneven **handkerchief hem** maximizes the movement created when walking. The matte neck edge and skirt border define the shape.

A high-waisted, gathered, baby-doll dress with a bib front yoke. The **folkloric influences** are apparent in the skirt's floral lace print in black on a white ground. The **bib front** has contrasting braided patterning, white on black, edged with a gathered black-and-white frill. The opposite black-frill underskirt emphasizes the black-and-white contrasting theme. A brocade waistband completes the look.

Petticoat

The special-occasion petticoat dress is a more deluxe version of the sundress petticoat style. It is regularly translated in luxurious layers of translucent fabrics such as lace, silk, and chiffon, often with a high-shine or low-luster finish to the fabric. The general feel of this style can be light and slinky, taking inspiration from lingerie, slips, and nightwear styles to inform fabric choices, silhouettes, detailing, and pattern shaping. The petticoat style is an ideal choice for evening wear and red-carpet dressing.

Bias cutting, pioneered in the 1920s and '30s by Madeleine Vionnet, is a popular feature of this style, skimming the body's contours and accentuating its lines and curves while enabling the fabric to drape softly to the hemline. Details are consistently delicate, such as fine spaghetti or ribbon straps, keyhole openings with rouleau fastenings, pin tucks, fine pleats, fragile frills, lace inserts, ribbon trimmings, and embroidery. Dress lengths can vary from very short, echoing the voluminous negligee, to floor length, and trailing. Necklines are open, exposing the chest and décolletage, with bare arms and shoulders often accentuated with scalloped edges and lace trim. The petticoat dress can often adopt two distinct looks, depending on its historical inspiration, such as a more elaborate translation with frills and flounces reminiscent of nineteenth-century dress and, in contrast, the more seductive and elegant body-conscious styles evocative of 1930s glamour.

This baby-doll-style dress has a printed-chiffon **tiered miniskirt** that is circular cut and gathered into the waist seam to achieve a full, flounced skirt. The delicate straps and neckline have been trimmed with a **circular frill**, with an additional frill left loose to fall over the upper arms. A satin ribbon fastens the bodice.

The **draped-cowl** neckline of the lace bodice contrasts with the transparent **chiffon layers** of the handkerchief-cut skirt with an asymmetrical hemline. The skirt of the dress has a ballet-inspired aesthetic, offering an alternative to the petticoat dress.

KEY CHARACTERISTICS

- ☑ Luxurious layers of translucent fabrics
- ☑ Inspiration from lingerie and nightwear
- ☑ Light, slinky, delicate, feminine
- ☑ Open neckline, bare arms and shoulders

1 Paneled lace over a nude-color underlayer suggests transparency. Puffed sleeves are edged with layers of lace; the same lace accentuates the V paneling that points to the waistline.
2 Full-length petticoat dress, bias cut from peach silk gives a nearly nude aesthetic. 3 Layering of contrasting fabrics give a range of tonal variations. The top layer of organza is scooped high above the bustline, revealing an underbra foundation. 4 Paneled transparent organza dress with flared hemline. A blue underskirt ensures a decorum of modesty, while the midriff is revealed. A lemon spandex, bra-styled underbodice balances the flash of color. 5 Self-fabric bands have been appliquéd onto the torso of this sheer chiffon dress to create a diagonal, crossover design. 6 Horizontal bands of lace wrap around the body and over one shoulder for a barely-there look. 7 This maxi-length chiffon dress is bias cut, with a deep V neckline that is echoed in the style lines. Full butterfly sleeves complement a flared hemline. 8 Bias-cut chiffon dress with a neckline plunging to the waist and a gathered bodice created by a drawstring neckline.

Petticoat (continued)

> Bias-cut, **simple**, unadulterated, white petticoat dress. The soft body-skimming silhouette is young and fresh, with **spaghetti straps** that require the absence of undergarments.

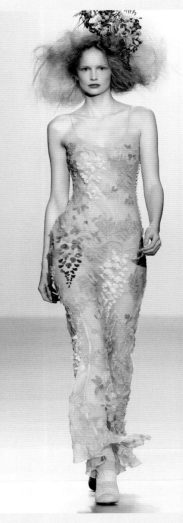

This sheer, spaghetti-strap maxi-length dress has allover wisteria **embroidery** that enhances the feminine and delicate feel of the design.

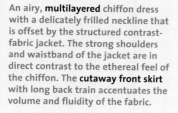

An airy, **multilayered** chiffon dress with a delicately frilled neckline that is offset by the structured contrast-fabric jacket. The strong shoulders and waistband of the jacket are in direct contrast to the ethereal feel of the chiffon. The **cutaway front skirt** with long back train accentuates the volume and fluidity of the fabric.

This simple tubular vest shape has added interest with the shaped and sheer **contrast yoke** that includes three-dimensional floral embellishments. The scalloped **dropped-waist seam** reflects the shaped yoke and complements the handkerchief hemline.

Alternative bodice: Wrap front with side tie fastening and spaghetti straps

Wide, scooped-neck chiffon dress with a cutaway skirt front and trailing back view. The **sheer**, delicate nature of the fabric is emphasized by the tonal silk flower embellishments that add **texture** to the design, graduating from the neckline to the hips.

Cocktail/prom

Usually thought of as dresses featuring frothy skirts in tulle or organza, with glistening embellishment and strapless, fitted bodices, the cocktail or prom dress remains an important component of a woman's wardrobe. Meant for mingling at a cocktail party or for young women celebrating their graduation from high school, the cocktail or prom dress is a lot less formal than the ball gown. Often designed shorter in length than the ball gown, falling just above or below the knee, or sometimes at calf length, the dress is meant to make the wearer feel glamorously attired yet relaxed and informal.

Created by Coco Chanel in the 1920s, the little black dress was an indispensable item of clothing for the cocktail hours, with dropped waistline and knee-length flounced skirt. The boyish shift silhouette created a blank canvas for trims and embellishment, while black was the acknowledged color for formal and semiformal occasions. During the 1950s, when cocktail parties were at the height of their popularity, designers such as Christian Dior, with his New Look, explored extreme puffball or bubble shapes—revisited in 1987 by Christian Lacroix's signature "pouf" silhouette—and re-established the cocktail dress as a timeless item of clothing. Contemporary cocktail and prom dresses have a multitude of design variations, from origami-inspired architectural dresses in structured woven fabric to slinky, sequined, silk-jersey alternatives.

Gray, geometric, constructed **squares and rectangles** inform the cut of this dress, from the square bib neckline and cutout armholes through to the square-cut seamed panel with inserted rectangles at the waist. The **split-front** straight skirt of the ankle-length dress completes the architectural forms.

Sleeveless, halter-neck slip dress. The drop-waisted bodice is fitted and heavily embellished with **sequins** to the seam just above hip level. The skirt is paneled and flares from the hip to knee length. The white net **underskirt** gives added volume at the hemline and helps to define the flapper style.

KEY CHARACTERISTICS

☑ Fitted bodice and full, gathered skirt, often with underskirts

☑ Short length—either just above or below the knee

☑ Slinky, seductive, and luxurious fabrics such as tulle or organza

1 Black-and-white tiered-effect dress with lace inserts and edging sewn to the dropped waistline and gathered to the hemline. 2 The bodice creates a blouson effect as it meets the waistband, and the skirt is gathered to the waistband. 3 Typical little black dress. The sweetheart-shaped neckline is accentuated as a small stand-up collar trims the neckline at shoulder level. 4 Ripstop fabric is taken out of a sportswear context to provide volume in the gathered skirt. The sheen accentuates the gathers and folds. 5 Unstructured slip-style shift dress in metallic foiled print to knee length. The simple sack-like shape is held up by braces. 6 Simple styling is the perfect canvas for the dense fringing of this mini shift dress. A high waistband stretches under the bustline, giving some definition. 7 The fitted bodice is transparent and the bra-shaped bodice of the underlayer defines the bustline. The skirt is cut wider at the waist than at the hemline and gathered to form a tulip-shaped skirt. 8 Fitted to the waist with a full skirt to calf. The bodice is drawn to the center and gathered into a fake knot, which ties under the bust.

Cocktail/prom (continued)

> This dress is constructed from separate bodice and skirt tubular panels that have been **folded**, to create fit and shaping, and fixed into the waistband seam. The **bodice** stands away from the body at bustline. The contrast, sleeveless round-necked underbodice is cut separately and is also fixed at the waistband.

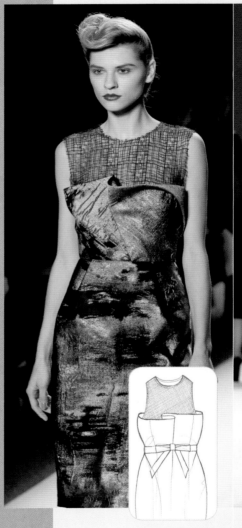

Alternative bodice detail: Self-fabric structured bow accentuating waist

Contrasting fabrics and color blocking define the pattern pieces within the dress. The V-neck sleeveless bodice has **lingerie references,** with black constructed paneling to mimic bra shaping. The fitted bodice dips to a V shape at the dropped waistline. **Accordion pleating** in metallic silver and a contrast-pleated panel in gold and skin tone give an elongated column effect.

The round-neck, sleeveless **shift dress** features strategic diagonal and horizontal seaming that incorporates excess fabrics grown into the center-front skirt panel, and diagonal to side seams that pleat and fold to form t**hree-dimensional** structures.

This bold, graphic-printed floor-length chiffon dress has a contradictory relaxed aesthetic, with a loosely fitted **wrap-front bodice** and low waistline. The bodice slightly blousons over the waistband, leading to a **full, gathered skirt**, which softens the geometric style of the print.

A simple, jersey, vest-shaped dress that is an ideal canvas for embroidery and sequin **embellishment**. The dropped waistline and fringed, beaded hem is inspired by the **Charleston era**. The asymmetric waistband complements and informs the design of the embellishment while also creating an informal balance.

1 Embroidered, sheer dress with halter neckline inserted into a narrow stand around the neck. A corseted, strapless foundation bodice gives structure and modesty. **2** Multilayered tulle dress with a ruched center-front bodice that creates an inverted V-shaped waistline, complementing the generous godet skirt. **3** Metallic fit-and-flare dress with contrasting matte gathered and frilled hemline. Contrast-fabric neckband and side panels define the shape of the neckline and bodice and balance the high-shine fabric. **4** The bodice is tipped with a wide stripe that reflects the solid-color band of the empire line. The skirt and fitted hemline create a puffball effect. **5** A deep V neckline is edged by a continuous band placket. A deep waistband accentuates the waist. Long set-in sleeves and a peplum overskirt complete the look. **6** A classic 1950s-inspired cocktail dress with an open neckline, grown-on cap sleeves, wide waistband, and full skirt. **7** A deep V neckline directs the eye to a flared, circular-cut peplum and straight knee-length skirt. **8** Quintessential strapless cocktail dress with faux bow-effect bodice detail.

Cocktail/prom (continued)

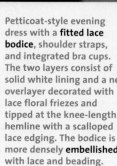

A pretty, layered, shift-style minidress with a 1970s retro, **hippie influence**. The crochet cotton-lace underpetticoat has a scalloped hemline that mirrors the scallop of the **transparent overlayer.** The chiffon dress is embroidered and trimmed with tiny beads. A trim mocks a dropped waistband. The halter neck dangles to hemline after tying at the neck, and is trimmed with beads and feathers, emphasizing the hippie look.

Petticoat-style evening dress with a **fitted lace bodice**, shoulder straps, and integrated bra cups. The two layers consist of solid white lining and a net overlayer decorated with lace floral friezes and tipped at the knee-length hemline with a scalloped lace edging. The bodice is more densely **embellished** with lace and beading.

Transparent **organza** shift dress, gathered at the waist by a self-fabric tie, drawn through a casing, to give a **ruched effect**. Long set-in sleeves are slightly gathered at the deep cuff. The funnel-neck collar stands high to cover the neck. French seams join the garment pieces and a back placket with covered buttons continues the **covered look**. The silver-foiled brocade print decorates the yoke, collar, and sleeve heads. The garment is worn over a small underslip for modesty.

Cocktail/prom (continued)

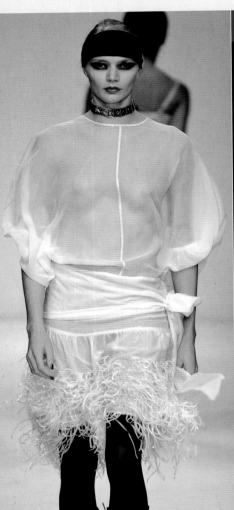

No side or shoulder seams, and integrated dolman sleeves gathered at the elbow, subvert conventional cutting. The **seaming** of the transparent fabric cuts the bodice at center front and center back. A blouson effect is created as the bodice is attached to the deep dropped waistband. The skirt is softly gathered from the hip and attached to the waistband, and the hemline is decorated with fringes that diffuse the boundaries. A self-fabric **cummerbund** ties at the side.

Shaping in the bodice is achieved by pleating and gathering into the seams, and **knotting** at the bustline creates a curved silhouette. Circular cutting creates a **puffball** shape, where the voluminous overlayer is seamed to a tighter underskirt in the same fabric

Alternative neckline: Ruched, one-shoulder strap

Border-printed chiffon dress with **plunging V neckline**, solid-color contrast border, and dropped waistband. The fine chiffon skirt is gathered into the waist seam to achieve a full, **maxi-length** skirt, maximizing the print design.

1

2

3

4

5

6

7

8

SPECIAL OCCASION

1 Textural minidress with a fitted silhouette and short set-in sleeves. **2** Off-the-shoulder dress with fitted bodice and cutout V-neck detail. The multilayered tulle skirt epitomizes this traditional cocktail style. **3** Boatneck sleeveless minidress with tiered fringing completely covering the shift shape. **4** Extreme plunging V neckline to the waistband creates a sexy feel to this otherwise strong and graphic silhouette. The notched shoulder straps complement the square-shaped skirt sides. **5** Long-sleeved jersey body-stocking foundation with self-color, high-shine rayon fringing overlay that creates a flirty feel, generating movement when walking. **6** Round-neck sleeveless dress with semifitted bodice and full gathered miniskirt. Self-fabric petals give a textural, three-dimensional effect. **7** High-contrast black-and-white embroidery, beads, and fringes in horizontal bands decorate this pretty shell-pink dress fitted to the waist and gently flaring to just above the knee. **8** Asymmetric, taffeta structured minidress with a strapless foundation. The wide double-fabric sash adds depth to the design, creating an oversized-bow effect.

1 Capped-sleeve, V-neck, semifitted dress with self-color mini frill embellishment on the bodice front. 2 With a fitted bodice and tiered, multilayered tulle skirt, the delicate matte fabric is contrasted with sequined shoulder straps. 3 Slash-neck, long-sleeved minidress. The intricately patterned bodice contrasts with the ostrich-feather stole-effect skirt, creating empire-line proportions. 4 Origami-inspired symmetrical tucks and folds give this sleeveless minidress a three-dimensional effect. 5 The metallic-woven fabric provides a high-luster sheen. The shoulder yoke and flared sleeves suggest epaulettes and, with the circular neckline, give a regal feel to the slim-line silhouette. 6 Strapless sundress with a fitted bodice with integrated bra foundation and shaped bustline. A full skirt is gathered into a high waistband. Gathered, layered petticoats increase the volume. 7 Gold sequins on a black ground, the luxurious fabric highlights the diagonal, fluid drape that crosses the body. 8 Elastane knitted bodice that accentuates the bustline. Knitted strapping trimmed with metallic hardware defines the waist, center-front, and side-bodice panels.

9 Metallic fabric, spaghetti-strap dress with slip-styling influences informing the bra cup and waistline seaming. **10** Full knee-length skirt and wide set-in sleeves are finished with a circular bias-cut frill. The round neckline has a center-front placket to the waist seam, with a single button fastening at neckline. **11** The elaborately sequined lace fabric is the main focus of this design, with its simple slashed neck, elbow-length set-in sleeves, and full skirt. **12** Silk-velvet dress with a shapeless tubular bodice leading to a V-shaped dropped-waist seam and full circular-cut skirt. **13** A structured and strapless foundation is completely covered in tiers of ostrich feather. Delicate, sheer neck yoke and sleeves are covered with a floral embroidery design. **14** Sunray-pleated metallic minidress with crossover bra cups and halter-neck straps. **15** Intricate, laser-cut pattern applied to an organdy base to create a structured front panel. The organdy skirt has large tucks into the waist seam to create fullness at the sides. **16** Single-sleeved asymmetric dress with generous folds on the right side seam that create diagonal drapes across the skirt.

Ball gown

With its heritage in couture dressmaking and bespoke tailoring, the modern-day ball gown assimilates traditional techniques of dressmaking, such as draping, fitting, and spiraling, to create monumental works of contemporary glamour.

Ball gowns are worn to red-carpet events and charity balls, and imply a grandness and sense of occasion like no other garment, dramatizing the female form and showing off skillful craftsmanship. Traditionally supported by complicated foundation garments and often including bust pads, grosgrain waist tapes, and tulle underskirts, the ball gown is a vehicle to show rich embellishments and ornate fabrics.

Rejecting the complex seaming and overt structure of traditional ball gowns, in the late 1950s/early 1960s, Hubert de Givenchy, under his brilliant mentor and friend, Cristóbal Balenciaga, set about redefining the customary cut of women's garments through the minimizing of seaming to create fit. Givenchy's minimalist endeavor, though simple on the surface, was innovative in its cut and construction, and was offset by feminizing his designs with embellishment and ornamentation, creating perfectly balanced aesthetic marvels.

With the emergence of charity balls and the rise of interest in celebrity, the traditional ball gown has evolved to reflect the changes in society, though it still remains at the core of a designer's vision, communicating the essence of his or her collection. Nowadays, the red-carpet dress is the most important platform for many designers' work, and the loyalty of a fashionable and famous client can sustain a designer's popularity.

This floor-length ball gown has an **asymmetric design** with a bodice single shouldered on the right side balanced by a diagonal sash on the left. The front skirt is wrapped with a shorter panel to knee length inserted underneath, creating a split to the hem. The skirt **fishtails** at the back.

This **simple, strapless, floor-length** sheath dress has a slight fishtail. The blank canvas of the architectural **column silhouette** is broken by an embroidered knotted string, from bodice to calf, seemingly tied to an appliquéd pebble motif.

KEY CHARACTERISTICS

- ☑ Full-length
- ☑ Grand sense of occasion
- ☑ Rich embellishments and ornate fabrics

1 Chiffon floor-length dress with a wide neckline and fitted bodice. The fit-and-flare skirt incorporates solid-color godets that increase the hem's circumference. **2** Fitted strapless bodice with baroque-inspired embroidery that contrasts with the tiered and chaotic floor-length skirt. **3** A figure-hugging silhouette with a fishtail to floor length, this ball gown is topped with a crisp white shirt-neck detail at the bust. Layers of gathered net give volume to the hemline. **4** A stretch, body-conscious foundation with demure turtle neckline and short sleeves contrasts with voluminous, chiffon floor-length godets. **5** Floor-length ditsy-print dress with a dirndl elasticized bodice. **6** A swathe of ombré pleated chiffon is fixed at the right shoulder and left to fall over the strapless foundation garment. **7** Fitted strapless dress that flares below the knee. The front panel below the waistband seam is slightly gathered to give a flattering shape to the stomach and hips. The wrap across one shoulder falls at the back of the dress to meet the long train behind. **8** The strong, square-shouldered, metallic-leather bodice juxtaposes the sheer chiffon, voluminous skirt.

Ball gown (continued)

> This sleek, contemporary ball gown has a **sporty aesthetic,** with a slashed neckline and cutaway wrestler-form armholes. The shaped armholes reflect the **body-conscious** waist-defined torso, which gradually leads to the full skirt with thigh-high split and train.

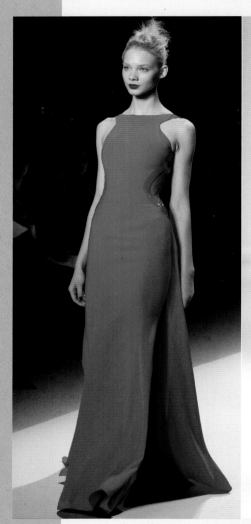

This bold abstract print is engineered to complement the garment design. The **graduated color** of the bodice contrasts the more dynamic use of color at the **hemline**, emphasizing the hem's generous cut and swing.

A strapless **corseted bodice** creates a strong base for this maxi-length column dress with flared, paneled overskirt. The **overskirt** leaves the front view exposed to reveal the gold sequined motif.

Alternative bodice detail: Turn-back cuff along neckline

The subtly graduated color of this contemporary ball gown gives a young, fresh appeal. The high neckline and **cutaway armholes** have a sporty feel and contrast nicely with the **heavily tucked** floor-length skirt.

Grecian-inspired one-shouldered chiffon dress with draped crossover front bodice. The skirt is double layered and cut circular to achieve a **generous hem.**

1 Circular-cut floor-length skirt and circular, asymmetrically frilled neckline. The bodice is wrapped and gathered into the neck edge with a side panel. 2 This strapless dress uses contrasting color inserts and folds to achieve an asymmetric sunburst effect that incorporates the shaping of the bodice and flare of the skirt. 3 Folklore-inspired lace bodice with scalloped lace straps and a gathered, voluminous taffeta skirt. 4 Marble-effect print reflects the flowing shapes of the chiffon-layered dress. Grecian toga styling is seen in the deep V and large armholes with dropped shoulder line. 5 Silk habotai has been swathed around a structured, strapless foundation to create an asymmetrical draped neckline and multilayered, wrapped floor-length skirt. 6 Low V-neck sleeveless dress with exaggerated dropped waistline and tiered skirt, reminiscent of traditional flamenco costumes. 7 Wide, V-neck dress with full circular-cut skirt gathered into the waistband, maximizing the fluidity and drape of the fabric. 8 Voluminous, lightweight silk skirt. The bodice is cut generously in order to create a soft fullness above the separate tied waistband.

Ball gown (continued)

The proportions of this single-shouldered dress create a strong silhouette. The diagonally draped fabric incorporates the bust and waist suppression enhances the **asymmetric bodice**. The diagonal waist seam mirrors the shoulder design and is offset by the **gathered, tiered** floor-length skirt.

Extreme fishtail silhouette with a long-line fitted bodice and defined bra cups. The fishtail skirt is achieved through multiple godets and is in stark contrast to the **body-conscious bodice**. The garment is softened by a sheer overlayer draped from the shoulders.

This strapless corseted bodice with full floor-length paneled skirt is a classic ball gown design. The **sweetheart neckline** reflects the shaped waist, with the self-fabric frills on the neck edge accentuating the overall shape. The **generously cut skirt** maximizes the impact of the busy allover print and allows for a modern interpretation of this design.

Ball gown (continued)

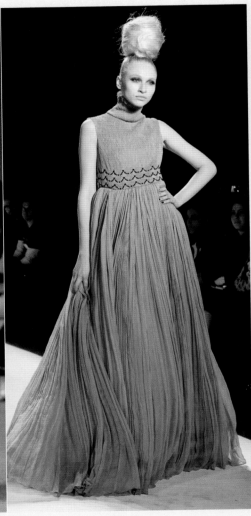

This simple floor-length, long-sleeved dress makes a good blank canvas for the pretty floral print with beaded accents. The **translucent fabric** exposes a hint of bare arms and chest, and is layered over a white slip dress. The round neckline and set-in sleeves give **maximum cover,** making the dress ideal for a more formal occasion, where showing too much flesh is inappropriate.

This dress evokes red-carpet glamour, with nearly nude body-conscious bodice and **long sleeves** covering the shoulders and arms but revealing and hinting at transparency at the bustline. Structure is achieved with a foundation built into the dress, giving a basis for the **draping** at the front of the skirt.

The voluminous skirt of this finely **knife-pleated dress** is in contrast to the simple sleeveless bodice with demure **turtleneck.** The high waistline is emphasized with a scalloped, smocking embroidery, and the pleated bodice overlay conceals the bodice's fit.

1

2

3

4

5

6

7

8

1 The floor-length lace hemline is raised at the front to reveal the calf. The high-necked sleeveless bodice is fitted to the waist. **2** The draped bodice contrasts with the box pleating of the skirt. The brocade fabric allows for both a soft drape and a sharp, defined pleat. **3** The simple cap sleeves, round neckline, and floor-length body-defining silhouette shows the allover metallic-sequined fabric to its full potential. **4** The deep scoop neck of this long-sleeved, bias-cut dress draws attention to the bustline. The body is emphasized by starburst shaping in transparent insert panels. **5** Strapless long-line bodice with metallic-lace overlay that contrasts with the multilayered tucked tulle skirt. A horizontally striped organdy full skirt defines the silhouette. **6** A strappy flapper-style dress, slashed from hemline to hip with fringes that reveal a flash of leg. **7** The juxtaposition of masculine and feminine, with tuxedo-styling references and soft gathered lace, are evident in this dress. **8** The body-conscious sheath shape, with high halter neckline and long billowing train, is achieved by the fine crystal pleating of the metallic fabric.

1 A strapless bodice is used as a foundation for this intricately tucked and draped dress. The symmetry of the draping and engineering of color placement brings a formality to the design. 2 The expansive A-line skirt acts as a canvas for the textural three-dimensional rosettes that cover the skirt's surface. 3 Sunray-pleated, floor-length chiffon dress. The high halter neck with extralong self-fabric tie fastening is left to hang to the hemline. 4 The loosely fitted bodice blousons over the skirt and leads to a gathered full skirt. The uneven hem with cutaway front view accentuates the skirt's volume. 5 Floor-length, fitted, fishtail ball gown. The grown-on, draped, asymmetric, strapless bodice balances the skirt's train. 6 Body-conscious column dress accentuated by horizontal silver and white stripes. The tubular bodice is broken up by Y-shaped shoulder straps. 7 Delicately embroidered and appliquéd chiffon sleeveless dress layered over a simple, solid lining. The scalloped edges are left to blur the outline of the armholes and neckline. 8 A sheer sleeveless bodice is offset by black floral appliqué and a monochrome, feathered straight skirt.

9 The fitted bodice in black transparent chiffon contrasts with the white satin of the full skirt, cut from circular panels. **10** Striped fabric has been manipulated into pleated frills to create a tiered skirt that contrasts perfectly with the simple strapless bodice. **11** The ornate embroidery of this strapless corseted bodice leads the eye down to a heavily embellished border that gives structure to the hemline while accentuating the fullness of the skirt. **12** An off-the-shoulder corseted bodice has been extended over the upper arms to emphasize the exaggerated A-line floor-length skirt. **13** A circular cut gives a waterfall drape at the front skirt, extending to a longer train at the side of the dress. The extended front bodice stands away from the body. **14** Square shoulder and a body-conscious silhouette, flaring from hips to hemline, give a contemporary take on 1940s-inspired glamour. **15** A sleeveless tulle floor-length dress with nude jersey lining. A concentration of embellishment on the left shoulder is balanced by a half-belt on the opposite side. **16** The high-stand neckline, cutaway armholes, and body-skimming bodice all create a strong, dramatic silhouette.

Wedding

Designers use the wedding dress as a vehicle to showcase their talents and epitomize their vision for that season's collection. Always the statement piece on the runway, the wedding dress often reflects the current trends and is adapted to work across a variety of silhouettes, lengths, and styles.

The traditional white dress was established as a status symbol by the late eighteenth century, because it would only be worn once. The white dress now symbolizes purity and chastity. Romance and nostalgia were the main inspiration for design throughout the Victorian and Edwardian eras, and they continued to inspire through to the 1950s, when bridal dresses became more demure and sophisticated, echoing evening wear styles. In the early 1960s, wedding dresses became more clean-cut, with no frills and minimal seaming. Often the waistline was seamless and the straight or bell sleeves cut in one piece with the dress or seamed straight, like a caftan. The simple dresses were often accessorized with elaborate headdresses. As the decade progressed, a feeling of nostalgia and romance returned, with lace, appliqué, and embroidery making a comeback. This romanticism continued well into the 1970s, restrained at first, then blossoming into a retro revival in the 1980s, with bridal designs referencing historical and romantic influences.

The contemporary wedding dress is a melting pot of design, absorbing historical and cultural references and depicting current fashion trends. With civil weddings and less formal ceremonies becoming more popular, bridal wear has become more relaxed.

Edwardian meets the 1960s in this wedding dress. The demure Peter Pan collar and long **puff sleeves** are offset by the cream antique-effect lace strapless bodice and **A-line miniskirt.** The uniformity of the striped chiffon yoke and sleeves complements the intricately detailed lace fabric.

An elegant dress created with soft lines on the bodice leading to a sinuous, flowing, **full skirt.** The sheer chiffon overlayer obscures the sharp edge of the **strapless bodice,** and the dropped shoulder seams create a graceful silhouette.

KEY CHARACTERISTICS

☑ **White statement dress**

☑ **Focus on back and front views**

☑ **Duchess satin, tulle, lace and brocade**

1 Bias-cut silk-velvet dress. The asymmetrical style lines are reinforced by the diagonal neckline and single sleeve emphasized by the elaborate bow-tie shoulder. **2** The column silhouette is created by this long, silk-spandex-mix jersey dress that skims the floor and hugs the contours of the body. **3** 1950s-inspired dress in duchess satin. A fitted, darted bodice is embellished by fine beading.

The waist is enhanced by a self-fabric sash tied in a large bow. **4** Floor-length wedding dress influenced by baby-doll lingerie, with empire-line, fitted lace bodice and shoulder straps. **5** Knitted dress in fine-gauge silk and elastane yarn. The illusion of a dropped waist is created through the change of knit structure. An oversized keyhole neck detail continues into a slash neckline.

6 A pin-tucked bib bodice resembles a Victorian nightgown, but the primness is counterbalanced by a short hemline. **7** Slip dress with integrated strapless bodice and fitted mini-length skirt and an overlayer of lace. A deep satin bow with floral corsage emphasizes the dropped waistline. **8** A strapless bodice foundation with a lace halter-neck overlayer and tiered bell-shaped skirt.

Wedding (continued)

> Body-conscious strapless dress with built-in corset to give structure and emphasis to the **fitted waist**. The **side seams** are brought forward, giving the illusion of a slimmer silhouette. The scoop-front, tiered fishtail skirt features layers of circular-cut frills that contrast with the restrained bodice.

Edwardian-inspired floor-length wedding dress with substantial **scalloped lace train**. The dress is waisted with a godet-paneled skirt that gives flare from the hip. The scalloped hemline is echoed in the demure cape-like **stole overlayer** that is inserted into the boatneck.

This satin-backed crepe **body-conscious** wedding dress has an elegant and sophisticated appeal. The cummerbund **asymmetric sash** and multiple rouleau loops and covered buttons on the sleeve add design interest to this overall simple silhouette.

Contrasting matte and shine **floral brocade** in a traditionally styled dress. The fitted bodice has a dropped-waist seam, though a sash defines the waistline. The plunging V neckline reveals a solid-color underbodice. The shoulder seams have been grown on to form the stand neckline. The volume in the skirt is created using **net petticoats**.

Empire-line dress with a deep waistband and **pleated bodice** overlay that stands proud from the strapless foundation. This is reflected in the **gathered peplum**, contrasting with the elongated floor-length fishtail skirt. The bustle-effect train complements the bodice detail, creating interest at the back view.

Wedding (continued)

Housecoat-style wedding dress in silk-satin fabric. The bust suppression has been manipulated and gathered into a curved yoke at the shoulders, creating drape at the **front wrap opening** and drawing the eye to the ornate buckle. The sweeping A-line floor-length skirt is split to the thigh, echoing the V of the neckline.

This **shirt-waisted dress** has a 1950s influence. Common to the period, it has a self-fabric-covered **belt and buckle.** The strapless bodice foundation has a short-sleeved, shirt-style overbodice made of self-color lace. The neckline, shoulder, and upper arms are covered to give a demure appearance.

Strapless wedding dress with a relaxed, unstructured draped bodice and skirt. The **deconstructed hemline** reflects the casual aesthetic, giving the impression of a wrapped toga style. The underskirt is layered and uneven with ethereal **Grecian qualities.** Disguised within this relaxed exterior is a structured foundation.

1 Flamenco-influenced dress with asymmetric, tiered fishtail hemline. A self-fabric band that extends over the right shoulder trims the neck edge. **2** Duchess satin dress with a boatneck and inverted V-shaped notch that mirrors the curve of the waistband, which extends into the back train. **3** Strapless corseted bodice with a circular, sunray-pleated, multilayered floor-length skirt. A delicate pleated peplum frill has voluminous pleated ties that sweep to the floor. **4** Heavy duchess satin gives volume to the long A-line silhouette. Design interest is achieved through the diagonal gathered panel. **5** The decorative waistband is the focus of this dress, with the bust and waist tucks, and angled pockets, all pointing toward the center front. **6** Fishtail silhouette with corseted bodice emphasizing the hourglass figure. A lace-appliqué overgarment becomes the focus, suggesting a yoke. **7** The bodice is darted to the waistline with an extended fitted hip, which flares to the knee. Voluminous layers of net fall to the floor. **8** Slip-inspired dress that follows the contours of the body. The high waistline is defined by a tie belt and corsage.

Wedding (continued)

> Tailored, round-neck, collarless coatdress with a formal aesthetic. The curved yoke extends to full-length magyar sleeves with a seam that extends from shoulder to cuff. The concealed-button **front placket** extends from neck to hem, adding to the **minimal look.** Patch pockets at hip level give a simple decorative and functional addition.

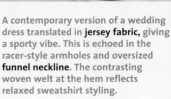

A contemporary version of a wedding dress translated in **jersey fabric,** giving a sporty vibe. This is echoed in the racer-style armholes and oversized **funnel neckline**. The contrasting woven welt at the hem reflects relaxed sweatshirt styling.

Slash-neck wedding dress with combined center-front panel and grown-on cap sleeves that are designed to restrict movement. The V-shaped bodice lines lead to a defined waistline then open out to the inverted, **multipleated panel** at the center-front skirt. The side seams of the skirt are displaced to match the bodice style lines and create more volume at the back view.

Gossamer-light silk performs well to achieve the **envelope shapes** created by geometric deconstructed cutting. The asymmetric style lines on the bodice complement the **draped skirt,** with integrated pockets set into the cowls at the sides, avoiding the need for seams.

Tiered gathered layers are strategically stitched to create an asymmetrical skirt that curves up the right-hand side seam and falls as layers on the opposite side. The **unfinished edges** of the fabric suggest fringes, with a play on direction in order to define the bodice.

1 Traditional ball-gown styling with horizontal deep tucks that add structure to the wide crinoline-style skirt. 2 This dress wraps the body, creating an envelope shape and requiring minimal seaming. Layers of tulle petticoat emerge from the hemline. 3 This bias-cut dress has a cowl neckline that falls to create a handkerchief shape with a beaded fringed trim. Accessorized with a cap sleeve and beaded silver vest. 4 Mini-length dress with a deep-sliced center-front V. The semifitted bodice contrasts with the fullness of the unpressed box-pleated skirt. 5 Duchess-satin-silk fit-and-flare dress with a Peter Pan collar, capped set-in sleeves, and ballerina-length skirt. Decorative vertical tucks create the only decorative element. 6 Crepe dress with cowl neck exaggerated at the back giving a deep backless view. 7 Silk-satin, bias-cut dress with set-in leg-of-mutton sleeves. The bodice seam is shaped as an inverted V under the bustline and decorated with beaded embroidery. 8 A drop-waist bodice is cut straight across the bustline. A halter-neck strap is attached to transparent raglan sleeves. Tucks run vertically down the front of the bodice.

Wedding (continued)

Traditional prom style with **sweetheart-shape neckline** and a strapless and corseted bodice. The waistband has a **chocolate-box bow** that cinches the waistline. The midi-length A-line skirt has a tulle overlayer heavily embellished with lace, appliqué, and beading.

Dress featuring two layers. The top chiffon layer has a **shirt neck** and button-placket opening ending just below the bust. This is fitted to the waist, then extends to a peplum at the front, dipping at the back to **form a train** at the ground. The fitted lace underdress has a shaped bra cup then clings to the body and flares from the knee to the floor-length hemline.

An **exaggerated A-line** silhouette continues from the strapless bodice neckline to the hemline. Layers of **chiffon tiers** cover the entire surface area of the design, offset by the sheer single-layer neck yoke. The hem is cut away at the front, emphasizing the long train on the back view.

INNOVATIVE

This category includes dresses that question conventions and push the boundaries in terms of fabric, cut, form, and construction. These are examples of visionary dresses that pave the way for future mainstream fashion.

Subverts the intrinsic qualities of lace with the juxtaposition of a hard black overlay of laser-cut black leather appliqué. A dress that is both fragile and feminine in coral pink, is contaminated and infected in a surreal and sinister manner. The nearly nude underlayer, with a foundation of boning, allows the black filigree to seemingly tattoo and engrave the body.

In context

Utilizing advances in science, engineering, and technology shaping the future, fashion designers are at the forefront of ground-breaking invention.

Collaborations between textiles, science, fashion, and technology allow for pioneering research and cutting-edge developments. Wearable technology—incorporating sensors, circuit boards, and power sources in textiles or garments—creates an interface between the dress and the computer. Light-emitting textiles and robotic articulation allow the transformation of the dress, no longer an inanimate object that purely interacts with the wearer.

The fashion laboratory can be evidenced in the 1920s, when Elsa Schiaparelli collaborated with industry, using innovative fabrics, borrowing scientific images, and embracing surrealism to design the modernist dress. Influenced by space travel and science fiction in the 1960s, Pierre Cardin experimented with vacuum-formed and molded textiles, André Courrèges explored bonded jerseys and synthetic fabrics, while Paco Rabanne developed metal chain-mail dresses. Contemporary designers such as Walter Van Beirendonck, Rei Kawakubo for Comme des Garçons, Maison Martin Margiela, and Hussein Chalayan challenge the perceptions of the body, and design fashion beyond the constraints of the fashion establishment. Japanese designers Junya Watanabe, Yohji Yamamoto, and Issey Miyake master and dissect traditional craft methods, pushing the boundaries of fashion and textile design.

Using innovative fabrics and styling in the late 1960s, Pierre Cardin was ahead of his time. Here, vacuum-formed and molded plastic and coated fabrics create textured surfaces and a minimal, architectural aesthetic. Revolutionary at the time, Cardin has set an example for the fashion designer's aspiration for new trends and innovation.

INNOVATIVE

Design considerations

Fascinated by materials and structure with an alchemist approach to fashion, Iris Van Herpen creates garments defined by innovation and craftsmanship. Inspired by architectural forms and natural organisms, she collaborates with artists, architects, and researchers to produce garments composed of materials such as copper, resin, silicone lace, UV-cured polymer, acrylic, and leather, combining the technology of 3D printing and hand-assembled craftmanship.

Understanding of fundamentals
Innovative dresses require new ways of looking by the designer in order to express creative ideas beyond the consideration of normal or mainstream. Understanding the fundamental traditions of fashion and textile craft and basic principles of techniques allow for rules to be broken and boundaries to be pushed.

Industry collaboration Collaboration is paramount in order to cross the individual specialist areas between textiles, technology, art, architecture, medicine, and science.

User considerations Consideration of user needs and environmental concerns can take precedence over seasonal trends, offering greater credibility and longevity with sustainable consequences.

Fabrics Added value can be achieved with the choice of high-tech fabrics and finishings for original appearance, handle, and high performance. For example, fabrics that appear light and delicate yet are durable and hard wearing, or breathable and waterproof, combine functionality with aesthetic without simply conforming to a fashion- or trend-led agenda.

Hussein Chalayan is known for his highly conceptual and thought-provoking work, which is at once beautiful to look at as well as technically advanced. A central theme to his work is the passage or perceptions of time and place. By a series of battery-operated pulleys, the dress transforms the silhouette from one era to another. Inherent in the presentation is the acknowledgment of our reliance on past style ideals, despite our technological sophistication.

Pattern cutting New ways of pattern cutting can be explored to minimize waste, allowing for a more ethical and considered approach. Digitally printed fabrics can be engineered to fit the pattern pieces, enhance the cut, and reduce the need for style lines in order to create design interest. Reducing the need for style lines, darts, and seaming, reductive pattern cutting strips away unnecessary detail but still maintains a strong silhouette and perfect fit.

The pared-down aesthetic hides a very complex and advanced form of cutting. An abstracted silhouette can be achieved through the use of subtraction pattern cutting pioneered by Julian Roberts.

The business end Innovative garments are not necessarily designed to be commercial—they often represent ideas in their purest form, which are then adapted and refined into a more marketable item. If or when garments are for ready sale, they may require different marketing strategies. Point-of-sale labeling may require additional information that explains the fabric content or care requirements. New symbols may need to be created in order to describe new functions and end-of-life disposal. The traditional runway show may no longer be appropriate, and the seasonal fashion calendar may not be applicable.

INNOVATIVE

Pattern cutting

Subverting shape and form through creative pattern cutting can redefine the relationship between the dress and the body, and the expectations of beauty and aesthetic. Notions of antifashion, or garments that defy trend and the established fashion hierarchy, can liberate the designer to challenge expectations and conventions.

Borrowing from sportswear requirements, cutting for movement can add a new dimension to traditional pattern cutting, increasing the functionality of the design and, in turn, improving quality of life. The design and construction of sculptural forms, much affiliated to architecture and engineering, are more likely to result in unconventional outcomes.

Japanese fashion design in the 1980s paved the way for a new approach, with designers such as Rei Kawakubo for Comme des Garçons, Issey Miyake, Yohji Yamamoto, and Junya Watanabe mixing science and art with fashion and using techno fabrics and inventive construction. Deconstructivist designers, such as Hussein Chalayan, Martin Margiela, and Ann Demeulemeester all take an intellectual approach to the design of the dress and push the boundaries of pattern cutting, starting with recognizable shapes and subverting them to disobey the principles of traditional cutting. Distorted proportions and body-defying shapes can blur gender and disregard function. This radical approach requires a cutting-edge approach to production and marketing, finding new ways to communicate and target the customer. Translated into a more accessible and commercial product, innovative cutting can be less overstated while still maintaining its originality.

The shape of the dress has been cut to suggest the **wrapping of a garment** around the waist. Integrated into the seams, the **mock sleeves** wrap and tie at the center front, with deep side pockets disguised within the garment. The end result is a soft, relaxed aesthetic.

Laser-cut leather gives a lace effect to the skirt. The softness and transparency is contrasted with the harder-edged, sculptural shapes at the neckline and bodice. The wide shoulder line and peplum effect help to disguise yet accentuate the waist, to enhance the **hourglass figure.**

KEY CHARACTERISTICS

☑ Subverting traditional pattern-cutting techniques

☑ Distorting proportions

☑ Consideration for user needs

1 Cocoon-like shape with rounded forms curves forward at the shoulder line, creating a cape effect. 2 Mélange wool in a constrained garment builds architectural forms with the precision of origami. Sleeves are open underarm to expose the undergarment, allowing articulated movement. 3 A side panel curves into a cape sleeve emphasized by contrast lining. The opposite shoulder is cut asymmetrically to a yoke. 4 Abstracted shapes show feminine curves, influenced by modern art, sculpture, and architecture. Minimal materials and enveloping forms, inspired by Balenciaga and Cardin. 5 Bold techno-cotton dress with origami folds and 1980s power-dressing influence. A nipped-in waist and front split reveal the feminine form. 6 Abstraction of space reveals the body, hinting at feminine curves. Fabric drapes blur the boundaries. 7 Asymmetrical shape with a casual, oversized silhouette and emphasis on the shoulder. Abstract shapes create a canvas for color blocking. 8 Soft curves have been used to inform a strong structured shape. The padded seam and integrated curved zips are functional and create design interest.

INNOVATIVE

Pattern cutting (continued)

> Aquatic theme with fantasy **mermaid** references: Fish-scale layers of **silver foil** on pleated shells cascade to a fishtail at the hemline. The fabric grows into a fitted metallic bodice that forms a deep halter neck.

Defying conventions and **questioning functionality and wearability,** this conceptual dress explores the boundaries between fashion and art. The drop-waist pleated dress has multiple personalities, with **conjoined triplicate dresses** attached to the back.

The pattern pieces of the dress have been **folded** like the stages of an origami puzzle in a luminous, Lurex, **brocade fabric**. The skirt, bodice, and collar are all integral components of this complex pleated structure.

Mixing circles and rounded curves with straight lines and diagonals, this dress consists of sculptural shapes and forms. The neckline stands high away from the neck, creating a straight line at the shoulder, forming a **rectangular silhouette** that contrasts with the skirt, which narrows to the hemline, creating diagonal lines edged with **circular ruffles**.

Unmistakeable **shirt references** are exaggerated and subverted to create dynamic **sculptural forms** that challenge the preconceptions of fashion. Using layers of multiple shapes to reinforce the pattern pieces and details of the shirt, the showpiece creates a strong, bold statement that evokes the concept behind the collection and presents the climax to the grand finale.

INNOVATIVE

Fabrics

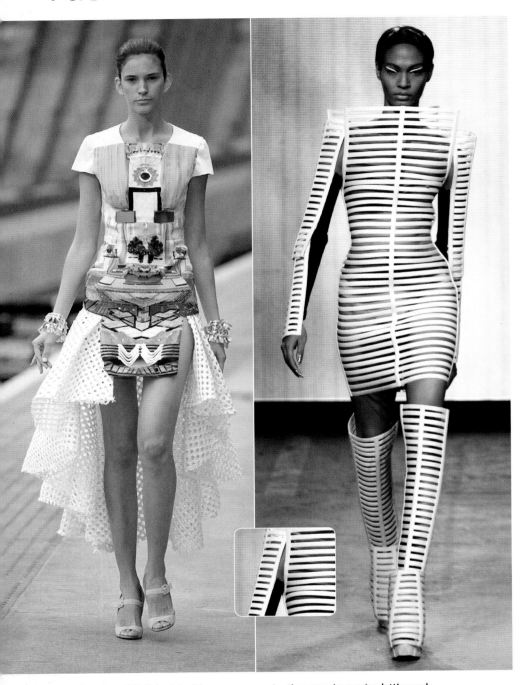

Is the future of the dress as simple as a spray of fibers directed at the body from an aerosol can? Scientific research, developed by Manel Torres in the form of the Fabrican, has made this a possibility.

Textile technology is moving at a fast pace, and innovations and new ideas are moving out of the laboratory and onto the catwalk. State-of-the-art textiles are often key to the development of original dresses, and sourcing interesting fabrics can be a challenge.

High-performance fabrics adapted from the military, space travel, and extreme sportswear can be translated into wearable fashion. Advanced synthetics, interesting mixed fibers, and ingenious fabric treatments offer the designer greater choice in terms of performance, handle, and visual aesthetic. Fabrics treated for crease resistance, water or stain repellency, or fire retardation offer added performance value. The customer's well-being can also be considered, such as when using fabrics with bacteria-fighting properties, wicking characteristics to allow breathability, reflective qualities for high visibility, or cloth that hardens on impact for physical protection. Sculptural shapes can be created using heat-set and molded textiles that interact and shift with the body. Bonding and layering and new fiber combinations and surface treatments create hybrid textiles. Mixed-media techniques, combining digital print with digital embroidery or laser cutting, welding, bonding, polychromatic printing, and heat-setting are only the tip of the iceberg in terms of potential embellishment and fabric manipulation.

A combination of digital print with embellishment creates a surreal interpretation of **interior scenes,** focusing on windows, lampshades, pelmets, tassels, and chandeliers. Digital printing allows for a photo-realistic approach and, together with three-dimensional pattern cutting, creates a **trompe l'oeil effect.**

Leather cage dress using **latticework construction.** The body-conscious silhouette with funnel neckline encases the form in a conceptual dress combining art, fashion, and architecture. It is zippered into place to **reveal and protect,** and questions notions of wearability.

KEY CHARACTERISTICS

- ☑ High-performance fabrics and fabric-surface treatments
- ☑ Use of new technologies and construction methods
- ☑ Consideration of user needs

1 Pinafore-style dress with ribbed hem and yoke mimicking knit but created by heat-molded techniques. Embellished with embroidery and appliquéd print for maximum pattern and texture. 2 Metal-chain fringes are set into the seams and draped over a wool-jersey dress to give a Gothic-inspired look. 3 The dress is a commentary on the objectification of women. The plastic is molded to portray breasts and hips with layers of horsehair similar to the ponytail reminiscent of a prize-winning horse. 4 Neoprene-effect leather, molded in chevrons for a constricted body-conscious look. Directional striping defines and softens the rounded shoulder panels. 5 The digital photo-realism within the print complements the structure of the pattern-cut shapes. 6 Latex rubber with laser-cut edges and circles that reveal layers underneath. Seams have been heat sealed. 7 Concertina effect created by heat-forming pleats and rounded shell-like curves. Allows the fabric to move with the body. 8 A vest bodice in high-gloss rubber and a full skirt pleated into the waistband. Accessorized with heavy-leather bra and wide belt.

INNOVATIVE

Fabrics (continued)

> Jewel-encrusted and heavily embellished **organic shapes** that resemble elaborate butterflies. A strong net foundation is the base for **laser-cut** multicolored leather shapes, layered to form strata and manipulated and curled to create complex, three-dimensional forms.

Manipulated, soft-fabric horizontal and vertical strips are attached to create a **wide open mesh** that reveals the body but can be worn over contrasting layers. The deep cowl-neck collar folds over to create a drape at the neckline.

Sprayable, nonwoven fabric, patented by Fabrican, creates an instant dress directly from an aerosol can onto the body. Cross-linking fibers form a fabric, liberating designers to create new and unique garments **without the need for seams** and lending the ability to incorporate fragrances and active substances.

In homage to the House of Rabanne's founder, the dress is made of **pearls and chain links** constructed to create a stripe pattern. The body is at once exposed and protected.

Silk layered on white organza and cut and frayed between vertical rows of stitching to create a subverted pinstripe, in keeping with the **exaggerated shirt styling.**

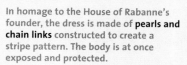

INNOVATIVE

Glossary

Angora Fleece from the Angora rabbit spun to create a soft yarn for knitting or weaving. Also describes the Angora goat, whose fleece is used for mohair.

Aran Originating from the Aran Islands off the coast of Ireland, a style of knitted patterns in natural yarn combining cables and decorative raised stitches and twists.

Argyle pattern Diamond-shaped pattern that originated in Scotland. Two or more colors are used to knit sweaters or pullovers often adopted by golfers and used in sock patterns.

Art deco Originating in Paris in the 1920s, an artistic style featuring streamlined shapes and geometric patterns inspired by aerodynamic machines and sunburst motifs.

Astrakhan Lambskin from the astrakhan region of Russia. Also used to describe woven fabric designed to imitate the lambskin effect.

Baby-doll Very short minidress similar to a young girl's dress. Also describes a flimsy, short, and sheer nightdress often worn over matching panties.

Bateau neck See *boatneck*.

Batwing sleeve See *dolman sleeve*.

Bellows pocket Type of patch pockets with expanding sides, commonly used on a Norfolk jacket.

Bell sleeve Sleeve that fits closely to the armhole and to mid-upper arm then flares widely to the wrist.

Bias The diagonal line that runs across the grain of the fabric at a 45-degree angle to the warp and weft. Cutting on the bias allows stretch in a garment.

Bishop sleeve Sleeve made from light fabric, widening from the shoulder and gathered into a cuff at the wrist.

Blanket stitch Decorative embroidered stitch originally used to edge blankets.

Blouson Short, loose-fitting men's jacket with gathered sleeves and cuffs. The term also describes the same gathered effect in a dress, for example, when a loose bodice is gathered into a waist seam.

Boatneck Shallow, curved neckline almost extending from shoulder to shoulder.

Bolero Inspired by traditional Spanish men's jackets, a short, cropped, open jacket, often worn over a dress.

Bombazine Twill fabric with a silk warp and a worsted weft, dyed black. Traditionally used for mourning garments.

Boning Originally strips of whalebone, and later covered flexible steel or plastic, inserted into stitched channels of fabric in garments, such as bodices or corsets, to help create shape, form, and fit.

Bouclé Looped or rough-textured yarn, knitted or woven to create a fabric with a knobbly surface.

Box pleat Pleat created by two folds facing outward and toward each other, then pressed flat.

Braid Strands of thread corded and woven together to create a ribbon effect. Used to decorate the surface or create an edging to a fabric.

Brocade Luxury woven fabrics, often using silk or metal threads, with an extra weft added to create a raised surface pattern.

Broderie anglaise Whitework embroidery creating decorative patterns—usually floral—combining pierced holes with satin stitch.

Bustle Padded shape worn under the dress at the back or sides to create volume underneath and support the outer skirt. Can be a metal frame or padded fabric forms.

Cable knit Knitted technique to create a vertical braided effect. Stitches are crossed over adjacent stitches, alternating over and under using plain and purl to define the cables.

Cheesecloth Thin, loosely woven cotton cloth originated from India. Also known as muslin.

Chenille Velvety cord with a tufted surface, made from silk or synthetic yarn, used to create a soft woven or knitted fabric of the same name.

Cheongsam Close-fitting Chinese women's dress with mandarin collar and side splits. Often fastened at the neck with frogging.

Chiffon Sheer, delicate, woven fabric using twisted silk or synthetic yarns for a grainy surface.

Chintz Glazed cotton printed with bright patterns—often floral. Originally imported from India.

Corduroy Cotton fabric with soft pile of parallel ridges in various widths to create variations, such as needlecord, jumbo cord, or elephant cord.

Corset Undergarment composed of a boned bodice covering bust to hips that is drawn and laced, or fastened with hooks and eyes, to create a defined and narrow waistline.

Cotton Fibers from the seed capsules of the cotton plant are spun and woven into fabric. First used in the Americas and Asia.

Couched work Decorative embroidery technique. Thicker threads are laid down on the face of the fabric then secured with stitches from finer contrasting threads, worked in and out of the fabric over the surface thread.

Couture Creation of high fashion, custom made-to-measure garments. French word for "sewing."

Cowl neck Large, deep, softly draped collar giving a feminine aesthetic.

Cravat Originating in Croatia, a patterned necktie with a pleated section to go around the neck, leaving a wider section to fold and drape at the front.

Crepe Thin, gauze-like woven fabric. The threads are first twisted to give greater elasticity. Crepe de chine and crepe georgette are typical fabrics.

Crew neck A round, close-fitting neckline.

Crinoline Large caged frame to create an underskirt or petticoat.

Crochet Using a hooked needle to pick up yarn or thread to make loops in decorative formats creating an openwork lace fabric as an alternative to knitting.

Cummerbund Wide satin sash worn around the waist.

Cutwork Holes cut in fabric creating decorative motifs and patterns that are edged and filled with embroidery and appliqué.

Damask Satin-weave fabric in cotton silk or linen thread in monochromatic colors to create decorative patterns. The contrast of the face and reverse of the satin weave is alternated, creating the pattern on both sides.

Dart A stitched fold on the inside of a garment to create shape and fit.

Décolletage A low-cut neckline on a woman's dress.

Deconstruct To challenge traditional concepts in fashion, for example leaving raw edges unfinished, distorting shapes, or using unorthodox fabrics.

Denim Cotton twill fabric made from one colored thread and one white thread. Used to make jeans and hardwearing work wear.

Devoré Decorative technique often seen in velvet fabrics. Areas of pile are burned away to leave a transparent pattern.

Dinner jacket Men's jacket for formal evening wear, often with satin- or silk-faced lapels.

Dirndl Traditional Austrian dress with lace-up bodice and full gathered skirt and apron.

Dolman sleeve Sleeves cut as part of the bodice panels, deep at the armhole then tapering toward the cuff.

Double-breasted Garment with front opening panels that overlap and fasten with two vertical rows of parallel buttons.

Double-faced A term used for fabric that has a finish on both sides, allowing the fabric to be reversible.

Drawn-thread work Warp and weft fabrics are removed, and the remaining laddered threads are pulled together and decoratively stitched to form a pattern.

Drill Linen or cotton woven twill used for its hardwearing qualities.

Drop waist A waistband on a dress that falls lower than the natural waistline.

Duchess satin A heavy and luxurious silk satin with a lustrous sheen.

Dyes Natural or synthetic pigments used to color fabrics.

Embroidery Decorative stitching applied as ornamentation to fabric using self-colored or contrast-colored threads, such as silk, linen, cotton, and rayon.

Empire line High-waisted bodice and long, slimline skirt originating from nineteenth-century dress.

Epaulettes Originated from military uniform, detachable flaps, or ornamental shoulder decoration.

Ethnic dress Traditional clothing from different cultures adapted for Western dress.

Eton collar Large, stiff, starched detachable collar derived from the uniform at Eton, the British public school.

Eyelet Hole made in fabric for a ribbon or lace to pass through, often reinforced by stitching or strengthened by metal rings.

Facing Attaching a strip of fabric, for example, at the neckline of a garment, where a duplicate shape is cut then stitched around the neckline and turned back to line and enclose the raw edges, in order to give a neat finish.

Fagoting The decorative joining of two fabrics by a series of embroidered patterns leaving a small gap in between the stitching. This can also describe the decorative embroidery between drawn-thread work where threads are removed across the warp and the weft then tied in bundles.

Fair Isle Technique originating from the Scottish island of the same name. Several colored yarns are knitted in turn to create a repetitive horizontal series of motifs or patterns.

Felt Fabric made from woolen fleece bonded together by heat, moisture, and friction. Felting can also be achieved by boiling and friction after weaving or knitting the fabric.

Flannel Woolen fabric with a plain or twill weave and a slight nap on both sides.

Fly front A fold of cloth on pants or skirt opening that covers a row of buttons or a zipper.

French seam A seam used to join transparent fabrics where the seam will be seen from the outside of the garment. The raw edges are sewn right sides together then folded back and enclosed within the second seam.

Frock Term for an informal gown or child's dress, used as an alternative for the term "dress."

Frogging A decorative braiding formed to create a closure and fastening, often on the opening of a coat. The frog button created by the braid passes under the braided loop.

Gabardine A wool or cotton worsted twill with diagonal ribbing. Invented by Thomas Burberry to make the famous Burberry raincoat.

Gathering A series of running stitches at the top edge of the fabric that is bunched together in order to decrease the width. Often set into a seam creating fullness at the other edge.

Georgette A lightweight sheer fabric of silk or synthetic fibers woven with a crepe texture.

Gigot See *leg-of-mutton sleeve*.

Gingham Plain-weave cotton fabric with different-colored warp and weft threads that create a check pattern.

Godet Triangular panel inserted into the seams of panels in a skirt to create a fluted, flared shape at the hemline.

Gores Panels of a skirt tapering from the hips out toward fullness at the hem, giving a close fit at the hip and a flared hemline.

Grain The direction of a fabric that affects how a garment will hang. The warp is the vertical, lengthwise, or straight grain. The weft is the horizontal, crosswise, or cross grain. The diagonal is the bias, which gives stretch. The selvage runs along the vertical edge of the fabric.

Grosgrain Heavy silk fabric or ribbon with a ribbed surface.

Gusset A piece of fabric, usually triangular in shape, inserted into a seam to give additional width in order to improve the fit.

Habotai silk A lightweight silk originating in Japan.

Halter neck A sleeveless bodice with straps that extend and tie around the back of the neck.

Herringbone A twill weave where a zigzag pattern is formed in the diagonal.

Houndstooth A type of check pattern with broken-edged squares or rectangles creating a four-pointed shape created as a twill weave.

Ikat Originating in Indonesia, the term describes the tie dying of yarn or thread that is then woven to create a blurred pattern.

Intarsia Technique used in knitting. A number of different-colored yarns are knitted to achieve patterns across a garment. Usually used to create bold areas of color where a single, non-repeating image is required.

Interfacing A bonded fabric used to strengthen or stiffen, giving structure to the outer fabric. Can be stitched between the lining and fabric or be bonded.

Inverted pleat The reverse of a box pleat, with the folds turning inward pointing together with the fullness behind.

Jabot A ruffle or frill at the neckline extending down as a waterfall effect.

Jacquard A fabric with a pattern woven into it, such as a damask or brocade, or knitted, such as Fair Isle. The pattern is achieved through holes punched in cards.

Jersey Knitted stretch fabric in different gauges from lightweight to heavyweight.

Kick pleat An inverted pleat at the hemline of a tight skirt, with the folds pointing inward to give ease of movement.

Knife pleat Pleats that face one direction around a garment.

Lace Decorative fabric woven or knitted to form patterns of open web-like structures creating contrasting areas of density and openness resulting in a delicate, transparent cloth.

Lamé Fabric woven with metallic threads, often gold or silver.

Lapels The turned back folds at the front of a jacket or shirt. The lapels can also be attached to the collar.

Lawn Linen or cotton with a fine weave giving a semitransparent appearance.

Leg-of-mutton sleeve A set-in sleeve gathered to the armhole and full to the elbow, then fitted from elbow to wrist. Also known as a gigot.

Liberty print Originally hand-printed floral or paisley patterns on silk, but more recently cotton or tana lawn, created by Liberty of London.

Linen A strong fiber taken from the stem of the flax plant and woven into a fine-, medium-, or heavyweight fabric, or spun and used as yarn for knitting.

Lingerie Underwear usually made from fine fabrics, such as silk. Can be decorated with lace of frills.

Lining The inside layer of a garment that adds finish, hiding elements, such as seams and raw edges. The lining gives comfort and can be used to add extra warmth or to give added benefits, such as breathability.

Lurex Trade name for a synthetic fiber yarn coated with aluminum or metallic fabrics to create luster and sparkle.

Lycra Trade name for spandex.

Magyar sleeve Used to describe a sleeve cut from the same pattern piece as the front panel, with Hungarian origins. The sleeve can be designed to be worn at varying lengths.

Mandarin collar A stand collar with a center-front opening, Chinese in origin.

Maxi skirt Skirt worn to ankle or floor length. The term was devised in the 1960s to differentiate between the midi and the mini.

Merino Wool spun from the fleece of the Merino sheep and woven or knitted to form a very good-quality cloth with a soft hand.

Micro mini Very short version of the mini-length skirt, worn pelmet length above the thigh.

Midi skirt Term used to describe a skirt to calf length, differentiating between the mini and the maxi length.

Miniskirt Short skirt worn above the knee to thigh level, popularized in the 1960s by British designer Mary Quant.

Miter The corners of a join where the seam is stitched on the diagonal to the point.

Mohair The hair of the Angora goat, sheared, carded, and spun then woven or knitted to create a fabric with a long or short fluffy pile.

Moiré Fabric with a watermark appearance created by a wavy pattern made by wetting and heating the fabric before running through heavy ribbed rollers.

Moleskin Cotton with a tight weave and short, soft pile giving a suede-like appearance and hand.

Muslin Lightweight woven cotton or linen with a semitransparent open weave.

Nappa leather Fine, high-grade, supple leather suitable for garments that require a soft hand. Used for gloves.

Negligee Dressing gown of transparent or lightweight fabric with a glamorous aesthetic.

Nehru collar High, round-neck stand collar with a split center front worn by the Indian leader Jawaharlal Nehru. Adopted by the hippie movement and popularized by the Beatles.

New Look The silhouette created by Dior in 1947, showing full skirts with wide hemlines from nipped-in waistlines. The look was the antidote to post-war austerity.

New Romantic Street style adopted by the youth of the late 1970s to mid-1980s. Inspired by eighteenth-century dress and created at home, adopting frills, laces, theatrical makeup, and unisex dressing. The style, integral to music and the club scene, soon became embraced by mainstream fashion.

Notch Markings on a pattern to define the point where one pattern piece matches the other. Shown as a triangle shape on the pattern and cut out of the fabric.

Nylon Trade name for synthetic fabrics with a wide range of weights, properties, and hands for a wide range of garments, particularly stockings traditionally known as nylons.

Ombré Fabric or thread dyed to give a graduated tonal effect. Often dip dyed.

Organdy Fine cotton or synthetic light gauze finished to give a crisp hand.

Organza Woven fabric using silk, cotton, rayon, or polyester to create a light, transparent fabric with a crisp hand.

Orientalism Interpretation of Asian and Middle Eastern styling in fabrics and garment shapes, adopted by Western fashion.

Paisley pattern Decorative pattern adapted from the Indian teardrop motif, taking its name from the Scottish village where imitation Kashmiri scarves and shawls were woven, popularizing the pattern. Liberty of London adopted the pattern in their prints, reviving its popularity.

Panné velvet Velvet with a high-luster surface created by the directional pressing of the pile in order to achieve a soft hand.

Passementerie Term often used to describe ornamental furnishing trims, braids, and tassels, but can also apply to fashion trimming. Often silk, gold, or silver threads, the decoration is luxurious and sumptuous.

Patch pocket A cut-out, shaped fabric applied to the surface of the garment to form a pocket. The sides and opening can be stitched for reinforcement or decoration.

Patchwork Small pieces of fabric sewn together in a jigsaw pattern to form a fabric and create a decorative effect. The pattern can be complex and intricate with geometric combinations, or with patches connected in random formations. Often using small-scale prints, the color and tonal values are key to the creation of repetitive, modular, interconnecting shapes.

Patent leather Coated leather with a lacquered finish to give a high-gloss sheen.

Pencil skirt Tight-fitting skirt to the knee or calf length, often with a split or pleat at the center-back for ease of movement.

Peplum Short overskirt sewn at the waistband of a garment to give a short overlayer or edging to a garment and a flounce at the hip. The peplum can be gathered into the seam, or cut circular or paneled and sewn in straight but flaring to the hem.

Peter Pan collar Traditionally seen in women's or children's clothing, a collar with rounded edges usually applied without a stand and turned down to give a soft effect.

Petticoat Undergarment worn as a foundation beneath a dress or skirt. It can function as layers or tiers to give volume to the skirt, or as a full garment from shoulder to hem to provide modesty under a transparent or lace fabric. The petticoat can be reinforced with a frame to give additional volume.

Picot Ornamental decoration created by braids, ribbons, or lace with a small loop of twisted threads forming a pattern at the edge.

Pile Extra yarn added to the surface of the woven fabric and cut to form a raised surface, such as corduroy or velvet. The nap of the fabric must be cut directionally, otherwise the pile will create a different sheen when stitched parallel.

Pin tucks Parallel lines of stitched tiny pleats for decorative effect, for example, vertically down the yoke of a bodice or vertically around the hemline of a skirt.

Piping A decorative edging or seam created by the insertion of a cord covered by a strip of fabric. The fabric will need to be bias cut if the piping is intended to fit around a curve.

Piqué Woven cotton fabric with a raised surface design, such as a honeycomb, check, or diamond pattern.

Placket The opening at the neckline of a garment that allows the garment to be taken on or off with ease. The placket is often fastened with buttonholes, though alternative fastenings, such as snap poppers can be used.

Plaid Woven twill cloth in a check or checkerboard with stripe pattern in vertical and horizontal crossing formations giving endless variations in color and size. Traditionally worn in Scotland as tartan.

Pleat Folded fabric in parallel lines to give a concertina effect, with varying combinations of formats, such as box pleat or inverted box pleat. The fabric can be heat treated for permanent pleating, or pressed and repressed after laundering. The pleat is generally fixed at one end to hold firm, with the other end flaring out, or fixed

at both ends to create areas of control or for decoration. Sometimes soft pleats can be used for gathering and drape.

Polyester Synthetic fibers made into threads and woven or knitted to form fabrics that have easy-care properties that can be crease resistant or fast drying. The fabric can also be heat set to form permanent pleats or folds.

Pom-pom A decorative ball made from yarn wound repeatedly and tied, then cut. The pom-pom can also be made from fabric or feathers clumped together.

Poncho Woolen cape made from a rectangular piece of cloth with a central hole for the head, worn with the corners at center front and back.

Poplin Traditionally a woven fabric with a silk warp and a cotton weft with fine crosswise ribs, creating a strong fabric. The fabric is now made from a combination of manmade fibers, sometimes mixed with cotton.

Power dressing Defined by the strong masculine silhouette of the 1980s, with wide padded shoulders mixed with feminine flirty nipped-in waistlines, peplums, gathers, and pussy-cat bows. Short pencil skirts and high heels help to create a powerful, business aesthetic.

Preppy style American student-inspired casual dressing with chinos and blazers, Fair Isles and pleated skirts, creating an aspirational, sporty, affluent feel.

Princess line The bodice and skirt are cut in one piece with darts at the waist and gores in the skirt to give fit and flare. The waist is defined, and the hemline has volume.

Psychedelic Brightly colored swirling patterns, sometimes with optical illusions. Also describes the hippie style of the 1960s and 1970s.

Puffed sleeves Short sleeves gathered at the sleeve head into the armhole and gathered at the lower edge to create a puff shape.

Punk style Street style created in the 1970s that subverted the conventions of fashion and society to establish a new wave of culture, invented by the disenfranchised youth. Heavily influenced by the music scene, fashion was home grown and involved distressing, ripping, and embellishing with safety pins and provocative slogans to create anti-establishment, anti-fashion statements.

PVC Stands for polyvinyl chloride, which forms a plasticized fabric or a coated surface that creates a waterproof, high-gloss surface.

Quilting Layers of fabric consisting of an upper fabric and lining sandwiching a batting, with lines or patterns of stitching through top to bottom. The padded effect creates surface decoration and can be used to reinforce areas of the garment or to create insulation.

Raglan sleeve Running diagonally from underarm to neck edge, the sleeve avoids the need for shoulder seams.

Ra-ra skirt Worn by cheerleaders and popularized in the 1980s, a short frilled or gathered tiered skirt.

Rayon A silk-like fabric made from cellulose fibers from plant extracts, ideal for lingerie-inspired dresses.

Retro Used to describe designs inspired by and referencing the fashion styles of previous decades.

Revers Describes the turned-back side of the reverse of the garment and, in particular, to describe the lapel of the collar.

Rhinestone A cut stone applied as a decoration to add glitz and sparkle.

Ribbing Knitted pattern, alternating sequences of plain and purl, mostly in vertical lines, used to create a stretch fabric often utilized as hems, cuffs, collars,

and plackets, or simply to give contrasting areas of definition within the garment.

Roll collar A collar that rolls without the use of a sharp crease or fold.

Rolled hem A very narrow hem, ideal for fine and delicate fabrics, used on scarves and lingerie and perfect for bias and circular hemlines. The fabric edge is folded or rolled several times and has a very discreet stitch, picking up minimal fabric, disguised within the rolls. This is usually hand rendered as a couture technique.

Rouleaux Strips of bias-cut fabric stitched and turned inside out to create spaghetti tape or ribbons that can be used as straps or loops for button fastenings or edgings.

Ruching Strips of fabric gathered in the center and attached to the garment to create a decorative frilly embellishment. The term can also describe the technique of gathering the edges of fabric, for example, at a neck edge.

Ruff A pleated collar, often detachable and can be layered and concertinaed. Made from linen or lace, the collar is starched to give shape and structure.

Ruffles Gathered frills or flounces, often running around the edges of cuffs and collars or down the front of a bodice or yoke.

Running stitch The thread is sewn in and out of the fabric creating a simple stitch that is often straight but can be used to form decorative patterns.

Sari Traditional Indian garment formed by a length of fabric wrapped around and pleated at the waist, then crossed and draped over the shoulder. Worn over a choli, which is a short fitted bodice.

Sarong Traditional Indonesian garment worn around the waist and wrapped or tied. Can also be worn underarm above the bustline. An ideal shape for beachwear.

Sash Deep belt around the waist or worn diagonally across one shoulder to opposite hip. Often self-fabric or ribbon, the sash can be tied or pinned.

Sateen Satin-weave cotton fabric with a luster on the surface of the fabric.

Satin Fabric with a smooth shine on the surface and a dullness on the underside. This is created by warp threads crossing over a number of weft threads at a time, or vice versa.

Scoop neck A round neck cut low, and sometimes wide, revealing varying degrees of décolletage.

Seersucker Fabric with a puckered surface created by different tensions in the warp before weaving the fabric. Using cotton or synthetics, this is an ideal fabric for the sundress.

Selvage The edge of the fabric either side of the warp when woven. The finished edge is created when the warp threads are looped back into the fabric during the weaving process and stops the fabric from fraying or raveling.

Sequins Cut disks of plastic or metal in various shapes and sizes with a hole to allow for stitching onto fabric. The disks can be finished to create luster and iridescence and be beaten to give texture.

Shantung silk Heavy slub silk with less-refined fibers to give a more uneven, textured surface.

Shawl collar A collar that travels around the neck increasing in width around the neck edge then tapering to the start of the "V" shaping at center front. The collar is turned or rolled back.

Shirring Parallel rows of tiny stitches gathered to pull in the fabric and create areas of constriction. Sometimes shirring elastic is used to create stretch.

Shot silk Woven with different colors in the warp and weft to give an iridescent sheen and a two-tone effect.

Silk Made from the fibers of the cocoons of the silkworm. The fine, lustrous fibers are spun and woven to create a luxury fabric.

Slash pocket A pocket with a slit opening with no covering flap, which can be set horizontally, vertically, or angled for variation in design.

Sleeve head The top part of the sleeve that is set or gathered into the armhole. The shape can vary considerably depending on the style of sleeve.

Slip A lightweight petticoat worn under dresses, sometimes acting as a layer under transparent fabrics. Can be adopted as a flimsy sundress or for special occasion dresses.

Smock Originally worn by farm laborers, the smock is a loose-fitting garment made from linen with a smocked yoke, often white on white. The style is adopted for childrens wear or for women's informal dress, ideal for maternity wear and great for larger sizes.

Smocking Decorative embroidered technique used to control and shape through a series of parallel stitches evenly gathered to form pleats, which are stitched on top to form patterns. The original gathers are pulled out once the embroidery is complete.

Spaghetti straps Very thin straps ideal for sundresses and special occasion dresses. The straps can be fixed or tied, or tightened through a clasp.

Spandex Synthetic fiber with stretch qualities that can be combined with other fibers, such as wool or denim, to give elasticity. Used in fabric for lingerie, swimwear, and sportswear to give a body-contouring effect.

Stand and fall collar A two-part collar with the stand rising from the round neckline and attaching to the fall—the outer visible layer that folds over.

Stand collar A collar that stands upright from the neckline opening. Variations in style include the Nehru collar.

Starch Treatment to stiffen fabric, either as a spray or washed with the fabric. Usually a plant extract although can also be chemical based. The starch can also be a coating inherent in the manufacture of the cloth, but is usually added after or during the laundry process.

Stole Worn around the shoulders like a wrap or shawl. Often using luxury fabrics for special occasion wear.

Stone washing The distressing and aging of fabric, such as denim or silk using a technique of tumble drying in vats with stones or pebbles.

Street style Originating on the street and created by young people in order to identify their version of popular culture. Adopted by designers and repackaged to recreate a more commercial version.

Suede The nap side of tanned leather, treated to give a soft textured appearance and hand.

Sweetheart neckline Copying the heart shape, this is a curved V neckline that gives a decorative feature to the top of the bodice.

Tabard A loose-fitting, open-sided garment worn over a dress or separates, sometimes as a protective layer.

Taffeta A silk or synthetic fabric with a heavy body, a glossy luster, and a crisp rustle, ideal for evening wear and special occasion wear.

Tail The long back of a man's dress coat or morning coat, or the longer hemline of a shirt designed to be tucked into pants. The tail can be a design feature that elongates a garment, sometimes squared or curved with split side vents.

Tank top A sleeveless pullover with a crew or V neck, knitted and worn over another garment layer. More commonly, a short garment worn with skirt and trousers, the tank can be elongated to form a dress.

Tatting The creation of a lace-like fabric or decorative border using a shuttle to make a formation of loops in a variety of patterns.

Tie dyeing Traditional African or Asian technique of dyeing after tying or knotting threads around the fabric in order to prevent the dye from absorbing, leaving the base fabric undyed in places.

Tiers Layers of gathered ruffles or flounces that overlap, often forming the skirt or petticoat of the garment.

Toga A Roman garment consisting of a semicircular piece of cloth draped and wrapped around the body and attached to form a garment.

Toggle Often worn on a duffle coat, a toggle is a cylindrical- or cone-shaped fastening traditionally made from horn or tortoiseshell and attached to a garment and fastened by a corded loop.

Train The back of the garment that falls to the floor and trails behind, originating from ceremonial costumes but adopted for evening wear and wedding dresses.

Trench coat Waterproof cotton or wool raincoat originally worn by military personnel with a caped shoulder, epaulettes, and belt, worn double- or single-breasted.

Tuck A folded section of fabric stitched in a straight line to create shaping or a decorative effect. Tucks are often stitched as a series running parallel.

Index

Tulip skirt With a petal-like quality, the tulip shape wraps around the body with a curve toward the hemline, giving a rounded silhouette.

Tulle Silk or synthetic net fabric used for petticoats or veils and common in evening wear. Generally a soft handle, the fabric can be starched for a stiff, more structured effect.

Tunic A short dress traditionally worn over trousers.

Turtleneck High, round-neck, close-fitting collar that turns back on itself.

Tuxedo Men's dinner jacket often with contrast satin- or silk-faced lapels, sometimes with a shawl collar. Worn for formal or evening occasions.

Tweed Woven, woolen cloth originating in Scotland in a plain or twill format, sometimes with a checked, dogtooth, herringbone, or alternative pattern in a variety of subtle to dynamic colorations.

Twill Woven fabric with a weave format where the weft crosses over and under one or more warp threads in a stepped formation to create a diagonal rib-like pattern.

Utility clothing Style of clothing that economized fabrics and manufacturing in response to a shortage of raw materials and rationing following World War II.

Variegated Often space-dyed threads are used to create a multicolored fabric with a patchy, inconsistent appearance, but sometimes dyeing the finished fabric can achieve the results.

Velvet Cotton, silk, or synthetics are used to create a fabric with a dense pile and a soft hand. The extra loops are creating in the weaving process then cut at the same length to give a visible luster and a luxurious feel. The nap is distinctive so the garment pieces need to be cut in the same direction on the fabric.

Vent Designed to give ease of movement, this vertical slit at the back or sides of a garment usually runs from the hem but can also be placed at the front.

Vest A sleeveless undergarment pulled over the head that has been adopted to describe an outerwear garment. Varying in lengths, the vest can been worn next to the body or layered over another garment.

Vintage clothing Clothes from a previous era with a nostalgic value, reused and reworn, and often mixed between decades and with modern-day garments to create a more contemporary aesthetic.

Viscose Made from cellulose plant fibers to mimic silk. Can also be described as rayon.

Voile Lightweight sheer fabric with a crisp finished surface. Traditionally made from cotton but can also be made from silk or manmade fibers.

Volant Used to trim or decorate, a flounce or frill with a wavy edge normally cut from a circle.

Waistband The band that circles the waist at the top of separates, such as a skirt, but can also be used to define the waistline of a dress.

Waist seam The seam that attaches the skirt to bodice around the waist of a dress.

Warp Threads that run vertically on the loom, parallel to the selvage edge, to create the basis for the interweaving of the weft.

Weave Describes the interweaving of the weft running horizontally between the vertical threads of the warp on the loom to form the cloth. Different woven structures and patterns are created by varying the number of over- and-under combinations.

Weft Threads that run horizontally, interlaced between the vertical threads on the warp of the loom to create a woven cloth.

Welt A strengthened or raised border on a garment. Also used to describe a pocket.

Whitework Embroidery using white thread on a white fabric background to create a subtle yet decorative effect. The term can also be used to describe broderie anglaise.

Wing collar Usually found on a formal men's dress shirt, a stand collar with the two end points creased and bent backward.

Wool Farmed from an animal, such as sheep, goat, or alpaca, the fleece is carded and spun, then knitted, woven, or felted to create fabric.

Yarn Thread made from natural or manmade fibers that have been spun or twisted. Used to create a knitted or woven fabric.

Yoke Pattern piece of a garment at neck, shoulder panel, or sometimes around the waist of a skirt, often fitted and attached to the lower parts of the garment.

Credits

Andrey, Degtyaryov, Shutterstock, pp.119tcr, 187tl, 195tcr, 195bl

Aronov, Sam, Shutterstock, pp.17bl, 47r, 49tcl, 65tcl, 101bcl, 132tr, 143tl

Atletic, Zvonimir, Shutterstock, pp.17tr, 33bcl/bcr, 43tr, 46tr, 56l/r, 58c, 64r, 80bl, 90l, 117bcr, 129tl/tcl, 135tl, 152bcl, 188br, 199bl, 200l/r, 201r, 205tl, 219br, 223bl, 226r, 230tcr, 241c, 247bl, 257tcr

aWear, pp.103tr, 107bcl, 119tr

Bae, Yeori, pp.22tl, 67tl, 202bcr/br

Berardi, Antonio, pp.19c, 21c, 91tr, 107bl/br, 118l, 119tl, 163bcl, 165r, 235l/r, 243bcl, 244tl, 247br, 264tr

Bloom, Shutterstock, p.102tcr

Bong, Selphie, p.203c

Borodina, Tatyana, Shutterstock, pp.48c, 247bcl, 249r

Catwalker, Shutterstock, pp.17bcr, 42r, 43tcl/tcr/bl/bcl, 45c, 50bl, 53bcr, 55l, 103tcr, 111bcr, 129bcl, 132l, 136c, 137l, 141c, 163tcr, 168l, 192l, 247tcl, 254tcr, 255br, 256l/r, 257tl/tr/bcr/br, 258l/r, 259l/c/r, 260l/c/r, 261tcl/tr/bl/bcl/br, 263l, 264tl/tcl/bcl, 265l

Corbis, pp.12, 13, 38, 39, 73, 124, 125, 158, 159, 121

Cousland, Neale, Shutterstock, p.105r

CyberEak, Shutterstock, pp.66, 91tl, 238l, 244tr

DIMITRI, pp.17tcl, 17br, 19l, 76, 77tcl, 79l, 110l, 113c, 115bl, 152tl, 163bcr, 185tcl, 189tcr, 190c, 191l, 193tcl, 195tcl, 197bcl, 220r, 239c, 243tl,tcr/bl

DIMITRI, Oliver Rauh Photography, http://oliverrauhphotography.blogspot.de, pp.171tr, 185tr, 203l

Dotshock, Shutterstock, p.187bcl

Efecreata Photography, Shutterstock, pp.61bl, 202tl, 264br

Fabrican, www.fabricanltd.com, Gene Kiegel, p.279l

Fahri, Nicole, pp.17bcl, 33tl, 62l

Ferry Indrawang, Shutterstock, p.121bl

Fowler, Holly, p.205tcr

Getty Images, pp.96, 97

Gitlits, Alexander, Shutterstock, pp.43bcr, 45r, 50br, 54tl, 67bl, 77tr, 102tcl/tcr, 111tr, 115tl, 117tcr, 119bl, 188bcl, 223br, 230bl

Glass, Abigail, pp.103br, 248r, 249c, 250bcr

Gromovataya, Shutterstock, p.53tcl

James, Edward, pp.11, 16r, 20r, 21r, 22tcl/tcr/tr/bl/bcl, 23l/c/r, 24l/r, 25tl/tcr, 26r, 27tcl/tcr/r/bcr, 29tcl/bcl, 31l/c/r, 32l/r, 33tcl/bl/br, 35bl/bcl/bcr, 37, 49bl, 50tcr, 53tcr, 57tl/tcl/tcr/tr/bl/bcr/br, 59l, 62r, 63l, 67tcl/tr/bcr, 69tr/bcr/br, 71, 83r, 84l, 85tl/tcr, 87tcr/tr/bcr/br, 88l/r, 91tcr, 92l/r, 93l/c/r, 95, 101bl, 102bcr, 105l, 108r, 109tcr/tr/bl/bcl/bcr/br, 114l, 115tcl/tr/bcr/br, 117tcl, 119br, 121tcl/tcr, 128l, 131c, 132bcl/br, 141r, 142l, 144r, 145tl/tcl/tcr/tr/bl/bcl/bcr, 146l, 147tr/tcr/tcl/bcr/bcr, 152bl/br, 153l/c, 157, 165l, 171tcr/bl/bcl/bcr, 173tl/tcl/tcr/bl/br, 175, 181tcr, 182r, 183c/r, 184r, 185tl/bcr/br, 195bcr/br, 197tcl/tcr/br, 198r, 199tl, 202tcl/tcr, 203r, 205bcl, 211, 221tcl/tcr, 223tcr/bcr, 224r, 232l, 233bl/bcr, 240tl, 243bcr, 244bl/bcr, 245bcr, 267, 272l/r, 273tl–r/bl/bcl/bcr, 274–275, 276l/r, 277tl/tcl/tr/bl–r, 278l/r, 279r

K2 images, Shutterstock, pp.100l, 181tl, 185bcl

Kallmeyer, Daniella, pp.26l, 28r, 115tcr

Kojoku, Shutterstock, pp.44l, 61tcr, 81r, 103bl, 108tc, 131r, 132tl, 169tcl/tr, 170r, 227bl, 241tr, 257bl

Mark III Photonics, Shutterstock, pp.51br, 69tcr, 77bcl/bcr, 80tcl/bcl, 85bl/bcl, 91bcl, 101tcr, 103bcl, 107tcr, 121br, 129tcr, 130r, 131l, 132tcl, 136r, 162l, 163tr, 167c, 230tl, 236l, 247tcr, 253bcr, 263c

Mikhaylova, Natalia, Shutterstock, p.65bcl

Miro Vrlik Photography, Shutterstock, pp.18, 102bl, 134l, 149br, 151c, 199bcr, 219tcr, 229c

Nomia Selects, pp.21l, 34l, 143tcl

Oparin, Anton, www.FashionStock.com, pp.19r, 22bcr/r, 25tcl/tr/bl/cl/cr/r, 27tl/bl/bcl/r, 29tl/tcr/tr/bl/bcr/br, 33tr, 42l, 43tl/br, 46tcr/bcr/br, 52l, 53tr, 55r, 57bcl, 60tl, 63r, 64tl, 65tr/bcr, 67tcr/bcl, 77tl, 85tr, 89r, 91tl/bcr, 109tl, 114c/r, 116l, 117tl/tr/bl/br, 121tl, 128r, 129tr/br, 133l/r, 135tcl/tcr/tr/bl/bcl/br, 138l, 139tl/tcl/bl/bcl/bcr/br, 140l, 141l, 143bcr, 145br, 147tr/bl/br, 148tcl, 149tcl, 167r, 169tcr, 171tcl, 172r, 173bcr, 181tcl/tl/bcr, 185tcr/bl, 187tcl/tcr/tr, 188tr, 189tcl, 193tcr/bcl, 197tr, 198tcl, 199tr/bcl/br, 202bl, 216r, 217bl/br, 220tl/tcr, 222r, 223tcl/tr/bcr, 227tcr/bcl, 230tcl, 232r, 233tl, 236r, 237l/bl, 239r, 240tcl/br, 241r, 242l, 244tcl, 245bcl, 253tr, 262l, 264bcr, 277tcr, 279c

Oparin, Anton, Shutterstock, pp.16l, 28l, 45l, 47l/c, 51bcl, 52r, 53br, 54tcl, 56c, 59r, 61tcl/br, 66c, 69tcl/bcl, 77br, 80tl, 81l/c, 82c/r, 85br, 87bl, 91bl/br, 101tr, 102c, 103tl/bcr, 104r, 105c, 106c, 111tcl/tr/bl, 121tcr, 129bl, 138tcr, 140r, 143bl, 149bcl, 152tcl/tcr/bcr, 155l, 162r, 163tl, 169bcl, 173tr, 194l, 195tr, 196r, 197bcr, 198l, 204l, 216l, 217tcl/bcl, 219tl/bcr, 221bl, 225l/c, 226l, 227bcr/br, 230tr/bcl, 231l, 233tcl/br/bcl, 234l, 237tcl/bcl, 246r, 247tl, 250tcl/tcr/br, 251c, 253bcl, 254tl/tcl/br, 255tl, 257tcl, 265r

Palomino, Elisa, pp.102tcl, 112bl, 202tr, 205bcr/br, 206l/r, 207l/c/r, 208–209, 216c, 223tl, 227tl/tr, 231c, 234r, 235c, 245bl, 263r

Photofriday, Shutterstock, pp.80tcr, 101tl, 102tl, 148r, 189bl, 190l, 202bcl, 250tl, 253tcl

Pyo, Rejina, p.197bl

Radin, Lev, Shutterstock, pp.17tl/tcr, 30r, 33tcr, 34r, 35tl/tcl/tcr/tr, 46tl/tcl/bl/bcl, 48l/r, 49tl/tcr/tr/bcl/bcr, 50tl, 51tl/tcl/tr, 53tl/bcl, 54tcr/tr/bl/br, 58l, 61tr/bcl, 63c, 64l, 65br, 68r, 69bl, 77tcr/bl, 78l, 79r, 82l, 84r, 86l, 87tl/tcl/bcl, 89l, 90r, 100r, 101bcr/br, 102bcl/br, 106l/r, 107tl/tcl/tr/bcr, 108l, 111tcr, 113r, 116r, 118r, 119tcl/bcl, 121bcl, 132tcr, 133c, 138r, 139tcr,

143tcr/tr/bcl, 146r, 149tl, 150r, 152tr, 154c, 163tcl/br, 164l, 166r, 172l, 180l/r, 181bl/bcl/br, 182l, 183l, 184l, 186l, 187bl/bcr/br, 188tl/tcr/bl/bcr, 189tl/br, 190r, 191r, 193tcl/tr/br, 194r, 195tr/bcl, 196c, 197tl, 198tcr, 201l, 204r, 205tcl/bl, 217tl/tcr/tr/bcr, 218l/c, 291tr/bl, 220l, 221bcl, 222l, 225r, 228l/r, 229l, 230bcr, 231l, 233tcr, 237tr/bcr/bl, 238l/r, 240tcr/bcr, 242c/r, 243tr, 244tcr/bcl/br, 245tl–tr, 246l, 247bcr, 248l, 249l, 250bcl, 251l/r, 252l/c/r, 253tl/tcr/br, 254tr/bl/bcl/bcr, 255tcr/tr/bl/bcl, 258r, 261bcr, 264tcr, 265c

Rex Features, pp.176, 177, 213, 268–269, 270–271, 273br

Roland, Stephanie, p.170l

Sermek, Gordana, Shutterstock, pp.54bcl, 65bl, 81bcr, 101tcl, 111br, 117bcl, 123, 189bcr, 243tcl/br, 261tl

Sha, Nata, Shutterstock, pp.35br, 44r, 49br, 50tcl/tr/bl/bcr, 51bl/bcr, 53bl, 54bcr, 60l/r, 61bcr, 65tcr, 66r, 67br, 68l, 69tl, 78r, 79c, 80bl, 82l, 85tcl/bcr, 86r, 89c, 104l, 110r, 111bcl, 112r, 120l/r, 121bcr, 132bl/bcr, 134r, 142r, 143br, 148l, 149tr/bcr, 151l/r, 153r, 154l/r, p.163bl, 164c, 166l, 167l, 169tl/bl/br, 173bcl, 186r, 189tr/bcl, 192c/r, 193bl/bcr, 196l, 218r, 219tcl/bcl, 221bcr, 224l, 227tcl, 230br, 233tr, 237tcr, 240bl/bcl, 241l, 253bl, 255bcr, 257bcl

Smith, Gina, Shutterstock, pp.113l, 264bl

Tan, Jordan, Shutterstock, pp.76r, 245br

UAL, pp.135bcr, 164r, 169bcr

Vortexdigital, Shutterstock, p.129tcr

Wachararwish, p.221br

Wilson, Rob, Shutterstock, p.262r

All other photographs and illustrations are the copyright of Quarto Publishing plc. While every effort has been made to credit contributors, Quarto would like to apologize should there have been any errors or omissions—and would be pleased to make the appropriate correction for future editions of the book.